Acclaim for
The 'One Thing' Is Three

The 'One Thing' Is Three is packed with deep theological insight, and while bursting with information, it is written from the heart and speaks to the heart in such a way that the reader is drawn into a greater realization about the nature, mission, and action of the Holy Trinity. I can think of no better timing than the Year of Faith for this book to be introduced. Fr. Gaitley has given us a great guide to help us in our knowledge and, therefore, our love for God the Father, God the Son, and God the Holy Spirit.

— **BISHOP DANIEL R. JENKY, CSC**
Bishop of Peoria, Ill.

Fr. Michael Gaitley's *The 'One Thing' Is Three* is nothing short of a popular synthesis of the great Catholic thought of our time. If you're asking yourself, "What's in it for me?" wait until you enjoy his combination of humor, passion, and brilliance rising to lyrical beauty. Analogies abound to help you understand truths you couldn't get your mind around for their abstractness or vagueness. Can a theology book be a page-turner? This one is!

— **RONDA CHERVIN, PH.D.**
Professor of Philosophy, Holy Apostles Seminary

Fr. Michael Gaitley, MIC, has a holy passion not only to contemplate the truth and beauty of the Trinity but to communicate it, which he does here with practical wisdom and spiritual insight. Readers will gain a new understanding and appreciation of the mysteries of faith, based on what the Church teaches about the highest and holiest Mystery of all: "The communion of the Holy Trinity is the source and criterion of truth in every relationship" (*CCC*, n. 2845). Both inspiring and illuminating, I highly recommend this book.

— **SCOTT HAHN, PH.D.**
Author, Speaker, Professor of Theology and Scripture, Franciscan University of Steubenville

In *The 'One Thing' Is Three*, Fr. Michael Gaitley, MIC, displays his extraordinary gift for expressing the most profound theological truths in simple, approachable, and attractive language. Father Gaitley shows that *communio* is a key that opens up virtually every mystery of the Christian faith — from the Holy Trinity to redemptive suffering, from the Sacraments to sexuality. Readers will find their understanding deepened and their faith enriched.

— **MARY HEALY, STD**
Associate Professor of Sacred Scripture, Sacred Heart Major Seminary

Once I started reading this book, I found it so enjoyable that I couldn't put it down. I congratulate Fr. Gaitley on a very fine work. I think not only beginners but many others will find inspiration in reading and meditating on this theological retreat.

— **FR. PETER FEHLNER, FI, STD**
Rector Emeritus, Shrine of Our Lady of Guadalupe, La Crosse, Wis.

This is a beautiful book of Catholic teaching with personal stories and practical instruction that can easily be applied to everyday life, especially in this Year of Faith.

— **TERESA TOMEO**
Syndicated Catholic Talk Show Host
Bestselling Catholic Author, Motivational Speaker

In *The 'One Thing' Is Three*, Fr. Gaitley offers the perfect resource for all those who desire sanctity and wisdom but who are busy just trying to keep up with life's constant demands. Whether you're new to the faith or a cradle Catholic like me, this book will unlock the treasures of Catholicism in a way that's clear, concise, and compelling.

— **LISA M. HENDEY**
Founder of www.CatholicMom.com
Author of *A Book of Saints for Catholic Moms*

The 'One Thing' Is Three

How the Most Holy Trinity Explains Everything

Fr. Michael E. Gaitley, MIC

MARIAN PRESS
STOCKBRIDGE · MA 01263

2016

Available from:
Marian Helpers Center
Stockbridge, MA 01263

Prayerline: 1-800-804-3823
Orderline: 1-800-462-7426
www.marian.org
www.thedivinemercy.org

Library of Congress Catalog Number: 2012945837
ISBN: 978-159614-260-2
First edition (4th printing): 2016

Cover Art: Photograph of the Church of the Holy Trinity mosaic,
Budva, Montenegro, by Paul Boyd. Used with permission.

Cover and Page Design: Curtis Bohner and Kathy Szpak

Editing and Proofreading: David Came and Sarah Chichester

† IMPRIMATUR †
Timothy A. McDonnell
Bishop of Springfield, Massachusetts
November 4, 2012

NIHIL OBSTAT	IMPRIMI POTEST
Rev. Mark S. Stelzer, STD	Rev. Kazimierz Chwalek, MIC
Censor Librorum	Provincial Superior
October 17, 2012	October 19, 2012

THEOLOGICAL NOTE: The subtitle of this work, *How the Most Holy Trinity Explains Everything*, is not meant to imply in any way that the mystery of the Most Holy Trinity is somehow conflated or exhausted by this or any other theological exposition. While God has revealed himself to man as one God in three divine persons, human reason cannot fully grasp or exhaust this most central mystery of Christian faith.

Printed in the United States of America

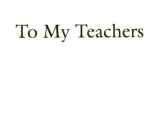

To My Teachers

You are
anxious
and
troubled
about many things;

one thing
is necessary.

~ Jesus

Contents

In Gratitude

A friend of mine teaches philosophy and religion at a Catholic high school in Southern California. One time, when I was in town, she invited me to speak to her students. I said, "Sure," and on the day we'd arranged, I gave a 40-minute talk to five class periods. At the end of the day, I was totally exhausted. Seeing this, my friend laughed and said, "Now imagine if you had to do this every day!"

After that one-day teaching experience, I have a new appreciation for the hard work and sacrifices of so many teachers. It is *not* easy. So, I'd like to begin by thanking all of my teachers, especially the ones who taught me so much of the philosophy and theology found in these pages. In particular, I gratefully acknowledge Fr. W. Norris Clarke, SJ; Dr. Peter Kreeft; Dr. John F. Crosby; Fr. Timothy Gallagher, OMV; Fr. Romanus Cessario, OP; Dr. Scott Hahn; Dr. Josef Seifert; Dr. Anthony Keaty, Dr. Kenneth Schmitz; Fr. Matthew Lamb; Fr. Thomas Weinandy, OFM, Cap.; and Dr. Michael Waldstein.

I'd also like to thank the young adult group, "Three," from my home parish, St. Peter Chanel, in Hawaiian Gardens, California. The members of this group graciously listened to lectures from me every Friday night during my first summer break from the seminary. (It was their Friday penance.) Those lectures and our subsequent conversations helped shape many of the ideas in this book.

On the book-preparation end of things, I first want to express my gratitude to those who proofread the manuscript and gave me their comments, especially David Came, Dr. Robert Stackpole, STD; Fr. Peter Damien Fehlner, FI, STD; Fr. Mark Stelzer, STD; William Perales, Erin Flynn, and Sarah Chichester, who has been a particularly big help. I'm also grateful to Curtis Bohner and Kathy Szpak for assisting with the cover and page design. I'd also like to thank all those who lifted me up in prayer during the time of writing, especially Mary Immaculate, my friends in the Hearts Afire parish-based programs; the Visitation Sisters in Tyringham, Massachusetts; the Norbertine Sisters in Tehachapi, California; the Oblate Sisters of the Most Blessed

Sacrament in Stockbridge, Massachusetts; the Sister Servants of the Eternal Word in Birmingham, Alabama; Mark Fanders, Maria Valentini, and Sr. Bernadette-Marie, FM.

For the opportunity to work on and publish this book, I thank my religious family, the Congregation of Marian Fathers of the Immaculate Conception. Finally, my deepest gratitude goes to God, the Most Holy Trinity: Father, Son, and Holy Spirit.

Fr. Michael E. Gaitley, MIC, STL
National Shrine of The Divine Mercy
Stockbridge, Massachusetts
October 11, 2012
Commencement of the Year of Faith

Acknowledgments

Permission to cite from the following is gratefully acknowledged:

The exit-return diagram of the *Summa Theologiae* from *Summa of Summa* by Peter Kreeft. Copyright © 1990 by Ignatius Press, San Francisco.

Excerpts from *Love and Responsibility* by Karol Wojtyła. Copyright © 1993 by Ignatius Press, San Francisco.

Excerpts from *On the Way to Jesus Christ* by Cardinal Joseph Ratzinger. Copyright © 2005 by Ignatius Press, San Francisco.

Diary of St. Maria Faustina Kowalska: Divine Mercy in My Soul, © 1987 Marian Fathers of the Immaculate Conception of the B.V.M., Stockbridge, MA 01263. www.TheDivineMercy.org.

Organizational chart of the *Summa* from the *New Catholic Encyclopedia*. Vol. 14 (Washington, DC: The Catholic University of America Press, 1967), p. 112. Reprinted with permission from The Catholic University of America Press.

"Holy Trinity" by Andrei Rublev (Scala/Art Resource, NY).

Special thanks to Paul Boyd for permission to reproduce the photo of the Trinity mosaic on the front cover.

INTRODUCTION

This book is for people such as my brother and sister. My sister has seven kids, homeschools, and doesn't have a lot of time to study theology. My brother also has a family and a demanding job — he, too, can't delve deeply into theology. Yet there's nothing more wonderful to study! So, I wrote this book for them, and if you're like my brother and sister, then I wrote it for you, too. Look at it as a kind of crash course in Catholic theology written for busy people and in a way, I hope, that's simple and easy to understand.

*T*HE 'ONE THING.' As I write, I'm a recently ordained priest, and before my ordination, I'd been not just a seminarian but a *professional* seminarian. I say "professional" because I ended up having more than 15 years of formal theology studies and preparation to become a priest. (Unless you're a Jesuit, this is *not* the norm.) During those many years of listening to lectures, reading countless books, and writing hundreds of papers, I was always looking for the "one thing" that could bring it all together, the one thing that could make it all simple, the one thing that could provide a key to the Church's wisdom. I figured that if I could find this one thing, not only would it make me happy, but then I'd have a much easier time sharing the Church's wisdom with others.

I believe I found it. The "one thing" is *three*. The one thing is the greatest mystery of our faith. And actually, the one thing is not really a "thing" at all but rather three divine *persons*: Father, Son, and Holy Spirit — the Most Holy Trinity. Now, unfortunately, this one thing is not so well known. It's often seen as esoteric, obscure, and outside of normal life. This book is meant to change that. It's meant to bring the Trinity home to our hearts, make difficult theology easy to understand, and share the highlights of a 15-year formal search for the one thing.

*S*IMILARITIES TO CONSOLING. The rationale behind this book is similar to that of my first book, *Consoling the Heart of Jesus*. Both books try to present a kind of key. *Consoling* is all about presenting a key to the spiritual life. After all, part of my many years in the seminary involved reading tons of books on spirituality. And during that time, I was always looking for the one thing, the "key," that could best help people to become saints — and I believe I found it. The key to becoming a saint is to focus on making all our actions aim at one goal: pleasing God, consoling the Heart of Jesus, and quenching his thirst for love and for souls. That's what *Consoling* was all about, namely, helping people discover this secret of the saints and a key to great sanctity.

This book is a bit different. While *Consoling the Heart of Jesus* gave a spirituality, the present work gives a theology. In other words, while *Consoling* aimed to help us become saints, this book aims to make us wise. Of course, sanctity and wisdom go together. (Saints often make the best theologians.) And this is so because of the connection between knowledge and love: The more we know God, the more we can love him. Therefore, this book serves as a kind of complement to *Consoling the Heart of Jesus*. It provides a big-picture vision of the theology that undergirds spirituality, and it helps us come to know and love God more deeply.

One other similarity to *Consoling*: The bold claim. In *Consoling*, I wrote that in some sense, it's easier than ever before to grow in holiness and that the book aimed to help us become "saints, great saints, and quickly." I felt confident to make such a bold claim because of the time we're living in. According to Sts. Faustina and John Paul II, ours is a "time of mercy," a time when God is offering us extraordinary grace and mercy.[1]

Well, because we're living in such an extraordinary time, I believe that God not only gives us a key to great sanctity but also a key to great wisdom. We find this key to wisdom in the theological term "*communio*," meaning "communion." This Latin word may be unfamiliar, but don't be afraid. The concept is simple and yet amazingly powerful for the way it helps us grasp some of the deepest mysteries of our faith.

*T*HE *SUPER-CONCEPT OF* COMMUNIO. Wait a minute. Didn't I say that the key to our faith, the "one thing," is the Trinity?

Yes, I did. And it's from the Trinity that we get the concept of *communio*, because this idea has its origin in the communion of love of the Most Holy Trinity. What's more, this idea of *communio* (communion) explains everything — as we'll see throughout the chapters of this book.

Before we turn to those chapters, I'd like to thank a certain group of people for pointing out to me this amazing super-concept of *communio*: The participants of the Second Vatican Council, particularly those who became Pope John Paul II and Pope Benedict XVI. It's their writings that bring this concept to the forefront of our minds. John Paul emphasized it over and over — in fact, it's a central concept to the *Catechism* he promulgated. Also, Pope Benedict was so moved by the idea that after the Council, as Joseph Ratzinger, he helped found a theological journal called *Communio*. (John Paul, as Karol Wojtyła, founded the Polish edition.) Finally, in 1985, the bishops of the Church, together with the Pope, reflected on the meaning of the Second Vatican Council and declared that the "ecclesiology of communion" is the central and fundamental idea of the Council documents.[2]

Again, the concept of *communio* (communion) is a special gift for our time. It helps us to interpret and understand our faith in a wonderfully new way. Of course, it's not something new in the sense that the Church has never heard of it. On the contrary, it's a concept that's been there from the very beginning — and I do mean *the beginning*: "In the beginning was the Word and the Word was with God and the Word was God" (Jn 1:1).[3] Indeed, it comes from the Trinitarian revelation of God in Jesus Christ, the Word become flesh. This ancient idea shines a powerful new light in our day, sparking renewal and spurring on a new evangelization.

Throughout the rest of this book, I'll be unpacking the concept of communion. Right now, though, I'd like to end this introduction by looking at how communion gets to the very heart of Sacred Scripture. For, again, communion is not something "new" as in "unheard of" — rather, it's a precious, rediscovered jewel at the center of Divine Revelation. It's the kind of beauty that St. Augustine famously described as "ever ancient, ever new."[4]

COMMUNIO *AND THE GREATEST PASSAGE IN ALL OF SCRIPTURE.* The greatest passage in all of Scripture? Obviously, not everyone will agree with me on this, but I've got a good reason for saying it. Here's how I came to discover this passage and how it's all about communion.

I began by asking myself, "If I could just memorize one great passage in all of the Bible, what would it be?" I didn't know. So, I began a process of elimination. I began with the broadest of choices: Old Testament or New Testament? Surely, "the greatest passage" would be in the New Testament, because that's where Christ is most fully revealed.

Next, I thought, "Okay, so what category of books in the New Testament are likely to contain the passage I seek?" That was also easy. Even though I love the Acts of the Apostles, St. Paul and his letters, and those of St. John, I knew that, as the *Catechism of the Catholic Church* teaches, "The Gospels are the heart of all the scriptures 'because they are our principal source for the life and teaching'" of Jesus Christ, our Savior.[5] So, I figured that the greatest passage must be located in the Gospels. Alright, but which one? Matthew, Mark, Luke, or John?

That was also an easy choice for me: The Gospel of John. The other three Gospels follow more or less the same story line (hence, they're known collectively as the "synoptic Gospels"). The Gospel of John is different. It blazes its own trail. And what a trail it blazes! A tradition in the Church gives it the symbol of an eagle, because it's the Gospel that soars. It's the last Gospel, written by the apostle who was "loved by the Lord above the others,"[6] a Gospel that's the fruit of his lifelong contemplation on the mystery of the Word made flesh. It's the Gospel recommended by great saints and mystics as containing the deepest riches of our faith and mysteries of Christ.[7]

Alright, so that narrowed it down for me. I'd find "the greatest passage" in the Gospel of John. But where specifically? John has 21 chapters, and they're all filled to the brim. Well, the

Gospel of John is divided into two major sections: the Book of Signs and the Book of Glory. The Book of Signs is about how Jesus reveals himself to the world and to "his own" and how they don't receive him. The Book of Glory is about how Jesus reveals his glory to those who do receive him. Of course, I want to receive him and behold his glory, so I chose the Book of Glory.

Now, the Book of Glory is divided into three sections: The Farewell Discourse, the Passion and Death, and the Resurrection. So, where's the greatest passage? I chose to look in the Farewell Discourse, which spans chapters 13-17. Why? Because that's where all the glory of the suffering, death, and Resurrection is explained. More specifically, it contains Jesus' last words to his disciples on the very night he was betrayed, right before he plunges into the dark "hour" of his suffering and death. In other words, it contains Jesus' precious last words, his "farewell" to his disciples — and he truly saves the best for last. Just as dying people often save their most meaningful declarations of love for the end, so also Jesus reserves his most sublime and intimate teaching for these chapters. For instance, in them, we find "the new commandment" (13:34), "the vine and the branches" (15:5), and "the way, and the truth, and the life" (14:6).

After I had already decided to limit my search for "the greatest passage" to the Farewell Discourse, I read something in the *Diary of St. Faustina* that seemed to confirm for me that this discourse truly hides a mystery that's unsurpassed in beauty. Referring to the place of the last discourse as the "Cenacle" (also known as the "upper room" of the Last Supper), the great mystic of Divine Mercy writes:

> Holy Hour. — Thursday. During this hour of prayer, Jesus allowed me to enter the Cenacle, and I was witness to what happened there. However, I was most deeply moved when, before the Consecration, Jesus raised His eyes to heaven and entered into a mysterious conversation with His Father. It is only in eternity that we shall really understand that

moment. His eyes were like two flames; His face was radiant, white as snow; His whole personage full of majesty, His soul full of longing. At the moment of Consecration, love rested satiated — the sacrifice fully consummated. Now only the external ceremony of death will be carried out — external destruction; the essence [of it] is in the Cenacle. Never in my whole life had I understood this mystery so profoundly as during that hour of adoration. Oh, how ardently I desire that the whole world would come to know this unfathomable mystery![8]

What is this unfathomable mystery? What is the great longing of Jesus? What is his profound conversation with the Father? I believe that this remarkable passage from the *Diary* is referring to the climax of the entire Farewell Discourse: Chapter 17. In my opinion, this chapter is the greatest in all of Sacred Scripture. Why? Because in this chapter, Jesus is no longer speaking his last, glorious words of love to his disciples. Rather, even more glorious still, he's speaking his last, glorious words of love to his heavenly Father. It's in this chapter that the veil is lifted, the veil that covers the eternal exchange of love of the Most Holy Trinity. It's in this chapter that, more than anywhere else, we get a glimpse into the fundamental longing of the Heart of Jesus, precisely as he ardently expresses it to his Father.

And what is it that Jesus longs for? What is his burning desire? *That we all be one.* He wants us all to participate in the communion of love of the Most Holy Trinity. Read chapter 17. It's all there. Jesus expresses his desire over and over in different ways, poetically weaving a kind of tapestry of communion and love. For instance, he prays to the Father, "that they may all be one; even as thou, Father, art in me, and I in thee, that they also may be in us" (vs. 21). The beauty of the expression in verse after glorious verse doesn't dilute the clarity of the desire: Jesus wants us to be one with him in the Most Holy Trinity.

But again, remember: My quest was to find one specific passage to memorize, not a whole chapter. No problem. The last verses of the chapter get to the heart of the matter, and they contain what I believe is the most beautiful passage in all of Sacred Scripture, a passage that reveals the mystery at the Heart of the Word made flesh and the deepest expression of communion:

> Father, I desire that they also, whom thou hast given me, may be with me where I am, to behold my glory which thou has given me in thy love for me before the foundation of the world. O righteous Father, the world has not known thee, but I have known thee, and these know that thou hast sent me. I made known to them thy name, and I will make it known, that the love with which thou hast loved me may be in them and I in them (Jn 17:24-26).

Let's now attempt to at least scratch the surface of this stunning passage.

First, it begins with Jesus expressing his desire. Think of it: What is the burning desire of the Heart of Jesus immediately before he enters into his Passion? (The very next verse begins chapter 18 and the Passion narrative.) He tells us right here. It's that we may be with Jesus where, he says, "I am." Actually, it might make more sense to write it as follows: "to be with me where I AM." This is because Jesus is using the divine name that's revealed in the book of Exodus, "I AM" (see Ex 3:14), and he wants us to be with him where "I AM" — in other words, where he is the eternal God in glory. In fact, he wants us to behold his glory that the Father gave him "before the foundation of the world." Put differently, he wants us to see and to participate in the eternal life and love of the Most Holy Trinity that was before the ages.

Jesus goes on in the next sentence to explain this desire not in terms of the divine name that he used in the previous sentence, the one from the Old Testament (I AM), but rather in terms of the divine name as he himself reveals it in the New

Testament: "*Father*." This is the name he means when he says, "I made known to them thy name and I will make it known." Jesus made his Father's name known to his disciples when he taught them how to pray, beginning with the words "Our Father" (Mt 6:9). And he fulfills his word "and I will make it known" immediately after the Resurrection, when he tells Mary Magdalene to tell the disciples (whom he significantly calls "my brethren"), "I am ascending to my Father and your Father" (Jn 20:17).

To reveal the name of the Father is, in a sense, the whole reason why the Word became flesh, as the very last verse of the prologue to John's Gospel suggests: "No one has ever seen God; it is the only-begotten Son, who is in the bosom of the Father, he has made him known" (1:18). Moreover, this "making the Father known" needs to be understood in the Biblical sense of "to know," similar to "Adam knew Eve his wife, and she conceived" (Gen 4:1). "To know" in the Biblical sense, expresses deep, life-giving intimacy and communion. Such "communion with the Father" is, according to Pope Benedict XVI, "the true center of [Jesus'] personality; without it, we cannot understand him at all."[9]

The communion of the Father, Son, and Holy Spirit[10] provides the background and meaning to everything we will now cover. To bring us into this communion is the deepest desire in the Heart of Jesus, and it explains *everything*.

THE THREE POINTS OF COMMUNION

In the introduction, I began by saying that I'm going to try to make this crash course in theology simple and easy. Well, you can't get much simpler than three points. In what follows, we're going to make a three-point meditation on what I call "the three points of communion." And these three points explain everything. Really. They're a kind of a summary of the *Catechism* and of the theology behind it. They're not a substitute for the *Catechism*, but chances are most of us aren't going to be reading that big book cover to cover anytime soon. I hope we will, but until then, here's a summary for us to reflect on:

> POINT ONE: Communion with the Trinity
> (Our final end)
>
> POINT TWO: Transforming Communion with Christ
> (Our immediate end)
>
> POINT THREE: Mission of Communion
> (Our mission)

Again, the rest of this book will simply be a meditation on these three points. That's all. So let's get started with the first one.

[By the way, I will frequently refer to each point of communion as a "part." For instance, I'll say something like, "Back in Part One, we learned … ." In this case, "Part One" would simply refer to "Point One."]

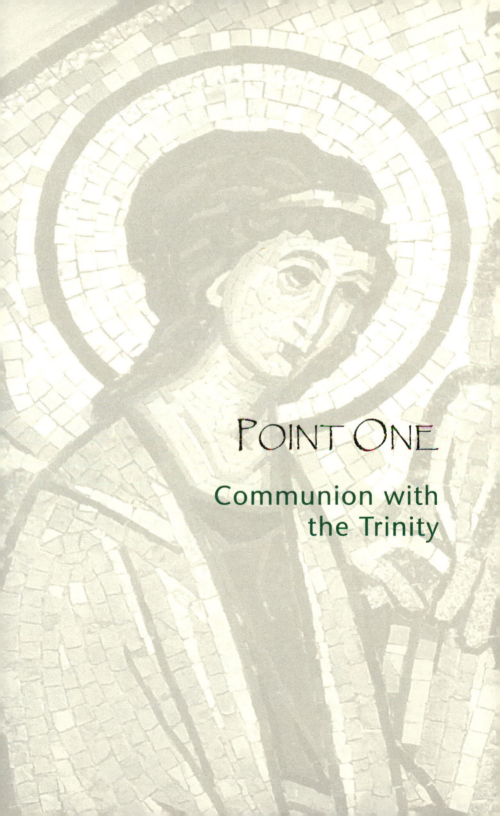

POINT ONE

Communion with the Trinity

The *Catechism of the Catholic Church* teaches that, by far, the most important mystery of our faith is the Most Holy Trinity:

> The mystery of the Most Holy Trinity is the central mystery of Christian faith and life. It is the mystery of God in himself. It is therefore the source of all the other mysteries of faith, the light that enlightens them. It is the most fundamental and essential teaching in the "hierarchy of the truths of faith."[11]

Since the goal of this book is to take us to the very heart of theology, it looks like we've come to the right place: The Trinity really is the "one thing." It's the mystery of our faith that's the source of all the other mysteries and shines light on them all. Alright, but what exactly *is* the Trinity?

The *Catechism* describes the Trinity as God's "innermost secret," which is that "God himself is an eternal exchange of love, Father, Son, and Holy Spirit … ." The *Catechism* then goes on to say something mind-blowingly amazing, "… and he has destined us to share in that exchange."[12] When this last line really hits home, it can transform our lives. We'll reflect on this powerful idea in due course, but first, let's try to appreciate the Trinity itself more deeply.

CHAPTER ONE

To Appreciate the Trinity

*P*ICTURING PAGODAS. In the introduction to his book *The Everlasting Man*, G.K. Chesterton makes a sharp observation: Because Christianity is so close and familiar to us Westerners, we've lost a sense of wonder for the sheer beauty of the story. In other words, we've heard so many times that God became man, seen so many images of Jesus dying on the Cross, and read so often that he rose from the dead that it doesn't always move us as it should. As Chesterton puts it, "It is almost impossible to make the facts vivid, because the facts are familiar; and for fallen men it is often true that familiarity is fatigue."[13] As an antidote to this ill, he proposes that we picture the story of Christianity in an unfamiliar context, such as in the midst of "Chinese pagodas." Thus, he writes:

> I am convinced that if we could tell the supernatural story of Christ word for word as of a Chinese hero, call him the Son of Heaven instead of the Son of God, and trace his rayed nimbus in the gold thread of Chinese embroideries or the gold lacquer of Chinese pottery, instead of in the gold leaf of our own old Catholic paintings, there would be a unanimous testimony to the spiritual purity of the story. ... We [would] admire the chivalry of the Chinese conception of a god who fell from the sky to fight the dragons and save the wicked from being devoured by their own fault and folly.[14]

Chesterton is right. We've gotten used to hearing the Christian mysteries, and we've lost some sense of awe for their greatness and glory. But while his proposal makes sense regarding the mysteries of faith that we can picture in our minds (the Incarnation, the suffering, death, and Resurrection of Christ), it doesn't work so well regarding the mysteries that are entirely spiritual. The Trinity is one such mystery.

So, if we can't picture the Trinity in the midst of Chinese pagodas, how do we take the step back from it that Chesterton recommends? How do we make the familiar idea that God is one-in-three seem not so familiar? How do we appreciate this mystery as if for the first time?

I propose that we imagine the alternatives, that we picture life without the Trinity. Specifically, I suggest that we put ourselves in ancient Greece and listen to the philosophers. They'll help us better realize the difference that one God in three divine persons really makes.

*T*HE GOD OF THE PHILOSOPHERS. It's 440 BC. We're right in the middle of the Golden Age of Greek culture. We've never heard of the Trinity, but we believe there is a God. We're wearied by the endless tales of Greek mythology that depict God as so many gods who, sadly, are just like us: imperfect, petty, and oftentimes tragic. Indeed, something inside us wants more than the jealousy of Hera or the arrogance of Zeus. So we go to the philosophers.

First, we go to Socrates, one of the greatest lovers of wisdom. We ask him about God, and he simply tells us about the gods: Zeus, Poseidon, Apollo, and Athena. As we begin to walk away disappointed, he calls out, "But there are also the Ideas, the greatest of which is the Idea of the Good." Hearing this, we turn back to him with full interest and attention. As he begins to speak to us about the Ideas, his face takes on an expression of reverence and awe, especially as he describes the Idea of the Good as

> ... the universal author of all things beautiful and right, parent of light and of the lord of light in this visible world, and the immediate source of reason and truth in the intellectual; and that this is the power upon which he who would act rationally, either in public or private life must have his eye fixed.[15]

"Ah, thank you, Socrates, so this Idea of the Good must be God, right?" Socrates remains silent. He doesn't say. He waves goodbye and walks away. Like so many of the other Greek philosophers, he seems reluctant to dispense with the gods he grew up with. No matter. The good news is that we're on to something here. We've now got a glimpse of something greater than the all-too-human gods of Greek mythology. So what's next? Well, let's fast-forward 100 years and speak with the other giant of ancient Greek philosophy: Aristotle.

It's now 340 BC. We're in Macedon at the palace of King Philip II, waiting outside the royal classroom. Inside, Aristotle is busy tutoring Philip's bright teenage son, Prince Alexander. When the lesson finishes, the future great conqueror of empires rushes out, passing us by in a blur of youthful energy. Then, Aristotle slowly emerges. Approaching him, we ask, "Excuse us, venerable teacher, but would you mind giving one more lesson today? We want to know about God, and we're wearied by the usual stories of the gods." With a gesture of his hand, he graciously welcomes us in.

Once inside, we explain what we've learned from Socrates, "He told us about the Idea of the Good, but he didn't tell us if it's God." Hearing this, Aristotle's face brightens with the pleasure of one who knows he's just won a debate as he says, "The Idea of the Good is not God, because there's something more than the Ideas. Ideas require a thinker, and God is a self-subsisting, solitary Act of thinking."

"And what does he think about?" we ask.

"Well, God thinks only of the best thing, which is himself."

"But does he think about us and the world?"

"No. He has no interest in us or the world."

Let's stop right there and reflect. Many would argue that Aristotle is the greatest philosopher in human history. (Even St. Thomas Aquinas, one of the greatest theologians in the history of the Church, gave him the compliment of calling him "The Philosopher.") So, one might say he represents the farthest that natural reason could take man in his attempts to know God. And what is the best that human reason could do? A solitary God who thinks only of himself.

Remember now, Aristotle's God is far more refined than the flippant gods of Greek mythology, and his theology even goes beyond that of Socrates's utterly abstract and impersonal Idea of the Good. Yet his theology poses a big problem. Why?

Because as the gods go, so we go. In other words, if they're capricious, fickle, and smug — so are we more likely to be. If God is solitary, impersonal, and aloof — so are we more likely to be. And moreover, it's all so sad. For just as a cold, dreary day can darken our mood and make us mean, so believing in a cruel or heartless God can make us constantly cower in fear and be bitterly harsh with others. On the other hand, just as a bright, shining sun high in the sky can lift our spirits and make us beam with joy, so belief in a warm, loving, benevolent God can make our joy complete and our hearts sing with a gratitude and love that overflows to others.

Despite the benefits that derive from believing in such a good and gracious God, the best human minds couldn't come up with it. They all came up short, and their gods ended up simply being reflections of themselves. God himself had to come to our rescue and reveal to us his "innermost secret." And what a secret! It goes well beyond our wildest dreams, perfectly satisfies the deepest longing of our hearts, and brightens our lives better than the Aegean summer sun. Let's now reflect on how this secret perfectly fits with our deepest desire and how it can make us truly happy.

*T*HE *GOD WHO IS A COMMUNION OF LOVE.* In our heart of hearts, what do we long for above all else? Love. We all want to love and to be loved. Specifically, we long for the communion of love. Look around — our culture makes it so obvious. Almost every song on the radio is about love (or a counterfeit of love). So much of what people say, do, and wear is really just an effort to be loveable, attractive, and accepted. Indeed, we hunger to be in communion with others and seek it out in so many forms, be they good or bad. For instance, we seek it in friendship, family, Facebook, fantasy, or fornication. With desire, we may run to these things while with fright, we run away from what seem to be the alternatives (loneliness and alienation).

Given our situation of being communion addicts, God is the perfect fit! He himself fits the hole in our hearts, for we pine for the communion of love, and God himself is the Communion of Love. We've often heard the "good news" that Jesus died for our sins — thank God and amen! But perhaps we haven't yet come to realize the good news that's just as good, namely, that *God is Trinity*. Put differently, he's the Communion of Love that we long for.

Let's think about this for a minute. Over and over, we've heard that the Trinity is a mystery. And many of us probably take mystery to mean "something we can't understand." Wrong. We can understand it, even if we can't *comprehend* it. In other words, the Trinity makes sense (we can understand it), but we'll never fully get to the bottom of the sense it makes (we can't comprehend it). We can always go deeper into the sense of the Trinity. Problem is, we often don't even try to scratch the surface of the sense it makes. But its sense speaks right to the core of our hearts, to our longing for the communion of love. So, we'd do well to reflect on the sense it makes, which has the power to make us mind-blowingly happy.

Now this makes sense: If we had to invent a God who would make us perfectly happy, we wouldn't invent the ancient Greek gods, and we wouldn't invent Aristotle's God. Rather, we'd invent the Trinity. Of course, nobody did (and actually, as the Church teaches, *nobody could have done it*[16]), but it's one of those things that in hindsight, might make us say, "Oh, yeah. That makes perfect sense. Why didn't Aristotle think of that?" Look at it this way, starting with the basic truth: We long for the communion of love. But a communion of love takes at least two. Thus, our "invented God" would need to be at least two. Problem is, God must be one (Aristotle figured that much out). Otherwise, we're left with the cartoonish Gods of Greek mythology — or worse, the stick-and-dirt deities of primitive religion.

Okay, so our ideal God must be one, but if he is Love itself, it would seem that he would also need to be at least two, for love is about relationship, and relationship involves more than one. Alright then, let's look at a God who is one-in-two, a "Holy Bi-nity."

On the one hand, this God is kind of disappointing, because relationships of two tend to be of the romantic kind, and those in such relationships often jealously guard their love. "Two is company and three's a crowd," as they say. Nevertheless, it would seem that a Holy Bi-nity would make us at least somewhat happy. It would give us the kind of contentment and warmth that some people feel when they watch a royal wedding. Of course, they're not actually involved with the royal couple, but as they watch the wedding on TV, they'll squeeze clenched hands to their hearts and get gushy about seeing the royals in love. So it would be with a Holy Bi-nity: We'd be glad to see that Mr. and Mrs. God are so in love with each other, but we'd still remain just outside observers.

Now here's an idea. What if our ideal God were not one-in-two but *one-in-three*? Okay, this gets us excited. It's kind of like the excitement people feel when, a few months after the royal wedding, they hear that a royal baby is on its way. Better yet, it's like the excitement when the baby finally arrives and people are gooo-ing and gaaa-ing over it, wishing they could hold it, and so on. It's especially the excitement of the grandparents who come rushing in. Of course, grandma and grandpa had loved seeing their child and his or her spouse happily married and in love, but when the baby comes, look out! Then they're over at the baby's house all the time. They want to caress the baby, kiss it, and give it presents.

In other words, while the intimacy of a husband and wife (marital love) is rightfully closed off to and exclusive of others, the intimacy of a mom, dad, and baby (family love) is rightfully open to others. This kind of family love is expansive and includes others, including other children. It's a fruitful love that multiplies. So, while a marital two is blissful, somewhat exclusive company, a familial three is a happy crowd that grows.

Thus, if we could come up with a God who would make us truly happy, our best bet would be to make one who is at least one-in-three. For, then, we'd have a God who is a Family of Love and whose love could reach out to us in our existential loneliness, saying, "Come, join the Family!"[17] Of course, this is as far as our hypothetical invention could go. We don't know that God would invite us to share in his inner life — and after the fall, it's definitely doubtful. But what if ... What if the God who is the Communion of Love invited us to join the Family? This would make us incomprehensibly happy.

Well, something beyond our wildest dreams is true: God is Trinity, an eternal Family of Love. What's more, he invites us to share in his own divine life. If we accept, we'll enjoy communion with him, and it will make us incredibly happy. In the next chapter, let's reflect more deeply on this wonderful news and soak in the joy.

CHAPTER TWO

To Share in the Trinity's Exchange of Love

Alright, now I don't mean to be a killjoy, but I think we should organize this section around a more formal theology lesson. Don't worry, though. It's a good one and not too complicated. In fact, it's one of the best lessons I ever learned during my marathon time in the seminary. It has to do with the meaning of salvation (or, as the *Catechism* calls it, "justification").

According to the Catechism, the gift of salvation is the "most excellent work of God's love," and in the opinion of St. Augustine, "It is a greater work than the creation of heaven and earth."[18] Again, as I said in the beginning, we're trying here to get to the heart of theology, and based on these quotes, it looks like we're on the right track. So what is salvation?

Salvation is two steps. The first is called *redemption* (or "restoration"). This is the part of salvation that has to do with the forgiveness of our sins and our restoration to a state similar to where we were before the fall. The second step is called *glorification*. This has to do with our being raised up to a state much, much higher than before the fall, a state of sharing in the Trinity's own exchange of love. To fully appreciate this second step, we need to come to better understand the first. So, let's start by looking at redemption.

*R*EDEMPTION. We're all sinners, born under the power of sin (see Rom 3:9-12). This power took hold of us because of the fall of our first parents, Adam and Eve. The *Catechism* describes their first sin as follows:

> Man, tempted by the devil, let his trust in his Creator die in his heart and, abusing his freedom, disobeyed God's command. This is what man's first sin consisted of. All subsequent sin would be disobedience toward God and lack of trust in his goodness.
>
> In that sin man *preferred* himself to God and by that very act scorned him. He chose himself over and against God, against the requirements of his creaturely

status and therefore against his own good. Created in a state of holiness, man was destined to be fully "divinized" by God in glory. Seduced by the devil, he wanted to "be like God," but "without God, before God, and not in accordance with God."[19]

As a result of this original sin, we all suffer its unfortunate effect, namely, *broken communion*. We find this break in communion in four different relationships: with God, with ourselves, with our neighbor, and with the rest of creation. The most fundamental break, the one that leads to everything else falling apart, is the break in communion with God.

One of my professors in the seminary, Peter Kreeft, explained this with an unforgettable image. He said it's like a set of iron rings suspended in the air and held together, because the first one is touching a powerful magnet, which represents God. When the first ring (man's soul, which includes smaller, interior rings) pulls away from the magnet, all the other rings (his other relationships) break away and fall to the floor. Let's now unpack this image.

Before the Fall   **After the Fall**

GOD

MAN'S SOUL

REASON, WILL, PASSIONS

MAN'S BODY

NEIGHBOR

REST OF CREATION

Man's soul is the first ring, and when, through sin, he pulls away from the magnet (God), he immediately suffers an effect in his soul. Not only does he lose the magnetizing energy of original holiness and divine friendship, but his heart itself becomes wounded. We see this wound in Adam and Eve right after the fall, "They become afraid of the God of whom they have conceived a distorted image — that of a God jealous of his prerogatives."[20] We see this false fear active in them when they run and hide from God as he comes strolling into the Garden (see Gen 3:8). We see this same false fear in ourselves when we, too, run from God and avoid him after we sin.

The loss of the "magnetism" of God's grace in our souls also makes our souls themselves begin to fall apart. It's kind of like there's a set of smaller rings suspended within the first ring of the soul. These smaller rings are our reason, will, and passions (appetites). Before the fall, all these smaller rings were joined together and remained in harmony and communion. After the fall, they're pulled apart: Reason becomes darkened such that it doesn't clearly see the good; the will becomes fickle and weak, and the passions become wild, unpredictable, and difficult to control. Describing this disharmony within him as "sin" and "the flesh," St. Paul unforgettably expresses the common experience of fallen humanity:

> I do not understand my own actions. For I do not do what I want, but I do the very thing I hate. … I can will what is right, but I cannot do it. For I do not do the good I want, but the evil I do not want is what I do. Now if I do what I do not want, it is no longer I that do it, but sin which dwells within me.
>
> So I find it to be a law that when I want to do right, evil lies close at hand. For I delight in the law of God, in my inmost self, but I see in my members another law at war with the law of my mind and making me captive to the law of sin which dwells in my members. Wretched man that I am! Who will deliver me from this body of death? (Rom 7:15, 17-24).

That last line leads us to the second ring: *the human body*. Before the fall, the body was to remain in communion with the soul (the first ring). In other words, if Adam and Eve had not sinned, they never would have experienced death, which is the separation of body and soul. But when the first ring (the soul) separates from the force of the magnet (the living God), it can no longer stay in communion with the second ring (the body). Thus, after the first sin, the body and soul begin to separate, which is manifested as aging and eventually death. Put differently, after the first sin, everyone must die a physical death of separation of body and soul. Worse still is the "second death," known as hell. In other words, unless God does something to bring us back into communion with himself before we die, then when we do die, we will also suffer the terrible second death: eternal alienation from God.

Next comes the third ring: *our neighbor*. What happens when the third ring breaks off from the others? Tension in human relationships. This includes the most intimate of human relationships, namely, that between man and woman. The *Catechism* teaches that, as a result of the fall, "The union of man and woman becomes subject to tensions, their relations henceforth marked by lust and domination."[21] All the other human relationships suffer as well. For, after man's break with God, so many forms of selfishness and egotism take over the human heart, causing division, injustice, misery, and war. Indeed, when man breaks communion with God, he quickly sets himself up as his own god and sees himself as the center of the universe, which causes a multitude of evils. As the earlier citation from the *Catechism* pointed out, this was the very reason why man chose to break from God, "He wanted to 'be like God,' but 'without God, before God, and not in accordance with God.'"

The fourth ring is the *rest of creation*. The *Catechism* observes that now, as a result of original sin, "visible creation has become alien and hostile to man."[22] Instead of the original harmony with creation, now wild animals maul men, men torture animals and pollute the environment, and natural disasters destroy life and property. The earth still sustains humanity, but it yields its fruit only through the sweat of toilsome labor and by the blood that flows from the pricks of so many forms of "thorns and thistles" (see Gen 3:18).

What a mess! Seven rings scattered on the ground in a mix of blood, sweat, and tears. But thanks be to God, for Jesus Christ our Redeemer forgives us our sins, restores us to communion with God, and gives us the grace to re-enter into communion with ourselves, our neighbors, and even with the rest of creation. In later sections, we'll look more closely at how this restoration is accomplished. Right now, let's turn our attention to the second part of salvation.

*G*LORIFICATION. The second part of salvation is called *glorification*. Unfortunately, this part is often overlooked, and I think it's because *redemption* often gets all the attention. Don't get me wrong, we surely should rejoice that Christ heals us and forgives us our sins, but there's more to get excited about — much, much more.

When I was a child, I remember being taught in my Catechism class that if we follow the commandments and love God with all our mind, heart, soul, and strength, then we'll get to go to heaven and behold God in "the Beatific Vision." On hearing this, I pictured heaven as all the saints sitting on some massive grandstand, looking up in the sky at the greatest fireworks display in the cosmos. In other words, I figured that heaven would be a spectator sport: us watching God do what God does. Well, it's not that. Heaven is our *participation* in the very life and love of the Most Holy Trinity. So, we won't simply be "watching the game." We'll be playing in it — or, as C.S. Lewis puts it, we'll be in the "Great Dance" with God and with one another.[23] The point is, we'll literally be part of the action.

I have to admit that back when I was a child, I wasn't quite satisfied with the idea of heaven as a spectator sport. Later in life, I read a passage from an essay by Lewis that spoke directly to my dissatisfaction:

> We do not want merely to see beauty, though, God knows, even that is bounty enough. We want some-

thing else which can hardly be put into words — to be
united with the beauty we see, to pass into it, to receive
it into ourselves, to bathe in it, to become part of it. ...
At present ... [w]e cannot mingle with the splendors
we see. But all the leaves of the New Testament are
rustling with the rumor that it will not always be so.
Someday, God willing, we shall get in.[24]

Specifically, we will get "in" *on the action*. Again, in heaven,
we'll literally be part of the glorious action that we'll also behold.
And what is the glorious action of the Trinity? As we've already
heard from the *Catechism*, it's an "eternal exchange of love."
The Father eternally pours himself out in a total gift of self-giving
love to the Son. The Son eternally receives that love from the
Father, beholds his caring countenance, and responds with his
own act of self-giving love to the Father. Meanwhile, the
proceeding love between the Father and the Son is the Holy
Spirit. So, we'll be participating in this eternal exchange of
mutual, self-giving love. Indeed, God "has destined us to share
in that exchange."[25] He desires to make us partakers of his
own divine nature (see 2 Pet 1:4). He wants to fully "divinize"
us in glory.[26]

Unfortunately, many Christians have never heard of this
"divinization" idea before, and it may seem too good and
glorious to be true. Well, it is true. It's been the teaching of the
Church from the very beginning. In fact, a major theme in the
writings of the early Fathers of the Church is the "divinization"
of man, the idea that in saving us, God wants to make us share
in his own divine life. In fact, the theme was so pervasive in the
teachings of the early Church that it was incorporated into the
Liturgy,[27] and theologians coined a Latin phrase to describe it:
admirabile commercium, meaning "the marvelous exchange."
This exchange is indeed marvelous as is clear from the famous
expression of it by St. Athanasius (296-373), "God became
man that man might become god."[28] It's summarized by the
words of St. Paul, "That though he was rich, yet for your sake
he became poor, so that by his poverty you might become

rich" (2 Cor 8:9). And it's most beautifully expressed by this poetic passage penned by St. Gregory of Nyssa (335-394):

> Man, as a being, is of no account; he is dust, grass, vanity. But once he is adopted by the God of the universe as a son, he becomes part of the family of that Being, whose excellence and greatness no one can see, hear, or understand. What words, thoughts, or flight of the spirit can praise the superabundance of this grace? Man surpasses his nature: mortal, he becomes immortal; perishable, he becomes imperishable; fleeting, he becomes eternal; human, he becomes divine.[29]

If this idea of our divinization doesn't make us shake in our shoes with joy, we haven't quite gotten it yet. That's alright. This idea is a tremendous weight for our minds to try to lift: the awesome weight of our hope of glory. But we should strive to lift it. We should ponder it in our hearts. For, as the gift offered becomes more and more real to us, we'll occupy ourselves less and less with the petty distractions of life that currently hold so much of our attention.

In his marvelous essay, *The Weight of Glory*, C.S. Lewis invites us to make it real, to consider "the staggering nature of the rewards promised in the Gospels."[30] Yet, knowing that we do not consider these promises enough, Lewis gently chastises himself and us:

> We are half-hearted creatures, fooling about with drink and sex and ambition when infinite joy is offered us, like an ignorant child who wants to go on making mud pies in a slum because he cannot imagine what is meant by the offer of a holiday at the sea. We are far too easily pleased.[31]

Now, someone might say, "Yes, I may be too easily pleased, but at least my little mud pies are right here before me, and they keep me quite contented. I'd rather have them than the pie in the sky that I can't eat until I die." There's a problem with this objection. The "infinite joy" that Lewis is talking about isn't just pie in the sky. The joy he means seeps in *now* as the greatness of the gift sinks into our minds and hearts. We drink deeply of it as our prayer matures, and life becomes bathed in a peaceful light. But this takes time and the discipline of prayer, and we may not be there yet. Not to worry. Even if we don't quite get it yet, the angels do, and they thank God on our behalf while he patiently waits for us to realize the gift he offers. Moreover, their example helps us appreciate the gift and experience the joy.

*T*HE *ANGELS STAND IN AWE — THE DEMONS BURN WITH ENVY*. Regarding the example of the angels, I'm thinking especially of the angels of the Nativity. On that incredible night when our Savior was born for us, humanity didn't fully grasp what was happening. But the angels got it. First, an angel of the Lord announces the good news to the shepherds:

> Be not afraid; for behold, I bring you good news of a great joy which will come to all the people; for to you is born this day in the city of David a Savior, who is Christ the Lord. And this will be a sign for you: you will find a babe wrapped in swaddling cloths and laying in a manger (Lk 2:10-12).

Then, after this announcement, all the other angels can't seem to contain themselves. "Suddenly," the text says, "a multitude of the heavenly host" breaks forth from the heights and appears. At this moment, I imagine them as so many friends at the biggest surprise party in the history of the cosmos. For long millennia, they'd been hiding in the dark, impatiently waiting for just the right moment to let out an explosion of joy. Finally, the cue has come: the announcement of the birth of the Savior. And again, that's when *all heaven* breaks loose. A multitude of angels bursts into ecstatic song and praise, extolling the goodness of God who has descended not only to forgive the sins of humanity but to raise humanity up to God's own divine life. They must have been beside themselves with wonder and joy at the mercy of God. Marveling at how low

God stoops to save man, their song of praise and adoration rises up to heaven, "Glory to God in the highest!"

Now, what a gift we have in the Church that at every Sunday Mass (outside of the seasons of Advent and Lent), during the Gloria, we're reminded of the marvelous moment of the angels' joyful wonder at man's salvation, a moment that should rouse us from our spiritual slumber to rightfully respond to the "good news" of our salvation with our own joy. Again, this is the good news not only that God forgives us our sins (for good reason, the Gloria is preceded by the Penitential Rite) but that he raises us up to his own divine life and glory, to a place that's even higher than the angels!

That the angels rejoice in the gift of salvation given to man is a testimony to their humility. For, if we think about it, the extent to which God shows his mercy to humanity can truly be taken as a scandal. In saving us, God raises us higher than the angels. Think of this for a moment: higher than *the angels*. According to the natural order of creation, angels are vastly superior to human beings. As pure spirits, their intellects far surpass our own. Moreover, when they appear, they are so wonderfully terrible that we may need to be told, "be not afraid," and may have to fight the temptation to fall on our faces and worship them, mistaking them for God (see Rev 22:8-9). Yes, the angels are absolutely fantastic. Yet God wants to divinize man, not the angels. He has destined man alone to partake of his own divine nature, and this has potential for great scandal.[32]

Some theologians believe that man's glorious destiny was indeed a scandal. They say that the revelation of man's destiny is what caused, at the beginning of time, the fall of one-third of the angels. Such theologians speculate that before the creation of humanity, the angels were given a test. They were shown that the Word would become flesh, that he would become man, and that by doing so, he would raise up human nature even higher than that of the highest of angels. This struck the pride of the greatest of the angels, Lucifer, about whom Isaiah speaks:

> How art thou fallen from heaven, O Lucifer, who didst rise in the morning? How art thou fallen to the earth, that didst wound the nations? And thou saidst in thy heart: I will ascend into heaven, I will exalt my throne above the stars of God, I will sit in the mountain of the covenant, in the sides of the north. I will ascend above the height of the clouds, I will be like the most High. But yet thou shalt be brought down to hell, into the depth of the pit (Isaiah 14:12-15).[33]

Notice how Lucifer kept repeating in his heart, "I ... I ... I." It seems he was saying, "No! Not those puny creatures (humanity) but *me*! I want to be the one to ascend to the divine nature, I want to exalt my throne above the angels, I want to be the one raised up to take part in the divine action." And then, according to one tradition of the Church, Lucifer made one further "I" statement before being banished to hell: "*I will not serve.*" In other words, he decided he wouldn't humble himself to serve a creature of a lower order of creation than himself, even if that "creature" were really the Incarnate God himself. And again, a third of the angels (who are now demons) went down with Lucifer (who is now Satan).

The lesson of the fallen angels is a sobering gift for us. It should help us realize just how good and generous God is to us fallen human beings. It should remind us that Satan and his demons hate us and literally burn with hellish envy. It should remind us that in their rebellious rage, they would like nothing more than to have us lose the gift that they once coveted. It should remind us that they would like nothing more than to drag us down with them "into the depth of the pit," that they'd like nothing more than to get back at God by preventing him from raising us up to the thrones of glory that Lucifer had so perversely cherished.

I suggest that part of Satan's strategy is to make us never realize the good that God offers us. For instance, he tries to distract us from God's gift of glory with the promise of mere mud pies. On the other hand, I believe it's the strategy of the good angels to suddenly burst into song and remind us that we are called to "Gloria! Gloria! Gloria!" And it is all ours, if only we, unlike Lucifer, will love and serve God, who comes to us in the greatest humility.

COMMUNION WITH THE TRINITY: OUR FINAL, JOYFUL END. Thus, we have a choice before us: communion or alienation, life or death, eternal bliss or eternal hell. Do we want to serve God or serve ourselves? Will we do God's will or our own? Do we choose to be self-giving or selfish? The heart of the question really is this: Do we want to be truly happy?

During my senior year in high school, I experienced a profound deepening in my Catholic faith, a kind of conversion. Then, when I entered college, I spent a lot of time trying to put it all together, trying to figure out how to make what I'd discovered about Christ and his Church more fully the center of my life. This wasn't easy. I'd grown up in the fast-paced, fun-loving, and hedonistic culture of Southern California, and many of my thought patterns and attitudes didn't yet match my newly re-found faith. One day, one of my friends handed me a short book entitled, *The Gospel of Life*, by Pope John Paul II. Reading it totally changed my life.

I think what did it for me was that the Pope answered "the big question" in a simple and clear-cut way. He basically asked, "What is the meaning of life?" And then, he gave the answer: *self-giving love*. John Paul repeated this simple answer over and over throughout the book: "Life finds its meaning when it is given as a gift. The meaning of life is self-giving love." This struck me so profoundly because it was the exact opposite answer from what I'd learned from my Southern California culture. That culture, which John Paul would call "a culture of death," said that the meaning of life is found in selfishness, pleasure-seeking, and doing whatever you want. It said, "If you want to be happy, be selfish." On the other hand, John Paul was saying, "If you want to be happy, give yourself in love." Moreover, he added that this kind of self-giving living, when embraced by believers, would build true communion with others, a culture of life, and a civilization of love.

We'll have more to say about the culture of life in Part Three, but for now, I think the important point is for us to ponder more deeply the most crucial question: What is the meaning of life? What brings happiness? Selfishness or self-giving love? It's the latter. Look around. People who make selfishness the center of their lives are miserable. It doesn't work. It's never worked. For selfishness leads to the opposite of authentic communion, which is what we're really longing for. Yet people keep going down that road to hell.

On the other hand, people who make self-giving the center of their lives are almost always happy. Look around. The happiest people are the most generous in self-giving. It works. It's always worked, and it's how people find true communion and happiness. Simply compare St. Mother Teresa of Kolkata to a Hollywood glamor queen. Mother Teresa, who embraced a life of humility, self-giving, and sacrifice, radiated joy from within — despite her trials of darkness. The glamor queen who embraces power, pleasure, and possessions shines and sparkles on the outside but is often sad and hollow on the inside.

This life is a preparation for our final end, communion with the Most Holy Trinity. The Trinity itself is a communion of Self-Giving Lovers, and we're invited to spend eternity in their loving embrace, to share in their exchange of love. Are we ready? Probably not. That's okay, because the training time is now. The purpose of this life is to learn to love as the Trinity loves. It's the time to be trained in self-giving love. And the soul that accepts such training in this life will not only be filled with the joy that flows from giving, love, and communion, but at the end of life, they will easily enter into the overwhelming joy of the God who is Gift, Love, and Communion. On the other hand, the soul that has been confirmed in selfishness in this life just may come to see the self-giving love of the Trinity as a kind of torture. The brightness of Love will burn the eyes of that soul, and it may even prefer the dark sorrow and despair of hell, which just might hurt less.

Remember, this present, earthly life is a flash in the pan. Our time here is short. What is 80 years compared to eternity?

Close to nothing. So, we should use well the short, precious amount of time we have here and come to intimately know and love our final end: the Most Holy Trinity. That's what this point, Point One, was meant to help us do. The next point, Point Two, is dedicated to how we get there.

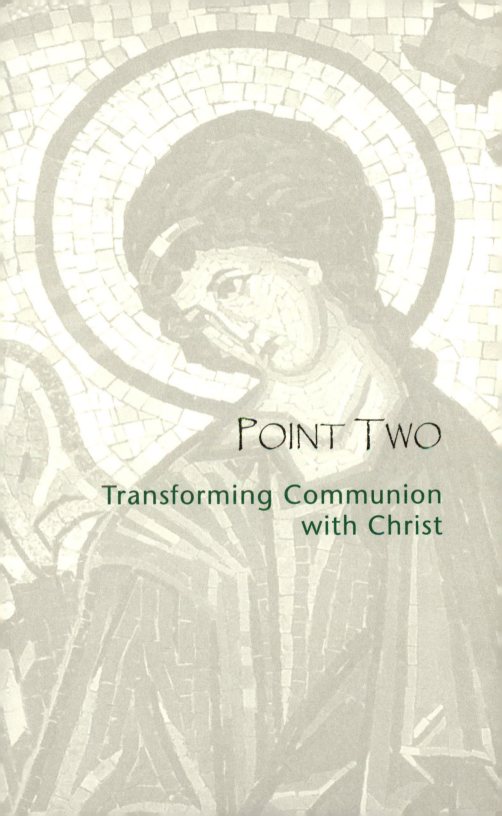

POINT TWO

Transforming Communion
with Christ

Let's review: Our final end is communion with the Trinity. In other words, our destiny is to share in the eternal exchange of love of Father, Son, and Holy Spirit.

Now, when saints make it to heaven — St. Mother Teresa of Kolkata, for example — does the Trinity suddenly grow in number? Does it become Father, Son, Holy Spirit … and Mother Teresa? In other words, if the saints are "divinized" (made to share in the divine nature), do the number of divine persons increase?

No. The Trinity remains three.

Okay, then where does Mother Teresa go? Does she take her seat on the great grandstand of the saints in heaven who fix their gaze on the Most Holy Trinity? Is heaven really a spectator sport after all?

No. While heaven is the Beatific Vision, it's also a participation in the Trinitarian action, the action of the Father pouring himself out in self-giving love to the Son, the Son responding in the same way, and then the Holy Spirit, who is Love, proceeding from the Father and the Son.

Alright, then where do the saints go? I mean, if the Trinity is still three, and the saints are sharing in the action, then where are the saints?

The saints are in Christ. He is our participation in the Trinity. In other words, our participation in the life of the Trinity is *to become one of the persons of the Trinity.* Specifically, we become "part" of *the Incarnate Son*, through the power of the Holy Spirit. When this happens, we don't become equal to Christ. Rather, we become members of his Body (see Rom 12:5; 1 Cor 12:12). Christ is the Head, and we are his members — not equal to him, but truly one with him, and we ascend through him, with him, and in him, in the unity of the Holy Spirit, to the Father. In short, we truly participate as "other Christs" in Christ's own eternal gift of self-giving love to the Father.

This chapter will focus on our transforming communion with Christ (by the power of the Holy Spirit), which brings us home to the Father. In particular, we're going to look at the ways this marvelous transformation in Christ takes place.

Now, to properly understand our transformation in (or *into*) Christ, it's helpful to see it in the context of a journey.

That's because our transformation in Christ takes us places; with Christ, we do some traveling; through Christ, we go back to the Father. Alright, but when we travel, it's often a good idea to have a map so as to know where we are and where we want to go. Therefore, before we begin looking at the ways by which we're transformed in Christ, let's first spend some time studying the map.

And by the way, while the journey surely involves some very deep theology, don't worry. For, as we walk this journey, we'll take small steps, and there's no fear of getting lost, because we'll have a clear and simple map.

CHAPTER ONE

Our Roadmap from the Trinity
and Back to the Trinity

*F*INDING THE MAP. After my first year-and-a-half in the seminary, I felt frustrated. The classes up to that point had largely been a hodge-podge of different perspectives on Catholic theology, and I couldn't make sense of them all. One professor taught this and another taught that, saying, "Rahner held this," and "von Balthasar held that." I knew it was important to know the different schools of theology and everything, but my mind was swimming in a hundred different theological opinions. So, I started a novena, and each day, I ardently begged God for wisdom, for the ability to see the big picture and not to lose the forest for the trees.

In the middle of the novena, I remember sitting in the seminary library, surrounded by books. I complained to the Lord, saying, "Lord, I don't even know where to begin. Look at all these books!" A whole shelf of books with similar spines suddenly caught my eye. I went over for a closer look. Two words jumped out at me, *Summa Theologiae.* "Oh, not that, Lord. Anything but that!" This particular version of the *Summa* was *60 volumes.* I had read short parts of this massive theological work of St. Thomas Aquinas before, and it was not easy going. Was the Lord now inviting me to dive in? After dismissing that frightening idea, I got up from my chair and went to one of the library computers. As soon as I moved the mouse, the blank screen popped to life, and I just about fell out of my chair. There on the glowing screen shined a beautiful, circular diagram that bore the heading, "Outline of the *Summa.*" Okay, I took this as a sign that I should start studying it.

The *Summa Theologiae,* meaning "summary of theology," is the greatest theological work of St. Thomas Aquinas, one of the Church's preeminent theologians. What makes it so great is not only its content but also its manner of organization. I had feared reading it so long as I simply saw it as so many thousands of pages of dense, dry, and outdated medieval theology. I came to love it as I got to know its brilliant organizational structure, known as the "The Great Circle of Being," which is what that diagram on the computer screen was all about.[34] I actually had encountered this circular structure several years before, but I think the shotgun blast of new theological perspectives blew it out of my mind. Anyway, I should say something more about that earlier encounter with the Great Circle.

While a sophomore in college, I was blessed to take the most meaningful course of all my studies. It was called "The Human Person: A Philosophical Exploration" and was taught by a visiting professor, Fr. Norris Clarke, SJ. After the first class, I knew there was something special about Fr. Clarke. Even though he was in his 80s, he had a sense of wonder like a child and an ardent love of wisdom that everyone in class seemed to recognize and appreciate. Therefore, years later, I wasn't surprised to read the following on the dedication page of a book written by one of Father's former students. It read: "*To Fr. Norris Clarke, SJ: More than a Thomist; a little Thomas.*" In other words, not only was Fr. Clarke a master of the thought of St. Thomas Aquinas, but he'd become wise like the saint. And if you asked this "little Thomas" what best summarizes and captures the essence of wisdom, he'd probably answer, "The Great Circle of Being," for he talked so animatedly about it during class. I'd now like to summarize this phenomenal idea that provides a mental map of all of philosophy, theology, and reality (as communion).

THE UNIVERSE AS JOURNEY. St. Thomas describes the idea of "The Great Circle of Being" as follows: "In the emergence of creatures from their first source is revealed a kind of circular movement, in which all things return, as to their end, back to the very place from which they had their origin in the first place."[35] In other words, all of creation (all beings) goes forth from God and then returns to God, making one big, circular movement. This circular movement, or Great Circle, can also be likened to a journey, the Great Journey, the great movement of all of creation from the Trinity and back to the Trinity.

Saint Thomas wasn't the first person to come up with the idea of "the Great Circle of Being" (or the universe as Journey). In fact, he borrowed the idea from a philosopher of late antiquity named Plotinus (205-270 AD). But even Plotinus wasn't the first to discover the idea. According to Fr. Clarke, no one person first discovered it, because it's a universal concept that everyone recognizes and expresses in various ways. He writes:

> [T]his basic image of the universe and all life, including human life, as a journey is a very old and very rich one, an archetypal image that shows up everywhere in cultures around the world, in their mythology, poetry, wisdom stories, art, philosophy, religion, etc. — and for very good reasons, since we all instinctively recognize the *journey* as the basic form of all human lives, a journey that can only be adequately described in a *story*. Thus in most religions throughout history first comes the story, only later come all the philosophical and theological reflections, commentaries, clarifications, explanations. Even in Christianity, first comes the Story, only afterwards the Creed. One of the favorite descriptions of the human being for St. Thomas and all medieval thinkers was *Homo Viator*, Man the Traveller.[36]

That last idea about "Man the Traveller" is something we may easily relate to because of its connection to another idea, namely, "pilgrimage." In St. Thomas's day, making a pilgrimage (going on a no-frills journey, usually on foot, to a sacred place or shrine) was extremely popular. It was so popular because a pilgrimage summarizes life, reminding the pilgrim that "here we have no lasting city, but we seek the city that is to come" (Heb 13:14), the New Jerusalem in heaven. In our own society, where we have a billion more comforts and luxuries than were available during the Middle Ages, it would seem that people would be less eager to be reminded that this life isn't all there is. Yet the idea of pilgrimage is still popular, at least among Catholics. At the National Shrine of The Divine Mercy, where I live, I'm amazed at the number of modern-day pilgrims who come to visit us throughout the year. Not surprisingly, the walking pilgrimage of medieval times has given way to the riding pilgrimage — usually on a big, air-conditioned bus — but people still come. For we all know deep inside that this life isn't all there is. We all know we're on a journey to the "something more" that truly satisfies, and the act of making a pilgrimage resonates with this reality.

But what about society as a whole? Is the idea of the universe as journey still widely recognized? I think so, at least by way of "story" in the sense mentioned by Fr. Clarke in the last citation, namely, that we all still instinctively recognize the basic form of human life as journey and story. Speaking of stories, I have one that illustrates this point from the days when I had the joy of listening to Fr. Clarke's enthralling lectures week after week.

One day, Father was speaking enthusiastically about the connection between the universe as journey and the human journey as story, and this is what I remember as the gist of the lesson:

> In every culture, in every society, in every family throughout history, people like to tell and listen to stories, but nobody likes a story without a point, and we love happy endings. That's because we all recognize deep inside that our lives are both gift and task, the task being that we're called to make our lives into good stories! That is, they should have a point to them, and we want them to have a happy ending.
>
> The way our lives become good stories and have happy endings is by doing God's will. God has a plan for our lives; there's a specific way that he wants us to help him bring all of creation back to himself, and our happiness comes from helping him do this according to our gifts and talents and in the way he wills for us.

One of the students, an unbeliever who heard Fr. Clarke speak this way, raised her hand and gave a remarkable response.

Here's my best attempt to repeat what she shared:

> Father, this makes sense, and painful sense. I don't
> feel that my life is a good story. Instead, it's more like
> the sitcoms I watch on TV. They're just a series of
> episodes. There's no real point to them as a whole.
> They just go from one stupid joke to another with no
> real end in mind. That's my life and the lives of so
> many of my friends: We just go around from weekend
> to weekend, doing our best to have "fun" so as to
> avoid the gnawing, inner ache of a hidden desperation.
> But you're right. There is indeed something else inside
> me that's crying out, "Make your life a good story!"
> And in my own small way, I want to help the cosmos
> return to its source.

I was deeply moved by this student's candor and openness,
and it helped me to recognize more clearly the truth of what
Father was saying. I realized that, yes, I, too, want to make
my life a "good story," or as Mother Teresa would say, "something beautiful for God." I, too, want to help God in the great
work of salvation. Yet I, too, had often found my life sadly
episodic and meaningless, and I wondered if it were already
too late for me. I thought to myself, "Could my life really become
a good story?"

I got an answer to this question the following semester
when I discovered the consoling message of Divine Mercy,
which emphasizes that *it's never too late* to say "yes" to God.
This message, which finds its basis in Sacred Scripture, teaches
that mercy can make all things new, that it can bring good out
of evil, and that it can even bring *an even greater good* out of evil.
But now I'm getting ahead of myself, so let's get back to learning about the journey and save Divine Mercy for later.

Okay, so there's this great, universal, and archetypal idea of
"the universe as Journey" that everyone seems to recognize, at
least intuitively. But perhaps the idea is still somewhat vague and
general. Well then, let's begin to home in on specifics, starting

with the point that there are two basic stages to the journey: first, *the journey out from God* and then, *the journey back to God*. In Latin, these two stages are known as *exitus* (exit) and *reditus* (return). Together, the "out and back," "*exitus* and *reditus*" make a circle, the Great Circle of Being. In what follows, we'll trace these two stages of the journey out from God and back to God.

*T*HE JOURNEY OUT. Why did God create? He surely didn't have to. After all, he was totally happy in and of himself, a perfect family of love: Father, Son, and Holy Spirit. Moreover, he knew that creating would add nothing to his glory, for it was already complete. He created, therefore, simply to share his goodness. As one beautiful line from the *Catechism* puts it, "Creatures came into existence when the key of love opened [God's] hand."[37] Now, what exactly is this love? Let's explore it.

I wonder if God's love when he creates is something like that of a young man and woman who are deeply in love. Sometimes, such a couple will take a step back from a tender embrace to gaze at each other, to take each other in with their eyes, before embracing again. We might see them do this, for instance, at a dance. There's a moment when, prompted by the man, the woman will playfully spin out from his arms — their hands still joined and eyes still gazing — and then she'll come twirling back into his embrace. There's something beautiful about that moment, as anyone who's danced with another well knows. I wonder if there was something like this going on during the act of creation.

Creation is an act of the entire Trinity: Father, Son (Word), and Holy Spirit. At the same time, each divine person creates according to his unique "property."[38] The *Catechism* sums up these "properties" by saying that the Father is the one "*from whom* all things are," the Son is the one "*through whom* all things are," and the Holy Spirit is the one "*in whom* all things are."[39] In light of these three properties and using the above analogy, we might describe creation as that playful moment at a dance where, to the music that is the Holy Spirit and prompted by the Father, the Word goes twirling out from the Father's loving embrace.

This "twirling out" of the Word to the music of the Holy Spirit from the arms of the Father causes *the procession of creatures from God at creation*. Such an image of creatures playfully and tenderly going forth from the Father, through the Word, and in the Love that's the Holy Spirit seems fitting to the imagery of Sacred Scripture:

> For as the rain and the snow come down from heaven, and return not thither but water the earth, making it bring forth and sprout, giving seed to the sower and bread to the eater, *so shall my word be that goes forth from my mouth; it shall not return to me empty*, but it shall accomplish that which I purpose, and prosper in the thing for which I sent it. For you shall go out in joy, and be led forth in peace; the mountains and the hills before you shall break forth into singing, and all the trees of the field shall clap their hands (Is 55:10-12, emphasis added).

> Before the mountains had been shaped, before the hills, *I was brought forth*, before he had made the earth with its fields, or the first of the dust of the world. When he established the heavens, *I was there*, when he drew a circle on the face of the deep, when he made firm the skies above, when he established the fountains of the deep, when he assigned to the sea its limit, so that the waters might not transgress his command, when he marked out the foundations of the earth, then *I was beside him*, like a master workman; and *I was daily his delight, rejoicing before him always, rejoicing in his inhabited world and delighting the sons of men* (Prov 8:25-31, emphasis added).

Together, these two passages reveal the *exitus-reditus* structure of reality as well as the intimacy, joyfulness, and delight that God finds in creating. They remind us that God did not have to create. Creation was a freely chosen overflow of love marked by, we might say again, a kind of playfulness. It really does seem like that moment of the dance, the moment of "twirling out." It also reminds us of that brief moment of the loving gaze, that moment to take the other in with one's eyes in a new light and, as it were, "from a distance." I wonder if part of the reason why God the Father created in the first place was to take a "step back" to admire the beauty of the Word in a new light, namely, *in creatures.* For all creatures are created according to the pattern of the Word, and it's the Word's reflection in creatures that causes the Father to gaze so lovingly upon them.

With this in mind, we can better appreciate that God the Father is like the young man at the dance who lovingly gazes on his beloved at mid-twirl, delighting in her goodness just before she comes twirling back to him. In other words, God the Father *beheld* the material creation that twirled out from him through his Word and in his Spirit, and while lovingly gazing on it, he saw that it was "good" (Gen 1:25). In fact, it was more than just "good." For, after he created man and woman, who reflect the beauty of the Word more than the rest of creation, he then saw that this work was "very good" (Gen 1:31). Next, he waited for this very good creation to come twirling back to him through the Word, with the Word, and in the unity of the Holy Spirit — but as we know too well, man and woman were not the best dancers. They chose not to return to God. They sinned.

Sin is bad news: The "very good" creation becomes badly broken. The good news is that the Word and the Spirit will see to it that creation is healed and gloriously returned to the Father.[40] For, as we already read in Isaiah, God says, "So shall my word be that goes forth from my mouth; it shall not return to me empty, but it shall accomplish that which I purpose, and prosper in the thing for which I sent it." Later in this chapter, we'll learn how the Word and the Spirit bring creation back to God after sin — "Plan B." In the next section, "The Journey Back," we'll see how creation was originally *supposed* to come back to God — "Plan A."

Before we turn our attention to this next section, there's one last point that will be helpful for us to consider here: Why does God create *so much?* Anyone who has ever sat quietly before a lake on a summer evening will know exactly what I mean. Remember how the seemingly tranquil scene suddenly came to life? Remember how you began to notice beetles buzzing about, fish nabbing flies with a "whirlp!" at the water's surface, leaves gently rustling in the wind, prickly weeds poking at your pants, and the billion blades of grass? Creation is full to the brim. Why? Why so much? Why did God create such a multitude and diversity of things, even encouraging such fullness with the command, "Be fruitful and multiply"? (Gen 1:28). The answer has to do with God's desire to see himself reflected in his creation, and St. Thomas gives this answer in what is probably my favorite passage in his entire massive *Summa*. He writes:

> Hence we must say that the distinction and multitude of things come from the intention of the first agent, who is God. For He brought things into being in order that His goodness might be communicated to creatures, and be represented by them; and because His goodness could not be adequately represented by one creature alone, He produced many and diverse creatures, that what was wanting to one in the representation of the divine goodness might be supplied by another. For goodness, which in God is simple and uniform, in creatures is manifold and divided; and hence the whole universe together participates [in] the divine goodness more perfectly, and represents it better than any single creature whatever.[41]

Marvelous. Absolutely marvelous. But why does St. Thomas say that God's goodness couldn't be adequately represented by one creature alone? Surely God's goodness could have been represented by a single creature. For instance, God could have created one white daisy, and the beauty of that little daisy would indeed have reflected and represented God's Beauty. But Thomas is right: It would have been inadequate — especially when you compare that one lonely daisy to a field of flowers of a thousand species planted near a wild ocean with the bright sun beaming in the sky and a family picnicking on a white, sandy beach, with their dogs playfully chasing the waves, while seagulls sail lazily on the wind like kites. Of course, our little, white daisy wilts in comparison to such a glorious scene, because such a scene *much* more adequately reflects God's infinite power, goodness, and beauty. Indeed, when it comes to finite creatures trying to represent the infinite Creator, St. Thomas is right: While they'll never do it perfectly, the more the merrier.

Yes, the more *the merrier*. The Father surely delights in his creation, because he delights in his Word (the Son) and in their Love (the Spirit), and the Word and Love put their own stamp on creation. So, as the Father lovingly gazes on this creation that brims over with the beauty of his Beloved, he then begins to tug on creation's hand to pull it back into the communion of his intimate embrace.

*T*HE JOURNEY BACK. Actually, the Father calls all of creation back to himself as soon as he sends it forth, but it takes time for creatures to respond fully. And how do they respond? By fulfilling their natures, by becoming what they were created to be. For non-human, material creation, this is easy. Animals, plants, pebbles, and streams blindly follow their natures according to the magnificent order of creation. Thus, rocks fall to earth by an unseen law, great oak trees grow with the cycle of the seasons, and squirrels store food by an invisible instinct. But man is different. For him, it's not so easy and automatic. He's not blindly guided as if by something from without. Rather, he can know and choose the order of creation by something from within. In other words, he can see the harmony of the Word in creation and freely choose to follow it. In this freedom is man's exalted dignity — and it also led to his shame.

As we read in the last chapter, man abused his freedom. Instead of choosing the Father's loving plan, he decided to do his own thing, and thus, he introduced so many terrible ruptures into the harmonious communion of original creation. But if God knew this could happen, why did he create man with free will? Why didn't he just force man into "autopilot," thereby making him as perfectly obedient as the rest of creation? Why such needless risk in making man free?

It wasn't needless. God wanted a free humanity so man could share in the Communion of Love, the Most Holy Trinity. (Authentic love requires real freedom, since robots and puppets on a string can't love.) Moreover, the rest of creation needed a free humanity, meaning that God created man to be the free and conscious savior of creation. Indeed, man's vocation was to bring the creatures of earth back to God, because they couldn't do it on their own. Yes, these creatures could follow their own natures and approach God, but on their own, they couldn't *fully* rise to glory. For that, they needed man.

An incredibly rich theme in the writings of the Greek Fathers of the Church is that man is a *microcosm*, a summation of all the orders of creation. At the highest order are the pure spirits, the angels. At the lowest order is non-spiritual creation: animals, plants, and the elements. Man stands in the middle of both of these orders, embodying them all. In fact, he's an *embodied spirit*. He's both spirit and matter, and for this reason, he sums up all of creation in himself and, therefore, is in the perfect position to raise the non-spiritual creation to the level of spirit:

> Man is the lowest of spirits and highest of animals.
> He is the center and bridge of the created universe.
> He is creation's priest, for when he offers his whole
> self to God he offers all creation, since he is in himself
> all that creation is: spirit (mind and will), which he
> shares with the angels; sensations and feelings, which
> he shares with animals; organic life, which he shares
> with plants; and physical matter, which he shares
> with chemicals.[42]

Now, the Trinity is pure spirit. So, how can non-spiritual creation return to the Trinity? It can't count on the angels, for they don't have a footing in the non-spiritual world. As pure spirits, they can't taste the sweetness of a grape, can't smell the perfume of a rose, can't hear the music of a lark, can't feel the

ground shake at the crash of ocean waves. Only man can help
the non-spiritual creation, for he's the being with a foot in both
the world of spirit and of matter. And from his foothold in the
world of matter, he can fling non-spiritual creation back to God
by taking it in through his physical senses, making it spirit
through conscious awareness, and then lifting it up to God
with praise and thanksgiving. With such songs of praise and
thanks, man gives spiritual voice to a spiritually voiceless creation.
Indeed, by his recognition of creation's power, beauty, and
goodness, he truly does spiritualize it and can offer it back to
God as a kind of cosmic priest.

    If this seems "new age" and flaky, it's not. It's as ancient
and as solid as the Old Testament. For example, take the beautiful
Canticle of Daniel (see 3:57-88, 56). For millennia, this song
of cosmic praise has arisen from the hearts of God's chosen
people. This same song flows into the hearts of the people
of God of the New Covenant as priests, deacons, religious,
and laity frequently sing it on Sundays and solemnities as part
of the Church's Liturgy of the Hours. I'll quote it now at
length, so we can see the full extent of what God meant when
in Genesis (1:28), he gave man "dominion" over all of creation:

> Bless the Lord, all you works of the Lord.
> Praise and exalt him above all forever.
> Angels of the Lord, bless the Lord.
> You heavens, bless the Lord.
> All you waters above the heavens, bless the Lord.
> All you hosts of the Lord, bless the Lord.
> Sun and moon, bless the Lord.
> Stars of heaven, bless the Lord.
>
> Every shower and dew, bless the Lord.
> All you winds, bless the Lord.
> Fire and heat, bless the Lord.
> Cold and chill, bless the Lord.
> Dew and rain, bless the Lord.
> Frost and chill, bless the Lord.

Ice and snow, bless the Lord.
Nights and days, bless the Lord.
Light and darkness, bless the Lord.
Lightnings and clouds, bless the Lord.

Let the earth bless the Lord.
Praise and exalt him above all forever.
Mountains and hills, bless the Lord.
Everything growing from the earth, bless the Lord.
You springs, bless the Lord.
Seas and rivers, bless the Lord.
You dolphins and all water creatures, bless the Lord.
All you birds of the air, bless the Lord.
All you beasts, wild and tame, bless the Lord.
You sons of men, bless the Lord.

O Israel, bless the Lord.
Praise and exalt him above all forever.
Priests of the Lord, bless the Lord.
Servants of the Lord, bless the Lord.
Spirits and souls of the just, bless the Lord.
Holy men of humble heart, bless the Lord.
Hananiah, Azariah, Mishael, bless the Lord.
Praise and exalt him above all forever.

[The Church adds the following conclusion
to the canticle in the Liturgy of the Hours:]
Let us bless the Father, and the Son, and the Holy Spirit.
Let us praise and exalt him above all forever.
Blessed are you, Lord, in the firmament of heaven.
Praiseworthy and glorious and exalted above all forever.[43]

In light of this canticle, it's helpful to reflect on words of
wisdom from a saint of the seventh century, Leontius of Cyprus,
who had no doubt about man's call to be a priest of creation:

Creation does not venerate the Maker through itself
directly, but it is through me that the heavens declare

the glory of God, through me the moon worships God, through me the stars glorify him, through me the waters and showers of rain, the dew and all creation, venerate God and give him glory.[44]

Indeed, it is "through me" (and you) that creation has its hope of salvation. What a responsibility God gave to man from the beginning! To fulfill his role, man not only had to be a material being but also needed the spiritual powers of knowing, loving, and choosing. Again, as we know too well, man abused these powers and all of creation suffered. Think of the horror of the non-spiritual creation when the indispensable link in the chain, man the microcosm, refused his service. Horror? Really? Well, maybe not horror, but St. Paul sure describes the "feelings" of creation in striking terms:

> For the creation waits with eager longing for the revealing of the sons of God; for the creation was subjected to futility, not of it's own will but by the will of him who subjected it in hope; because the creation itself will be set free from its bondage to decay and obtain the glorious liberty of the children of God. We know that the whole creation has been groaning in travail together until now; and not only the creation, but we ourselves (Rom 8:19-23).

So, what next? If the essential link in the chain that was meant to bring all creation back to God is broken, are we, therefore, without hope? Since Adam failed, is the Great Circle of Being to remain a pitiful *semi-circle*? Is it doomed to be in the image of a dimly lit half-moon? Is creation ever to rise again and complete the circle? Saint Paul is hopeful, and so should we be. For a second Adam, a new Adam, was sent to the world to complete the work that the first Adam failed to do. Moreover, thanks be to God, the new Adam doesn't leave fallen humanity out of the loop. Rather, in the most glorious "Plan B" ever imagined, the new Adam dusts us off, forgives us our sins, and invites us, with him, to take up again our failed task of bringing all of creation back to the Father.

Of course, the new Adam is Christ Jesus, our Lord. And as we said at the beginning of this chapter, the way we enter into the life of the Trinity is by becoming Christ — not by becoming Jesus Christ the Head of the Body but by becoming members of his Body. Now, if we're still following our map, all this reminds us that we need to return (*redditus*) to God and that this return is accomplished by a transforming communion with Christ. We'll say more about this in the next chapter.

Chapter Two

Transforming Communion with Christ through Faith and the Sacraments

One of the things I love about St. Thomas Aquinas is his conciseness and clarity. In a few sentences, he communicates what takes other theologians pages and pages to explain. For instance, right now I'm looking at a 450-page theology book on my desk that explains how we're transformed in Christ. Well, St. Thomas basically summarizes that whole book with the following sentence:

> The power of Christ's passion is joined to us through faith and through the sacraments, yet in different ways; for the contact which is through faith takes place through the act of the soul, but the contact which is through the sacraments takes place through the use of external things.[45]

If this sentence isn't totally clear now, don't worry. We're going to be spending the rest of this chapter unpacking its brilliance. Specifically, we're going to unpack its two main points: First, the Passion of Christ; and second, faith and the Sacraments. In other words, we're going to look at how our transformation in Christ is accomplished above all through the power of Christ's Passion, which we receive through faith and the Sacraments. So, let's first look at what Jesus has done for us in his *Passion*. Then, we'll look at how we receive what he has done for us through *faith* and *the Sacraments*.

1. The Passion of Christ

*W*HY THE PASSION? Saint Thomas emphasizes that of all the mysteries of the life of Christ, it's above all the Passion that causes our salvation. In other words, we have Jesus' rejection, condemnation, bloody scourging, crowning with thorns, carrying of the Cross, and violent death on Calvary to thank for saving us. Well, when it's put like this, the question may arise, "But why?" Why did Jesus have to suffer like that to save us? Couldn't God have just forgiven us our sins without having had his Son suffer so terribly?

Actually, *God could have simply forgiven us our sins.* He could have forgiven our sins without having his Son undergo the Passion for us. As St. Thomas says, God could have forgiven us without paying the price for our sins on the Cross, for a judge is free to forgive sin, and to do so is not unjust but merciful.[46] However, if God just forgave us our sins without his Son paying the price, we would not have been given the many benefits that flow to us from the Passion.[47] In other words, we would have been *redeemed* but not *glorified*. Yet God wanted us to be glorified in his Son, a desire that Jesus himself expresses with the words, "that the love with which thou hast loved me may be in them and I in them" (Jn 17:26). God wanted us to partake of his divine nature (glorification), which is a gift that goes beyond the forgiveness of sins (redemption). So, in an even greater act of mercy, God didn't dispense with the order of justice, and Jesus went to the Cross to pay the price for our sins, so we might have a destiny that's the envy of the angels.

*H*OW THE PASSION SAVES US. Okay, but how does this work? Why do we benefit more by Christ's indescribable suffering and torture? Jesus' words to his disciples at the Last Supper explain it best: "Greater love has no man than this, that a man lay down his life for his friends" (Jn 15:13). In other words, Jesus wanted to reveal to us the greatest love — and we needed to see it. Why? Because of the deep heart wound that all of us bear as a result of the fall of our first parents.

Remember how Adam's sin made him see God in a distorted way, as if God were mean, vindictive, and harsh? Remember how Adam and Eve hid from him after they sinned? Remember all those times when each one of us has hidden from God after our personal sins? Well, God wanted to convince us fearful, skittish creatures of his love for us, and by the Passion, he proves it. In other words, being fallen, wounded creatures, distrustful of God, we needed a dramatic revelation of God's love to convince us of it and to help us accept it. By Jesus' suffering and death, "Man knows," says St. Thomas, "how much God loves him, and is thereby stirred to love Him in return, and herein lies the perfection of human salvation."[48] Or, as another theologian puts it:

> In rescuing sinful man, God responded to man's needs. He took into consideration the sinner's distortions of divine reality, his suspicions, mistrust, and aggressivity towards the Divine. In this state man needed more than just a moral exhortation and a divine offer of grace to convert him. God's grace had to provide man with tangible evidence for the reality of his infinite compassion and of his holiness. ... [I]n this context, then, we begin to perceive why the Incarnation and the cross appear as the most appropriate way for man's rescue. ... In this way [Jesus' death on a cross] God showed man in a most convincing manner his own true nature that is pure love and mercy.[49]

So, God wanted to prove his love for us, and we needed to see it. This point helps us to understand that God the Father is not some bloodthirsty deity whose anger is only satisfied by the blood of his Son. He didn't need to see Christ's death. We did:

> God does not accept anything in exchange or relent on account of something which Christ does. If Christ substitutes for sinful man in the experience of his passion, he does so only to enable men and women themselves to experience again the compassion of God. It is not that God then resumes being compassionate; rather, the human person is then free to accept God's love. All in all, [salvation] changes us, not God.[50]

That last line is so important. Our salvation in Christ doesn't change God. Rather, it changes us. Furthermore, the way it changes us, the benefits of the Passion, are not just psychological. It's not that Jesus' suffering and death on the Cross simply wins our compassion and helps us to trust in him. There's more. The Passion of Christ, indeed, his whole Paschal mystery (Passion, death, and Resurrection), gives us a multitude of graces that cause a real transformation in us. How we receive these graces is what the next sections are all about. But before we get to those sections, I'm going to make one important point about the Paschal mystery that will be the key to everything that follows.

*A*N *EVENT THAT ABIDES*. We've been focusing on the Passion of Christ as the main event that saves us, which is true. But the larger picture is that *the whole Paschal mystery* also gets to the heart of what saves us. In other words, it's not just Christ's Passion and death that save us most especially — it's also his Resurrection. Now, all the mysteries of the life of Christ are salvific for us, but the Paschal mystery is the most central one for our salvation, and it's from the Paschal mystery that we most effectively receive God's saving grace. Alright, but how do we receive it? After all, the Paschal mystery happened 2,000 years ago. While this is true, it's also true that among all the events in history, the Paschal mystery is special, as the *Catechism* explains:

> His Paschal mystery ... is unique: all other historical events happen once, and then they pass away, swallowed up in the past. The Paschal mystery of Christ, by contrast, cannot remain only in the past, because by his death he destroyed death, and all that Christ is — all that he did and suffered for all men — participates in the divine eternity, and so transcends all times while being made present in them all. The event of the Cross and Resurrection *abides* and draws everything toward life.[51]

Think of it: All other events in human history "pass away" and are "swallowed up in the past." But the Paschal mystery of Christ — indeed, all the events of his life — "transcends all times while being made present in them all." This is amazing. The Paschal mystery, Jesus' suffering, death, and Resurrection, "abides."

Alright, but how do we get in contact with this mystery? How do we reach this event that extends out across the ages? Again, as I said at the very beginning of this chapter, by faith and the Sacraments. So, let's start with faith and how it brings us into this contact.

2. Faith and the Passion of Christ

A TALE OF TWO MOVIES. The best way I can think of to illustrate how faith brings us into contact with the Paschal mystery of Christ is with the help of two movies. The first, *Saving Private Ryan* (1998), is set during the Normandy invasion of World War II, and its opening scene is unforgettable. For 27 long minutes, the brutal morning of the U.S. Army's June 6, 1944, D-Day assault on Omaha Beach unfolds in what's widely regarded as the most realistic war scene ever filmed. It was so realistic that the Department of Veterans Affairs set up a special hotline to help the hundreds of former soldiers who were traumatized after seeing the film. One veteran who saw it simply said, "It couldn't have been more real." In fact, for those veterans who were willing to talk about it, the reaction was more or less the same, "They nailed it."

For all veterans who have suffered the experience of war, *Saving Private Ryan* has the power to bring them back. For the actual survivors of World War II, it can be overwhelming. At a private screening for such vets, a quarter of them left the theater just 10 minutes into it, and the projectionist had to stop the film several times to allow the men to compose themselves. The point is that the film had the power to bring these brave men back to the horrors of the war. Of course, the movie is not an actual time machine — it can't literally bring the soldiers back to the 1940s — but it does stir memories, and memories can make the past seem vividly present.

Let's now consider a second movie, *The Passion of the Christ* (2003). Here, we have another very realistic film. In fact, no other film even comes close to depicting the suffering and death of our Lord as graphically as does *The Passion*. Achieving

such realism was the intention of the director, Mel Gibson, who
said, "I really wanted to express the hugeness of the sacrifice,
as well as the horror of it."[52] The film does indeed capture the
violence done to Christ, but according to the actor who plays
Jesus in the film, Jim Caviezel, it's not without purpose or
meaning:

> No one has ever showed Jesus in this way before,
> and I think Mel is showing the truth. Mel hasn't
> used violence for violence's sake and it has never felt
> gratuitous. I do think the realism will probably shock
> some people, but that is why the film is so incredibly
> powerful.[53]

Pope John Paul II seemed to agree. After watching a private
screening of the film shortly after its release, he summed it up
in five words: "*It is as it was.*" Interesting. This sounds a lot
like the reaction of World War II veterans to *Saving Private
Ryan*, "It couldn't have been more real." But they could say
this because they were there. How could the Pope know? Was
he there at Calvary?

Let me try to answer this question by asking another one:
What has more "take-you-back-effect" (TYBE), watching the
movie *Saving Private Ryan* or *The Passion of the Christ*? I would
say that it depends. Specifically, it depends on who's watching
the movie. If we compare a war vet who watches *Saving Private
Ryan* to an unbeliever who watches *The Passion of the Christ*, then
the former clearly has more TYBE, because the vet has real
memories that the film can stir up. But nobody living today
was historically present 2,000 years ago at Calvary. Therefore,
The Passion can't evoke real memories.

Alright, but what if you compare a veteran of the D-Day
invasion on Omaha Beach watching *Saving Private Ryan* and a
Christian watching *The Passion of the Christ*. Which movie has
more TYBE? Well, if the Christian's mind and heart is moved to
faith and love, then undoubtedly the *Passion of the Christ* has far
more TYBE than *Saving Private Ryan*. The reason why has to
do with who Jesus Christ is.

Jesus Christ is true man. As true man, he was born at a specific hour, lived for a precise number of years and days, and died at a particular moment in history. Jesus Christ is also God, and as true God, he is eternal. So, what happens when the eternal God becomes incarnate and enters time as a man? Well, it makes the events in the life of such a man utterly unique. They become "God events" that happen in time but transcend all time. Therefore, what the *Catechism* teaches about the Paschal mystery actually applies to every event in the life of Christ. In other words, while all other events in history happen once and are then "swallowed up in the past," the events in the life of Christ "cannot remain only in the past." Rather, they "participate in the divine eternity" and "transcend all times while being made present in them all." Thus, all the events in the life of Christ "abide" and are a source of life and blessing for every one of us, so long as we can meet Christ there in the "divine eternity."

Unlike Christ, we're not "true God." But remember what we learned in the last chapter about divinization: We truly are called to share in God's own divine life. We're called to share in the divine eternity, and this eternal life begins with our Baptism, which we'll talk about more in the next section. Here, it's enough to say that at our Baptism, sanctifying grace is poured into our hearts, and we're then given supernatural powers, the most important of which are the theological virtues of faith, hope, and charity. Starting with faith, these virtues allow us to touch and enter the "divine eternity," the "eternal now" of God. In other words, they allow us to transcend time, and when they're active in our minds and hearts, we have a true contact with Christ. Let's go back to the example of *The Passion of the Christ*, which will make this clearer.

If an unbeliever watches *The Passion of the Christ*, he may be impressed by the acting, startled by the violence, and touched by the story. But unless he believes that Jesus Christ is the incarnate Son of God and confesses him as Lord and Savior, then he has no real contact with Christ by means of the movie. Indeed, for an unbeliever, the movie will have very little TYBE, because he wasn't there at Calvary 2,000 years ago. But if a believer is watching the film and his heart is moved with love for Jesus, who he believes is his Lord and Savior, then he has a real contact with Christ through the mystery of the Passion, which the movie serves to communicate. Watching the movie becomes an event that evokes faith and love in the heart of the Christian, and, therefore, it can occasion his being mystically transported to the abiding event of the Passion. In view of this, I think we can better understand the Pope's comment, "It is as it was."

Although Pope John Paul II was not historically present during Christ's Passion and death, he frequently was "mystically transported" there.[54] In fact, the Pope was a seasoned traveler when it came to mystical transportation. I say this because he prayed the Stations of the Cross every Friday, the Sorrowful Mysteries of the Rosary every Tuesday and Friday, and he offered Mass every day, which is a re-presentation of the sacrifice of Calvary. (More on this later). In other words, he was someone who had the reality of the Passion of Christ frequently before his mind, and he pondered it in his heart with faith and love. Therefore, in a very real sense, he spent more time at Calvary than the brave soldiers of the D-Day invasion spent on Omaha Beach. And even though John Paul was not historically present at Calvary during the Passion, he was truly present to Christ there in an even more real sense.

A "more real sense"? This may seem like an odd statement, but look at it this way. Who was more present to Jesus on Calvary: John Paul II praying the Fifth Sorrowful Mystery of the Rosary or one of the Roman soldiers who helped crucify Jesus? Well, it depends. If we're talking about St. Longinus, the Roman solider who pierced the side of Jesus and then believed, then he would seem to be the most present at Calvary, because he was present both historically (physically) and by faith (spiritually). However, if we're talking about an unbelieving Roman soldier and John Paul, then the Pope was present to Jesus on Calvary in a more real sense. And in fact, Jesus was also more present to the Pope — for this presence isn't just a one-way street.

As true God, Jesus Christ knows all things, and on the Cross, he knew and loved John Paul II, you, me, and everyone who ever lived, lives now, and will live in the future. He could see each one of us with his divine knowledge, and he loved every one of us with a human Heart. The *Catechism* says as much:

> Jesus knew and loved us each and all during his life, his agony, and his Passion, and gave himself up for each one of us: "The Son of God ... loved me and gave himself for me" (Gal 2:20). He has loved us all with a human heart. For this reason, the Sacred Heart of Jesus, pierced by our sins and for our salvation, "is quite rightly considered the chief sign and symbol of that ... love with which the divine Redeemer continually loves the eternal Father and all human beings" without exception.[55]

This love of Christ that reaches out to us through the ages is a key to having a living relationship with Jesus in the mysteries of his life. For, if we have faith, we can be truly present to him and meet his love as if we were living with him 2,000 years ago. Indeed, just as a divine power went forth from him and healed and blessed those who touched him during his earthly life, so we, too, can touch him and receive the same gifts of grace by faith. Having such a living relationship with Jesus, not as the man who lived way back in the past but as the one who is alive and present to us now, is a key to becoming transformed into him and to receiving his saving power.

Before closing this section on faith and how it puts us into a real contact with Christ in his mysteries, I want to briefly say something about faith and the other theological virtues, especially charity.

*W*HY *SUCH A FOCUS ON FAITH?* As I've been writing about faith, you may have been wondering, "Well, faith is just one of the theological virtues. What about the other two? What about hope and charity? Don't they also put us into a real contact with Jesus? And if so, why all this emphasis on faith?"

In emphasizing faith, I'm following the lead of St. Thomas Aquinas. Remember, he says, "The power of Christ's passion is joined to us through faith and through the sacraments." He doesn't say "through faith, hope, and charity." I often wondered why he just says "faith." Then, one day, I came across this masterful explanation by Abbot Anscar Vonier:

> It is a favorite idea with Saint Thomas, that faith is truly a contact with Christ, a real, psychological contact with Christ, which, if once established, may lead man into the innermost glories of Christ's life. Without this contact of faith we are dead to Christ, the stream of His life passes us by without entering into us, as a rock in the midst of a river remains unaffected by the turbulent rush of waters. This contact of faith makes man susceptible to the influences of Christ; under normal conditions it will develop into the broader contacts of hope and charity; but it is the first grafting of man on Christ which underlies all other fruitfulness. Till faith be established the great redemption has not become our redemption; the riches of Christ are not ours in any true sense; we are members of the human race, but we are not members of Christ.[56]

In other words, there's a primacy to faith. It's the beginning of our supernatural life and "underlies all other fruitfulness," meaning it opens us up to hope and charity and all the treasures of a spiritual life. It's like this: Faith, hope, and charity go with the movement of mind and heart, a movement where *knowledge goes before love*, a movement where faith precedes hope and love. To make this point as clear as possible, I should say something more about the movement of mind and heart and then the movement of faith, hope, and love.

Before we can love someone (or something), we first need to know him or at least to see him. When we know him or see him, then love begins to stir in our hearts ... or at least it *might* begin to stir in our hearts (whether or not it does begin to stir is a mystery of the heart, for as Blaise Pascal famously wrote,

"The heart has reasons of which reason knows nothing"[57]).
The mind is therefore like the eagle-eye of the soul, and the
heart wears coke-bottle glasses. In other words, the heart can
see, but not very well: It can only see and respond to the things
that the mind (and all the senses) brings right before it. And
without the eyes of the mind and senses, the heart remains in
the dark and paralyzed — paralyzed because it can't move
unless something lovable is presented to it. In sum, here's the
movement of mind and heart: The mind presents things to the
heart, and then the heart may or may not respond with love.

Now, faith, hope, and charity follow this movement of
mind and heart where *faith has to do mostly with the mind and
hope and charity have to do with the heart*. It's like this: Faith
gives the mind the ability to know God as he reveals himself to
us, and then, hope and charity are how the heart responds
when presented with this knowledge. Hope is the response of
the heart that says, "Wow! This God and the good things he
has revealed are *for me!*" (Many of those good things are in the
future, such as heaven and the rewards of heaven, which is why
hope tends to look to the future.) Charity (love) is the response
of the heart that says, "Wow! This God is Beauty, Truth,
Goodness, and worthy of all my love. I love him not *for my
own sake* but for who and what he is and deserves." So, that's
the movement: faith, and then, hope and love.

Now, in the following passage, Abbot Vonier tells us more
about the difference between faith and charity within the context
of our transformation in Christ, what he calls "incorporation
into Christ." Before you read it, I should warn you that it's not
so easy. Don't worry. I'll unpack it afterward:

> Incorporation into Christ, according to Saint
> Thomas, has a threefold degree; the first is through
> faith, the second is through charity in this life, the
> third is through the possession of heaven. It is true
> that the whole tendency of faith is towards charity,
> that ultimately faith without charity cannot save us;
> nonetheless, charity cannot exist in man without

faith, while there may be true faith in man without actual charity.

All this goes on to demonstrate that there is in faith an instrumental power, enabling man to open the door that leads to perfect union with Christ. We cannot speak of such instrumental power in charity, for charity is not a means towards the possession of God; it is, on the contrary, actual possession of God.[58]

Okay, so what I think he's saying here is simply a follow-up to what we covered regarding the movement of mind and heart. For faith gives us the knowledge of God, but charity gives us the actual love of God, which is God himself and perfect union with him. Now, since our purpose in this chapter is to explore *how we are transformed in Christ*, we're going to want to stay focused on the "how," the "means," the "way," the "instrument" that leads to our union with Christ, which is faith, and not so much on the end, which is love. For faith is the means, charity the end; faith is the way, charity the destination; faith is the instrument, charity the goal. Abbot Vonier summarizes the main point for us: "[T]hrough the possession of charity we do not only contact Christ, we are actually in Christ. Charity is not an instrument, while faith has primarily an instrumental role."[59]

So, we've been focused on faith as the way to our transformation in Christ. Or, to use Vonier's terminology, we've been focused on faith as having an *instrumental role* in forming us into Christ. But there's something else besides faith alone that has an instrumental role in bringing about our transforming communion with Christ — that something else is the Sacraments. And so, since our focus in this chapter is on how we're transformed into Christ, let's take a look at how the Sacraments do this.

3. The Gift of the Sacraments

*A*N EVEN DEEPER CONTACT WITH CHRIST. In the last section, we learned that faith — which develops into charity and hope — puts us into a real contact with Christ in his mysteries. In fact, faith is a supernatural power that allows us to transcend time and touch and enter the "divine eternity," the "eternal now" of God. This is amazing! Faith brings us into a real contact with Christ in his mysteries that took place 2,000 years ago.

Now, perhaps you think it's strange that I've been saying that, by faith, we have a real "contact" with Christ in his mysteries. After all, faith is something spiritual while contact is something physical. So, I must be speaking metaphorically, right? I mean, surely we don't actually *touch* Christ. Surely we're talking a spiritual, immaterial kind of thing, right? Well, yes and no.

When I'm praying the Rosary, meditating, for instance, on the Fifth Sorrowful Mystery, the Crucifixion, it's true that while I do "touch" Christ by faith, this is a wholly spiritual reality. However, when I'm at Mass and receive the Eucharist, "contact with Christ" takes on a new meaning. With the Eucharist (and the other Sacraments), we're talking more than a purely spiritual contact. For, with the Sacraments, the immaterial becomes material. The spiritual becomes bodily. Grace becomes, in a sense, incarnate. Such is the gift of the Sacraments! For God, knowing that we are both body and spirit, gives us two ways to touch him and receive his saving grace. One way is spiritual (through the virtue of faith) and the other way is both spiritual *and* material (through the Sacraments). On this point, recall the super-sentence of St. Thomas that began this chapter:

> The power of Christ's passion is joined to us through faith and through the sacraments, yet in different ways; for the contact which is through faith takes place through the *act of the soul*, but the contact which is through the sacraments takes place through the use of *external things*.[60]

An act of the soul (faith) is purely spiritual. The use of external things (in the Sacraments) is both spiritual and material. That God gives us a bodily means to enter into communion with him — the Sacraments — reveals his Fatherly care for us. Because he knows we're most at home with what we can see, hear, taste, and touch, he saves us by making use of material things in the Sacraments: water, oil, bread, and wine. And because the Sacraments reflect our human reality of body and spirit so completely, they can communicate to us even greater graces than faith alone. In fact, they can bring about an even more intense communion with Christ.

Of course, in exalting the Sacraments in this way, I in no way mean to diminish faith, which would actually be absurd because the Sacraments are grafted onto faith, presuppose it, and are essentially united with it. Indeed, St. Thomas Aquinas frequently calls the Sacraments "the Sacraments of faith" (*sacramenta fidei*). Still, my purpose here is to emphasize that the Sacraments really are crucial. For just as the fact that the Word became flesh is important, so also are the Sacraments important; *for the Sacraments are a continuation of the Word become flesh* (see Jn 1:14). Indeed, now that Jesus has bodily ascended into heaven, it's through the Church and the Sacraments that his bodily presence remains with us, though in a different way. During this "age of the Church," during this time of waiting until the Lord comes again, Christ himself acts (spiritually and bodily) through the Sacraments. What a gift!

Okay, but what exactly is a sacrament? We've learned that the Sacraments are essentially connected to faith, that they involve the use of "external things, " and that they're instruments of saving grace. Now, putting all this together (and then some), here's a concise definition of the Sacraments that's given in the *Catechism*:

> The sacraments are efficacious signs of grace, instituted by Christ and entrusted to the Church, by which divine life is dispensed to us. The visible rites by which the sacraments are celebrated signify and

make present the graces proper to each sacrament. They bear fruit in those who receive them with the required dispositions.[61]

Alright, there's a lot here. Let's try to get to the core of this definition by going right to the first sentence, "The sacraments are efficacious signs of grace." These words remind me of something my Sacraments professor in the seminary used to emphasize over and over. He'd say, "If you remember only one thing from this course, remember this: *The sacraments DO something!*" In other words, they're not just nice ceremonies. They're not just signs. They *effect* what they signify. They are efficacious — "efficacious" basically means that they DO something. And what do they do? They do what they signify. They actually do what they point to. So, for example, Baptism is a sign of washing, and it actually washes us. Specifically, it washes us clean of sin. Okay, but *why* are the Sacraments efficacious? Why do they have the power to DO what they are signs of? The *Catechism* gives an answer, "They are *efficacious* because in them Christ himself is at work: it is he who baptizes, he who acts in his sacraments in order to communicate the grace that each sacrament signifies."[62]

Christ acting in the Sacraments is not just pious language. It's not a throw-away statement. Jesus *truly* and *powerfully* acts in the Sacraments. As one theologian puts it, "At the moment of reception, Christ is thinking of the recipient, turning his redemptive love upon him, and reaching out to sanctify him."[63] This is an amazing thought. Jesus is looking at *me* whenever I receive a sacrament, pouring out his love upon *me*, reaching out to touch *me*. But how can this be? The answer is related to that earlier section where I was talking about the movie *The Passion of the Christ*.

*M*EETING CHRIST IN THE SACRAMENTS. Remember how, in an earlier section, we learned that Jesus Christ knew each and every one of us during his earthly life? Well, how was this possible? It was possible because Jesus is not just true man but also *true God*. As God, he could see all people of all time. And while he lived his earthly life and especially his Passion, he had each and every one of us on his mind. He was thinking of us. Not only that, he was giving himself to each one of us, individually and particularly, in the Sacraments:

> ... Christ, as he lived the mystery of his suffering, decreed that the sacrament which I receive on this particular day, twenty centuries after the event of Calvary, should forgive the sins of which I am at this moment guilty and should bring me the grace allotted me by God from eternity for today. ... [W]hat is happening is that the mysteries of Christ are here and now producing their predetermined effect in a particular member of Christ.[64]

Keep in mind that that particular member is each one of us. Jesus was thinking of you and me as he suffered and died for us, and he was mindful of every Sacrament we would ever receive throughout our lives. Even more, he was inviting us in each Sacrament that we receive "now" to be united with him in the mystery of his sacrifice "back then":

> [Christ is] constantly, from the first moment of the Incarnation, on Calvary, now in heaven, offering his life and death for each individual [person] and is directing that the sacrament which I now receive should grant me fellowship in his sacrifice. The mysteries of Christ are not simply events of the past ... . To receive a sacrament is to enter into communion with the act which made the events of Christ's life saving mysteries and which enfolds the whole mystery of the Church. To assist at Mass or to receive a sacrament fruitfully is to be drawn into union with Christ's saving act, accepting its benefits and making one's own it's God-centered worship. Christ's primary, interior mystery is unaffected by time; the sacraments incorporate us into it.[65]

This sounds like the passage from the *Catechism* that we read earlier, the one that described the Paschal mystery as transcending time. For, here, we read that "the mysteries of Christ are not simply events of the past" and that they are "unaffected by time." Moreover, this passage highlights the idea that by the Sacraments, we can touch these mysteries: We "enter into communion" with them, are "drawn into union" with them, and are "incorporated" into them. All this and the preceding citation should have us saying, "Wow!" Because what these passages describe is *totally awesome*. They're saying, "Yes, we truly touch Christ! We truly meet him in the Sacraments." They're saying, "Yes, Christ is truly thinking of me, reaching out to me through the ages, and loving me in every sacrament." What a wonder! What a gift! Indeed, writing on the topic of the Sacrament of Sacraments, the Eucharist, Pope John Paul II writes about the *amazement* we should have before the sacramental mystery, a mystery that brings about a "oneness in time":

> In this gift Jesus Christ entrusted to his Church the perennial making present of the paschal mystery. With it he brought about a mysterious "oneness in time" between [the Paschal mystery] and the passage of the centuries.
>
> The thought of this leads us to profound amazement and gratitude. In the paschal event and the Eucharist which makes it present throughout the centuries, there is a truly enormous "capacity" which embraces all of history as the recipient of the grace of the redemption. This amazement should always fill the Church assembled for the celebration of the Eucharist.[66]

Yes, and this amazement should fill us when we approach *every* Sacrament. For Jesus himself is attentively hearing our sins, encouraging us, and pouring out his merciful forgiveness in the Sacrament of Penance. Jesus himself is washing us in the water flowing from his pierced side in Baptism. Jesus himself is joining husband and wife together as one flesh in the Sacrament of Marriage. Jesus himself is stretching out his loving hand to touch the infirm with his strength, healing, and consolation in the Anointing of the Sick. Jesus himself is breathing out the Holy Spirit in the Sacrament of Confirmation. Jesus himself is receiving the humanity of broken men and using them as his instruments of salvation in the Sacrament of Holy Orders. Wonder of wonders! Jesus remains truly with us, not just in our minds through his Word, not just in our souls through faith and grace, but also *bodily* present with us in his Sacraments, where he continues to bless, forgive, cleanse, unite, heal, strengthen, and make all things new.

As we better come to realize what a gift we have in the Sacraments, we should be saddened that so many Protestant Christians don't appreciate the Sacraments, because their churches do not offer them. We should be even more saddened by the situation of some Catholic Christians who are offered the Sacraments but who still don't appreciate them.[67] To show God our thanks for the gift of the Sacraments, let's reflect deeply on the gift that they are, beginning with this beautiful reflection on their mysterious and awe-inspiring grace:

> Any effort we make in order to cultivate sacramental thought will be rewarded with precious fruits in our spiritual life; it will make us into true mystics. Our dear sacraments are truly a stream of life and light … .
>
> … The stream of sacramental grace is truly the flow of the Blood of Christ: in one way or another every sacrament is the fire of Christ's love when He was dying on the Cross.
>
> Perhaps the most satisfying line of sacramental thought is to visualize the sacraments as mysterious carriers of all the powers that are in Christ's death.
>
> … Sacraments are truly an energy that comes from Christ in person, a radiation from the charity of the Cross, a stream of grace from the pierced side of Christ.[68]

You will notice that a key theme in this reflection is the Passion of Christ. Thus, it serves as an important reminder to us that the Passion of our Lord, indeed, the whole Paschal mystery, is at the center of sacramental power. In fact, the Sacraments are a real contact with the Passion of Christ, "mysterious carriers of all the powers that are in Christ's death." To remind us of this reality, let's contemplate the following concise but extremely illuminating passage from St. Thomas Aquinas:

> It is manifest that the sacraments of the Church derive their power specifically from the passion of Christ, whose efficacy is linked to us, as it were, through the receiving of the sacraments. As a sign of this, from the side of Christ hanging on the Cross there flowed water and blood, of which the one belongs to Baptism and the other to the Eucharist, which are the two principal sacraments.[69]

Because this book is meant to be merely a crash course in theology, we don't have time to reflect at length on each one of the seven Sacraments (Baptism, Confirmation, the Eucharist, Penance, the Anointing of the Sick, Holy Orders, and Matrimony). So, we're just going to look at the two principal Sacraments that St. Thomas mentions, the two that especially flow from Christ's pierced side: Baptism and the Eucharist.

*B*APTISM. We walk into a Catholic Church, dip a finger in the Holy Water font, and bless ourselves in the name of the Father, and of the Son, and of the Holy Spirit. Why? Why do we do this? Is it just "one of those things" we Catholics do? Yes it is, and a great one, too.

We bless ourselves with Holy Water on entering a Catholic Church to remind ourselves of the most important day of our lives, the day of our Baptism, the day when the minister of the Sacrament poured water over our heads (or dipped us into a pool) and said the glorious words, "I baptize you in the name of the Father, and of the Son, and of the Holy Spirit." On that day, we were saved! On that day, the two stages of salvation began to be accomplished in us: redemption and glorification.

Baptism *redeems* us because it cleanses us of sin, both original (from Adam and Eve's sin) and personal (our own sins). It *glorifies* us because it brings about our transforming communion with Christ. In other words, it takes us from the sad state of being sinful, fallen creatures to actually becoming a new creation, a son or daughter of God. It's at our Baptism that the heavens open, the Spirit descends, and the Father says, "This is my beloved son! This is my beloved daughter!" It's at our Baptism that we truly become sons and daughters in the Son, heirs of the kingdom of heaven, and members of the Body of Christ, the Church. It's at our Baptism that we become temples of the Holy Spirit, are filled with the gifts of the Spirit, and receive the supernatural power to live in the spirit of faith, hope, and charity. It's at our Baptism that we are made sharers in Christ's priesthood and in his prophetic and royal mission. (More on this later.) What a divine blessing!

But how? How can so much good come from one little ceremony of pouring water and pronouncing words? As we learned earlier, its because Christ acts in the Sacraments — especially from the Cross. Indeed, the Sacraments are "mysterious carriers" of the power of Christ's Passion, flowing from his pierced side. Let's now reflect on how baptism in particular is a sharing in Christ's Passion, a real contact with him in his Paschal mystery, beginning with some stunning words of St. Thomas:

> The suffering of the passion of Christ is communicated to the one who is baptized inasmuch as he becomes a member of Christ, as if he himself had borne that pain, and therefore all his sins are remitted through the pain of Christ's passion.[70]

Did you catch that? See why these words are so stunning? According to St. Thomas, in Baptism, we get the same graces as if we ourselves had borne the pain of Christ on the Cross! Think about that for a moment. In Baptism, the Father sees us in the love of his Son on the Cross. He loves us as if we ourselves were obedient unto such a painful death. He loves us in the same way as if we ourselves had expressed the perfect act of love for humanity and for the Father. This is beyond generosity — it's amazing mercy! And in case we missed it, St. Thomas says it again, using different words:

> In Baptism man is incorporated into the passion and death of Christ, according to Romans 6:8: *If we be dead with Christ, we believe that we shall live also with Christ.* It is clear, then, that to everyone who is baptized the passion of Christ is communicated as a healing power, as if he himself suffered and died.[71]

Abbot Vonier, whom we heard from earlier, comments on these words of St. Thomas and seems just about as blown away by this idea as I am. He writes, "Could the sacramental grace be summed up more gloriously? The privilege of the baptized is 'as if he himself had suffered and died!'"[72]

It's not just the good Abbot and me who are astounded by this reality. Amazement at Baptism's power to give us a share in Christ's Passion — without our having to bear the pain — goes back to the earliest days of the Church. In fact, in the Office of Readings of the Liturgy of the Hours, there's an excerpt from one of the ancient catechetical texts of the Church in Jerusalem. The unnamed author marvels at the power of Baptism as a sharing in Christ's Passion:

> This is something amazing and unheard of! It was not we who actually died, were buried and rose again. We only did these things symbolically, but we have been saved in actual fact. It is Christ who was crucified, who was buried and who rose again, and all this has been attributed to us. We share in his sufferings symbolically and gain salvation in reality. What boundless love for men! Christ's undefiled hands were pierced by nails; he suffered the pain. I experience no pain, no anguish,

yet by the share that I have in his sufferings he freely grants me salvation.[73]

We've all heard the phrase, "There's no such thing as a free lunch." We've probably also heard, "No pain, no gain." Well, here we have much more than a free lunch: loads of goodly gain without any pain on our part. Of course, someone did pay the price, and he suffered horribly, terribly, incredibly. Jesus himself took it so we wouldn't have to. He embraced death so we wouldn't have to suffer eternal death in hell. He bore it all so we could be one with him in the unity of the Most Holy Trinity. And yet, as members of his Body, it's fitting that we resemble him in his suffering. It's fitting that we take up our crosses and follow him. But be not afraid! For our crosses are nothing compared to his, and he even gives us the grace to bear their weight. When we do accept our own relatively little crosses, he gives us the further grace of making us more deeply and gloriously transformed into himself.

In short, Baptism brings about our transformation in Christ, but it doesn't complete it. Our transformation is an ongoing process that involves prayer, following the commandments, carrying the cross, and frequenting the Sacraments. Perhaps nothing in this process helps us more than the Sacrament of the Eucharist, to which we now turn our attention.

*T*HE EUCHARIST. Recall the words of my professor in the seminary, "*The sacraments DO something.*" We just learned what Baptism does: It brings about a transforming communion with Christ, making us members of his Body. Well, the Eucharist sustains, deepens, and completes this transforming communion. Following on this idea, in this section, we're going to look at the Eucharist from two perspectives: as a sacrament of transformation and as a sacrament of communion. I believe that these two ideas, *transformation* and *communion*, get to the heart of what the Eucharist is all about.

(a) Transformation. Okay, so let's start with transformation. What's transformed in the Eucharist? Pope Benedict XVI teaches

that there are a series of transformations that take place in the Eucharist. The first and most obvious one is *the transformation of bread and wine into the Body and Blood of Jesus*, which is called "transubstantiation." This means that at the words of consecration, "This is my Body," and "This ... is my Blood," bread and wine are transformed into the Body, Blood, Soul, and Divinity of Jesus Christ. Commenting on this most fundamental transformation that takes place in the Eucharist, the Pope says:

> The substantial conversion of bread and wine into his body and blood introduces within creation the principle of a radical change, a sort of "nuclear fission," to use an image familiar to us today, which penetrates to the heart of all being, a change meant to set off a process which transforms reality, a process leading ultimately to the transfiguration of the entire world, to the point where God will be all in all (cf. 1 Cor 15:28).[74]

At different moments throughout the rest of this book, particularly at the end of Part Three, we'll be tracing this "process which transforms reality," this process that leads to "the transfiguration of the entire world," this process of *redditus* (return) back to the Trinity, "where God will be all in all." (I can hardly wait!) But for now, let's stick with the series of transformations that take place within the Eucharist itself.

The second transformation has to do with one of the signs of the Sacrament, namely, *death and violence*. Death and violence? Yes. Listen to the words of consecration: "This is my body, which will be *given up* for you ... . This is the chalice of my Blood ... which will be *poured out* for you." We hear these words all the time, so their graphic nature might easily be lost on us. But it *is* graphic. Having to give up one's body implies suffering and death. Moreover, blood being poured out usually means pain and violence — and that's exactly what they mean here. The celebration of the Eucharist is a re-presentation of the sacrifice of Calvary,[75] which is where Jesus hands himself over to hate-filled men who violently spill his blood, separating it from his broken body.

Alright, so where's the transformation here? First of all, man's hatred and violence toward the God-man is transformed by God into a perfect act of self-giving love for man, as Pope Benedict XVI says:

> [Jesus] does not counter violence with new violence, as he could have done, but rather he puts an end to violence by transforming it into love. The act of killing, of death, is changed into love; violence is conquered by love.[76]

The Holy Father goes on to say that this transformation of violence and hatred into love, this conquering of death by love, leads from death to life. In fact, he writes, "Death itself is transformed: love is stronger than death. It lasts."[77] And so, there is actually a third transformation taking place here: *death to resurrection*. The dead body becomes a risen body. A body "given up" and blood "poured out" as an act of love of the Son of God becomes a risen reality. Thus, the Eucharist truly contains the whole Paschal mystery: suffering, death, and Resurrection.

This third transformation from death to resurrection is, in fact, why the Eucharist is called "Eucharist" in the first place. For Eucharist means "thanksgiving." Now, is Jesus, at the Last Supper, thanking God for his approaching, violent death? Of course, not. Rather, he's thanking the Father beforehand for delivering him from the power of death (see Ps 16:10), thanking him in advance that his prayer for deliverance will be "heard" (Heb. 5:7). He's praising and thanking the Father for the future gift of the Resurrection.

Pope Benedict writes that it's on the basis of this advance thanksgiving that at the Last Supper, Jesus "could already give his body and blood in the form of bread and wine as a pledge of resurrection and eternal life (cf. Jn 6:53-58)."[78] So, an essential part of the third transformation — death to resurrection — involves the transformation of sorrow to joy and despair to hope.

Thus, while the Eucharist re-presents the sacrifice of Calvary, it also contains the hope of the Resurrection and a prayer of praise and thanksgiving for it. Pope Benedict refers to this prayer as the "essential thing"[79] and "fundamental element"[80] of the Last Supper. Therefore, the Eucharist gets to the very core of the Christian life, because it's a prayerful sacrifice of praise and thanksgiving, even and especially in the face of pain and suffering, because of our trust in our Heavenly Father's providential care.

The fourth transformation has to do with another sign of the Eucharist, namely, *food*. For, when the bread and wine are transformed into the Body and Blood of Christ, they still have the "accidents" of bread and wine. In other words, even though the Eucharist is no longer bread and wine, it still smells like bread and wine, feels like bread and wine, and tastes like bread and wine. Therefore, the Eucharist, the Body and Blood of Christ, can be eaten as food. However, this is no ordinary food. For, most food, when we eat it, becomes assimilated and is transformed into our bodies, but this food, when we eat it, assimilates and transforms us into it. Indeed, it transforms us more deeply into Christ, bringing us "into the very dynamic of his self-giving" love.[81]

In sum, the Eucharist is a sacrament of transformations: It transforms bread and wine into the Body and Blood of Christ; it contains the transformation of violence and hatred into self-giving love; it is the transformation of sorrow and death into the joy of resurrected life through the power of divine love; and it brings us into an even deeper transforming communion with Christ when we eat of it as Holy Communion. And speaking of Holy Communion, let's look more closely at the Eucharist as communion.

(b) Communion. Remember our key to this whole crash course in theology is the super-concept of *communio*. Well, according to Pope Benedict XVI, this concept refers first of all to the Eucharist:

> The concept of *communio* is anchored first and foremost in the most Blessed Sacrament of the

Eucharist, which is why, in the language of the Church, we still describe the reception of this sacrament today, and rightly so, simply as "going to communion."[82]

Let's now look at all the forms of *communio* (communion) created by worthily eating of the Eucharist, the Body of Christ.

First, as we've already mentioned, Holy Communion deepens the transforming communion with Christ caused by the Sacrament of Baptism. As I just mentioned, when we eat the Body of Christ, instead of it becoming part of us (like most food does), we become part of it. In other words, by worthily eating of the Eucharist, we become more deeply united to Christ and become Christ. There's a saying, "You are what you eat." Well, it applies here in a profound way.

Yet, when we receive the Eucharistic Body of Christ, not only are we brought into a deeper communion with Jesus Christ the Head of the Body, we're also brought more deeply into communion with one another, with the other members of Christ's Body. Pope Benedict explains this point with remarkable clarity and beauty:

> We all "eat" *the same man*, not only the same thing; in this we all are wrested from our self-enclosed individuality and drawn into a greater one. We all are assimilated into Christ, and so through communion with Christ we are also identified with one another, identical and one in him, members of one another. To be in communion with Christ is by its very nature to be in communion with one another as well. No more are we alongside one another, each for himself; rather, everyone else who goes to communion is for me, so to speak, "bone of my bone and flesh of my flesh" (cf. Gen 2:23).
>
> A true spirituality of communion, therefore, together with its Christological depth, necessarily has a social character also ... . For this reason, in my prayers at communion I must, on the one hand, look

totally toward Christ, allowing myself to be transformed by him and, as needed, to be consumed in the fire of his love. But precisely for this reason I must always realize also that he joins me in this way with every other communicant — with the one next to me, whom I may not like very much; but also with those who are far away, whether in Asia, Africa, America, or some other place. By becoming one with them, I must learn to open myself toward them and to become involved in their situations. This is the test of the authenticity of my love for Christ.

Whenever I am united with Christ, I am also united with my neighbor, and this unity does not end at the communion rail; rather, it is just beginning there. It comes alive, becomes flesh and blood, in everyday experience of being with others and standing by others. Thus the individual element in my going to communion is inseparably interwoven with my membership in the Church and my dependence upon her life.[83]

The heart of the communion with others that we experience in the Eucharist is summed up by one word in that last sentence: Church. In this paragraph, Pope Benedict focuses on our communion with the members of the Church on earth. But there are also members of the Body of Christ, the Church, *in purgatory* and *in heaven*. At the moment of communion, then, we are particularly united with all of them as well. For instance, we are united with our faithfully departed loved ones and with our Blessed Mother and St. Joseph.

Now, if we're united with all the members of the Church by being united to Jesus Christ in the Eucharist, wouldn't it be strange if we weren't also united with the Trinity? Sure would be. But, in fact, it's not strange, because the Eucharist also brings us into communion with the Holy Trinity. For, while each member of the Trinity is a distinct person, they also interpenetrate one another:

> [T]he Father is wholly in the Son and wholly in the
> Holy Spirit; the Son is wholly in the Father and
> wholly in the Holy Spirit; the Holy Spirit is wholly
> in the Father and wholly in the Son.[84]

So, when we receive Jesus in the Eucharist, the whole Trinity comes into our hearts. While only the Son, Jesus Christ, comes to us sacramentally as flesh and blood — after all, he's the only one of the divine persons who became incarnate — the Father and the Spirit are also truly present because of the presence of the Son. For, wherever the Son is, the Father and Spirit are there also.

I said that in the Eucharist, the Trinity "comes to us." Well, there's also a sense in which, in the celebration of the Eucharist, we "go to the Trinity." This happens during that remarkable moment when the priest at the altar takes the Body and Blood of Christ into his hands, raises it up, and prays,

> Through him, and with him, and in him, O God,
> almighty Father, in the unity of the Holy Spirit, all
> glory and honor is yours, forever and ever.

In that glorious moment, all the faithful lift up their hearts and gather their joys, sorrows, works, and sufferings and, with faith in the power of the Resurrection, unite these offerings and themselves to the Body and Blood of Christ at the altar. Then, through, with, and in Christ, we all go to the Father in the unity of the Holy Spirit. This is exactly a foretaste of the end of time when God will be "all in all" (1 Cor 15:28).

There is so much more we could say about the Sacraments, and especially the Eucharist, but we'll have to end here. Thankfully, there will be more time at the end of Part Three for us to take another look at the Eucharist. Before then, we still have some ground to cover regarding the first of the two ways that we are transformed into Christ, namely, faith. (The second way was the Sacraments.) Actually, before we begin, I can't resist saying just a few words about the Sacrament of Confession ...

Bottom line: Go to confession. Really. As Catholics, we're obliged to sacramentally confess our sins at least once a year, but I highly recommend going at least once a month. Why? First of all, it has the power to restore us to full communion with God if, sadly, we break this communion through mortal sin. Second, it has the power to renew us when we're weighed down with venial sin.[85] In other words, Confession is for *all* of us, no matter how ordinary or extraordinary our sins are.

It's sad that so few Catholics regularly avail themselves of this wonderful Sacrament of Mercy. After all, it's an incredible gift! But don't just take my word for it. Read St. Faustina Kowalska's words about Confession in this endnote.[86]

Okay, now back to faith.

4. Faith and Vatican II

Wait, we already covered faith. So why rehash that road again? We're doing it because of the Second Vatican Council (Vatican II), which took a new, deeper approach to the topic of faith. At least, that's the interpretation of one of the bishops who was at the Council, Karol Wojtyła. But why should we listen to him? After all, there were plenty of bishops at the Council and so many Vatican II voices with their own opinions and interpretations. Well, we should listen to Wojtyła because he became the Pope — and not just any Pope. As John Paul II, he led the Church through the tumultuous post-Vatican II times *for more than 26 years.* So, he especially knows what he's talking about. But before we get to his interpretation of the Council on the topic of faith (and how it deepens our transformation in Christ), let's first review some things about the Council itself.

A DIFFERENT KIND OF COUNCIL. The Second Vatican Council (1962-1965), which is the most important event for the Catholic Church in the modern world, was a different kind of council. Other councils in the history of the Church were dogmatic and apologetic in character — in other words, they defined and defended our Catholic faith, usually against the challenge of heresy. So, while Nicea had its Arius, Ephesus had its Nestorius, and Trent had Martin Luther, Vatican II had no such adversary, enemy, or heretic to oppose. Therefore, it didn't pronounce any condemnations and never intended to announce any infallible dogmas. So what did it do? What was its purpose?

Vatican II was called to respond to a problem, but it wasn't heresy. Rather, it was *duplicity*. In its own words, it calls out the great problem of Christians in the modern world:

> One of the gravest errors of our time is the split between the faith which many profess and the practice of their daily lives. As far back as the Old Testament the prophets vehemently denounced this scandal, and in the New Testament Christ himself with greater force threatened it with severe punishment. Let there, then, be no such pernicious opposition between professional and social activity on the one hand and religious life on the other. The Christian who shirks his temporal duties shirks his duties towards his neighbor, neglects God himself, and endangers his eternal salvation.[87]

Duplicity, the split between what one professes and how one lives, goes back as far as the Old Testament, and it's something that even Jesus himself railed against when he repeatedly blasted the scribes and Pharisees, "Woe to you scribes and Pharisees, hypocrites!" In fact, such duplicity is as old as human nature. Still, there's something about our modern situation that seems to have made duplicity and hypocrisy frighteningly widespread. For, even with all its blessings, the fast-pace of our contemporary society seems especially effective at pulling Christians away from living out the faith. Maybe it comes from being too busy? Maybe it's all the distractions? Whatever the reason, there's the huge problem, for instance, of the "Sunday Catholic" who simply goes to Mass on the Lord's Day and spends the rest of the week without giving a single thought to the Lord.

Despite its forceful language, the Council wasn't out to condemn the likes of "Sunday Catholics" but rather to help them (us?) bridge the divide between faith and life. Thus, it was the first "pastoral council." In fact, its whole purpose, according to Pope John XXIII, who called the Council, was "*aggiornamento*," which basically means "bringing up to date." In other words, the aim of the Council was to proclaim the ancient Catholic faith in a form that would make more sense to the people of today. So, it didn't formulate new doctrine so much as it attempted to express the doctrines of the faith in ways that people of the modern world could better understand and apply to their lives. It tried to answer modern man's burning questions about God, the Church, and man himself. Its goal was to help Catholics get to know and love their faith more deeply.

A DIFFERENT KIND OF CARDINAL. Cardinal Karol Wojtyła, who participated in the Council, wholeheartedly embraced its teachings and vigorously implemented them in his archdiocese of Kraków, Poland. And when he did, the Church fell apart: Religious fled their convents, priests abandoned their parishes, and the faithful left the faith in droves. Right? *Wrong*. The archdiocese of Kraków, unlike much of the rest of the Church, experienced lasting, fruitful, widespread renewal after the Council. Perhaps this was because Wojtyła got it so right. He did exactly what the Council called for by tirelessly helping the faithful in his archdiocese to assimilate its teachings into their lives.

How did he do it? Two steps. First, he wrote *Sources of Renewal: The Implementation of Vatican II*, a book that leads the faithful on an insightful tour through the documents of the Council with an eye to helping them apply its teachings to their lives. By writing it, Wojtyła said he was fulfilling a debt of gratitude to God who so generously spoke in and through the Council. Such a gift, he felt, required a response, and that response is *faith*. Specifically, it's a response of faith to the "word of the Spirit" given to the Church in the Council documents. As a bishop of the Church who personally witnessed the power of this word at the Council, Wojtyła felt a responsibility not only to give an ardent response of faith himself but to help the faithful to fully respond in faith as well. So, again, his first step was to write *Sources of Renewal*.

His second step was basically to implement the major theme of the Council, namely, *communio*. He did this by calling together the *communio* of a local Synod, which was like having a mini-Vatican II in his archdiocese. The heart of this "Synod of Kraków" was the *communio*-gatherings of the faithful in parish-based groups (more than 500 of them throughout the archdiocese) where they studied, shared, and prayerfully pondered the teachings of the Council. By all accounts, these groups were vibrant, dynamic, and cherished experiences of faith for most everyone involved. (As late as 1997, no less than 50 of them were still meeting!) Of course, the main textbook for these meetings was the Cardinal's book, *Sources of Renewal*, which the people loved — especially a curious concept that stood at the center of the book and that guided their whole experience: *the enrichment of faith*.

*T*HE ENRICHMENT OF FAITH. For Wojtyła, the response of faith we owe to the Council is not just any kind of faith but, specifically, the "enrichment of faith," which he sees as "the fundamental requirement for the realization of the Council."[88] To understand what he means by it, I'm going to contrast the enrichment of faith with a common understanding of faith prior to the Council.

Before the Council, if you were to ask most people what faith means, they probably would have said something like this: "The Church said it, I believe it, that settles it." Understood properly, there's nothing wrong with saying that faith means assenting in this way to the truths of the faith. But is this all there is to faith? No way. For Wojtyła and the Council, assent is just the beginning, and the response of faith should go deeper — much deeper. It should become an explicit act of the *whole person* (intellect, will, and heart) who makes the faith his own. Therefore, the teachings of the Church should not *simply* be assented to intellectually — "Yeah, I accept that, I believe that" — but taken deeply to heart such that they form one's conscious life and are expressed in one's attitudes. Indeed, the truths of the faith are not supposed to end in the abstract but are meant to become a concrete reality in the life and very being of the believer. And when this happens, we respond, "I *believe!*" We say, "I've experienced it! It's seeped deeply into my heart and into my very being. I love it, and I'm striving to live it." Without such a deep enrichment of faith, the tragic split between faith and life, between what we profess and how we live our lives, will sadly remain the norm for Catholics in the modern world. It's this norm of duplicity that Vatican II rightly aimed to break.

So, according to Wojtyła, the Council focused not so much on the question, "What should we believe?" but on the more difficult and complex question, "What does it mean to be a believer, a Catholic and a member of the Church?"[89] The difficulty and complexity of this question flows from the difficulty and complexity of being a human person. For we're more than just intellect (thinking) and acts of the will (doing). In fact, each human person is a world unto himself. His inner, conscious life is full of hidden depths and mysteries unknown, and these are definitely not easy to analyze. But the Council is calling us to go there! For the enrichment of faith is not simply about agreeing to the truths of the faith as if superficially from "the outside" ("I believe") but about bringing them to "the inside," that is, into our conscious life and into our hearts such that our inner life, attitudes, and actions are changed by the truths we have cherished within ("I *believe!*").

Thankfully for us, the Council took the more difficult road. It embraced the challenge of "giving Christians a life-style, a way of thinking and acting."[90] It did this not by making a list of rules to follow but by highlighting how to believe, how to bring the truths of the faith deeply into one's heart and into one's conscious life. It did this by describing the attitudes that ought to spring from such enriched faith. Moreover, the Council laid responsibility on the Christian himself to take the truths of the faith to heart, so he could judge everything in light of a *living* and *mature* faith:

> The Council outlined the type of faith which corresponds to the life of the modern Christian, and the implementation of the Council consists first and foremost in enriching that faith. What is needed is "the witness of a living and mature faith, one so well formed that it can see difficulties clearly and overcome them. ... This faith should show its fruitfulness by penetrating the whole life, even the worldly activities, of those who believe."[91]

Fostering such a "living" and "mature" faith, such enriched faith, was the goal of the whole Council. For from such a faith springs attitudes that express the faith amid "the whole of life," and according to Wojtyła, this becomes "true proof of the realization of the Council."[92] The task of forming such mature faith, such a well-formed Christian conscience that bears fruit in authentic Christian attitudes in daily living marks "the direction which should be followed by all pastoral action, the lay apostolate and the whole of the Church's activity."[93] Indeed, Wojtyła sees that the Council has "opened up a new chapter of the Church's pastoral activity."[94]

JOHN PAUL II AND THE ENRICHMENT OF FAITH. Alright, I hope your head is not spinning. That was a lot of deep stuff. If it's not all crystal clear now, don't worry. In this section, I'm going to try to make the idea of the enrichment of faith even clearer. To do this, I want to begin by highlighting a key point from the last section.

Notice that Wojtyła said something rather remarkable: Fostering the enrichment of faith is "the direction which should be followed by all pastoral action, the lay apostolate and the whole of the Church's activity." Well, now that's saying something. *All pastoral action should foster the enrichment of faith? All the apostolic work of the laity? All the Church's activity?*

That's a lot. That's a big deal. In fact, it's such a big deal that when I first read this statement of Wojtyła, I wondered if he forgot about it or backed off such a bold strategy once he became Pope John Paul II. I mean, did John Paul really see the enrichment of faith as the direction that should be followed by *all* the Church's activity? Yes, he did, and it is a big deal.

I first realized that fostering an enrichment of faith really was a key pastoral priority for John Paul II while I was in the seminary. During that time, I studied many of the Pope's writings. I read every major document he wrote and even learned some Polish, so I could delve more deeply into the original texts from before he became Pope. One thing that amazed me about John Paul is the consistency of his thought, specifically on this point of the enrichment of faith as the key pastoral priority. While I don't recall him ever using the phrase, "the enrichment of faith," as Pope, everything he did flowed from this idea. By this, I mean that he was constantly making the faith concrete and livable. He was constantly helping the faithful to bring the Gospel home to their hearts and into their lives.

To show how John Paul did this, I'd like to present three things in this section: (a) the related teaching of Blessed John Henry Newman, (b) several examples of how John Paul II promoted the enrichment of faith, and (c) the golden-key-example of how he did this. Let's start with John Henry Newman.

(a) John Henry Newman. Blessed John Henry Newman? Yes, it may seem a bit random. You may be asking yourself, "What does this 19th century Oxford scholar and English Catholic convert have to do with a 20th century council and a modern day Pope?" Actually, he has *a lot* to do with them. Regarding Vatican II, he's widely recognized as one of the main precursors to the Council. In fact, he's often called "the Father of Vatican II" in the sense that his writings anticipated its main themes. Regarding John Paul II, Newman shares with him the exact same pastoral priority: the enrichment of faith, except Newman doesn't call it this. What does he call it? Well, you're in for a treat — actually, a lot of treats.

Newman doesn't just give another name for the enrichment of faith. Rather, he gives a whole book that explains the entire concept, and it's a masterpiece. It's called *Grammar of Assent*, and while it's by far his most difficult work to understand, it rewards those who wrestle with it. By way of introduction to it, I'd like to contrast Newman with someone else whose writings especially reward wrestling — as in "*Summa* wrestling."

Of course, I'm talking about the author of the *Summa Theologiae*, St. Thomas Aquinas. He's the exact opposite of Newman, at least in this sense: While Newman throws himself into his writing such that you actually meet him there, St. Thomas runs and hides. Really. Besides his stock phrase, "I answer that," you'll be hard pressed to find one single "I" statement in the entire *Summa*, one single personal reference, one single autobiographical line. It's nothing personal, but Thomas isn't interested in being personal. He'd rather have us pay attention to God and theology, and he gets out of the way. One Newman scholar explains this curious difference between Thomas's approach and Newman's:

> Whoever reads Newman with sympathy and understanding cannot fail to be fascinated by the way he lives in his writings and speaks to his readers through them. If we think of St. Thomas Aquinas we right away notice the contrast to Newman. St. Thomas remains hidden behind the issues of which he treats; he practices a sober objectivity whereby he keeps his person out of his discourse; he wants to yield entirely to the truth that he serves and to let it speak for itself after he has presented it. But Newman serves the truth in a different way; in addition to uttering the objective truth, Newman is also present in his words, not only explaining how he personally came to the truth, but also giving witness to the truth. Yes, there is in all his religious writings this passion of a witness. The reader not only finds penetrating arguments and telling rebuttals, he also finds Newman solemnly bearing witness.[95]

So, Newman serves the truth in a different way. He doesn't throw himself into his writings out of some narcissistic need to be recognized but rather to serve the truths of the faith, to bring people to an enrichment of faith. Again, we can find the explanation of how and why this approach works in his *Grammar of Assent*.

The *Grammar of Assent* was something that had been on Newman's heart for more than 35 years before he wrote it. He envisioned it as "a work embodying all the principles I have implied in my books."[96] And, indeed, it really does contain the secrets to Newman's success. I mean that in this sense: When you read the *Grammar* after having had the pleasure of experiencing Newman's other writings, especially his stirring sermons, it suddenly hits you, "So that's what he was doing! That's why he's so moving! That's why his writing is so powerful!" The heart of this Ah-ha! moment comes down to the discovery of one word: *real*. What Newman means by this word is the key that unlocks the brilliance of his world, the key to fully understanding the enrichment of faith, and the key (along with the Sacraments) to our transformation in Christ. So, without any further ado, let's get *real*.

Actually, to get what Newman means by his use of the word "real," we need to contrast it with something else, namely, the word "notional," specifically, *notional knowledge*. What is notional knowledge? For Newman, notional knowledge has to do with "large principles," "general laws," and "common nouns, as standing for what is abstract, general, and non-existing, such as 'Man is an animal, some men are learned, … to err is human, to forgive divine.'"[97] In short, notional has to do with what's abstract, general, and not actually existing. (For all you sports fans out there, it's just about any post-game interview of a professional athlete — can you say, "cliché"? Can you say "sentence after sentence of clichés"? That's notional.)

Protestant Christianity in Newman's day was for him the epitome of what he means by "notional." He found the un-real of the notional in the old Anglican platitude-laden sermons that used so many words yet still said nothing. He even found it in the more lively preaching of the Evangelicals, which to him was "just flourishes" in which "the Lord's name" was used "as a sort of charm or spell to convert men,"[98] and he noted that the "recipients of [this] preaching became 'worn out.'"[99] The problem was that, for Newman, most everything Protestant was notional, meaning there was "nothing definite or tangible."[100] The preachers, he said, would speak in an "unreal mechanical manner"[101] and make "vague statements about [God's] love, His willingness to receive the sinner, His imparting repentance and spiritual aid, and the like." But vagueness doesn't move people, and he called such Protestantism "the dreariest of possible religions."[102]

It wasn't until he came into the Catholic Church, with its robust teaching on the reality of the Sacraments, especially the Eucharist, that he found not only his spiritual but intellectual home. Regarding this experience, he wrote:

> Now after tasting of the awful delight of worshipping God in His Temple, how unspeakably cold is the idea of a Temple without that Divine Presence [of the Eucharist]! ... [It helped to] produce the deep impression of religion of an objective fact. ... It is really most wonderful to see the Divine Presence looking out almost into the open streets from the various [Catholic] Churches. ... I never knew what worship was, as an objective fact, till I entered the Catholic Church.[103]

Here, we've stumbled on Newman's meaning of "real," as in "real knowledge." It's something like the Most Blessed Sacrament: a real, concrete, bodily presence, an "objective fact." As Newman describes it in the *Grammar*, real knowledge has to do not with common nouns but "singular nouns" where "the terms stand for things external to us, unit and individual, as 'Philip was the father of Alexander,' 'the earth goes round the sun,' 'the Apostles first preached to the Jews.'"[104] Knowledge of such *concrete things* is what Newman means by real. And while notional knowledge is important for life — for instance, we couldn't communicate without it — our lifelong task is to come to a real knowledge of the things that are most essential, such as the truths of our faith. Moreover, if our knowledge of these truths remains only on the notional level, then faith for us becomes hollow, shallow, and unreal. And then we find ourselves to be the kind of "Sunday Catholics" who embody the split between faith and life. Newman poured himself out in an effort to prevent this from happening. He was the great champion of the real in matters of religion.

Okay, but how did he do it? He did it, above all, by his preaching — whereby he always strove to keep it real. And what a lot of preaching he did! Newman's many volumes of collected sermons rival the size of Aquinas's *Summa*. Actually, it may be helpful at this point to contrast Aquinas and Newman again to better grasp the point of Newman's pastoral thrust.

Aquinas's *Summa* is the perfection of notional, theological knowledge. In it, he explains all things human and divine in a brilliantly logical, ordered, and intellectual way. His is a masterful treatment, and yet, he himself didn't think so, at least not after "the experience." During the last year of his life, while at Mass on the feast of St. Nicholas, he had a mystical experience of God that afterward made him say, "All that I have written seems to me like straw compared to what has now been revealed to me." Were his works really straw? Of course not. The *Summa* is one of the greatest works of theology. Yet the knowledge it gives, if it stays on the level of general notions, cannot reach the knowledge born of experience, what Newman calls *real* knowledge.

Newman's sermons are so many power-packed presentations communicating *real* knowledge. In each one, he doesn't attempt to treat everything. Rather, he covers one thing, one familiar topic, one single, theological point — He was scrupulous about this. And what wonders he works with a single point! Being one of the best prose writers in the English language, he unpacks his topic using all his marvelous powers of persuasion, rhetoric, and communication. He hammers on some poor, notional point until it bleeds the real.[105] This, he felt, was his solemn duty as a preacher: to bring his listeners to realize (as in REAL-ize) the point. And it worked. When you read Newman's sermons, you actually experience the faith. It comes across in the beauty of the language — read a Newman sermon out loud, it really is stunning in its sound; it literally sings! It comes across in the concreteness of the examples — Newman has the ability to paint a vivid, relatable picture, indeed! Above all, it comes across in the personal witness of Newman's own faith — you can tell that the truths he shares are deeply real to him.

That last point is key. When someone has real knowledge, he becomes a powerful tool for bringing others to the same knowledge. Such knowledge imparts to the one who possesses it

> ... a seriousness and manliness which inspires in other minds a confidence in its views, and is one secret of persuasiveness and influence in the public stage of the world. They create, as the case may be, heroes and saints, great leaders, statesmen, preachers, and reformers ... .[106]

Newman surely possessed this kind of knowledge, and therefore, he had great powers of "persuasiveness and influence." For example, we see it in a surprising Latin statement that was used by some of the undergraduates at Oxford who came under his influence, "*Credo in Newmanum*" ("I believe in Newman"). One of Newman's great admirers explains:

> This was not adolescent hype, ... this just expresses what all of us who are deeply indebted to Newman are willing to say. We have not only been convinced by Newman's teaching, but also convicted by his witness. He has appealed to our intellect, and he has appealed to our imagination. Mind has spoken to mind, and heart has spoken to heart. His influence on us has been intellectual, and it has been personal.[107]

It's interesting that the one who penned this paragraph, John F. Crosby, was one of my professors in college who greatly influenced me. He persuaded me to follow his philosophy (Newman's philosophy) not just through his arguments but above all through his personal witness. So, it went from Newman to Crosby to me, and now, I hope, to *you*! That's how it works. Enriched faith gets passed from one heart to another. I hope I can do it. Crosby sure did, and Newman was the expert. It's no surprise to learn that when he became a cardinal, he choose for his episcopal motto, "*cor ad cor loquitur*," that is, "heart speaks to heart." He chose well, for from the heart flows what is concrete, personal, and real — and this moves other hearts:

> ... deductions have no power of persuasion. The heart is commonly reached, not through the reason, but through the imagination, by means of direct impressions, by the testimony of facts and events, by history, by description. Persons influence us, voices melt us, looks subdue us, deeds inflame us. Many a man will live and die upon a dogma: no man will be a martyr for a conclusion.[108]

The young Karol Wojtyła, who pulled himself away from theatre and Polish literature to follow a vocation to the priesthood, would largely have agreed with these words. As an actor, he knew well the strength of the imagination to move hearts, the power of voices, looks, and direct impressions. Likewise, as a student of Polish culture, he knew well the power of events, history, deeds, and description.

The adult Wojtyła, Pope John Paul II, the history-making actor on the world-stage, also knew well the language of the heart — very well. In fact, he has enriched the faith of more than a billion Catholics and believers, as we'll now see.

(b) Pope John Paul II. It's October 16, 1978. You've just been elected Pope John Paul II, the 265th Pontiff of the Roman Catholic Church. You've spent the last 10 years overseeing what's probably the most successful implementation of Vatican II of any diocese in the world. You said at the beginning of that

implementation process that *all* the pastoral action of the Church, *all* its activity, should be directed to helping believers bring the faith more deeply into their lives — "the enrichment of faith," you called it. Blessed John Henry Newman expressed the same idea using different words, saying the Church's job is to help believers experience the faith as something concrete, personal, and real.

Of course, you're an incredibly consistent man. So, you're surely going to continue this task. You're surely going to help the whole Church implement the Second Vatican Council. You're surely going to go on to enrich the faith of believers throughout the world. So what do you do? How do you make the experience of faith concrete and real in our lives? Here are some suggestions.

First, *go out to all the world*. Look, nobody's faith is as deeply "enriched" as yours. After all, you've been slow-cooked in one of the deepest and richest Catholic cultures on earth. In fact, Polish culture is the very *definition* of "concrete Catholic faith." You were brought up singing *kolendy* (carols) at the Christmas "Wigilia," memorizing more than 600 of these faith-filled songs. All your life, Mass was standing room only. Each year, on All Souls Day, you'd spend the day *with the entire town* at the cemetery, hanging out at the graves of your loved ones surrounded by about a billion candles. You *know* processions. You're *all* about pilgrimages. Not only did you frequently visit the Shrine of Kalwaria Zebrzydowska near your home, but you would walk dozens of miles to the Shrine of Matka Boza Czesto-chowa (Our Lady of Czestochowa), who everyone in your country knows is the Queen of Poland. Oh, and you'd walk that pilgrimage with a huge part of the able-bodied population of Poland. Did I mention singing? You know thousands of Polish patriotic and religious hymns, which often go together. Did I mention poetry? You can recite hundreds of Polish poems by heart. Growing up, there seemed to be a church on every corner, a roadside shrine on every street. *Real saints* were buried in many of your Churches, often next to miraculous images — and yes, miracles really did happen in your town and throughout your country. They were a fact of life. You and your countrymen did *not* work on Sunday. You *did* pray the Rosary. Many of the people you knew personally were hidden saints who knew suffering and offered it up with Christ, because that's just what Polish people do. Yes, so growing up in your land and being such a conscientious believer slow-cooked you to Catholic faith perfection.

Okay, so now go out to all the world with your super-enriched faith. Remember, not everyone experiences the faith as deeply as you Poles. So go out there. Go out to Asia. Go out to North America, South America, Africa. Go to the rest of Europe and Australia. Go to every nook and cranny of the earth, and use your personal influence. Let us see the joy in your face. Let us experience the depth of your prayer. Let us feel your love for Christ. That'll do it. That'll enrich our faith. That'll be a concrete witness from the successor of St. Peter and Vicar of Christ on earth. That'll give us an experience of the Gospel and will encourage the brethren of believers. That'll make the faith real to us. You won't be some far-off and foreign Pope in Rome. You'll be our friend. We'll feel like we actually know you and that you know us. We'll see you looking directly *at us*, even amidst crowds of hundreds of thousands. We'll hear you speaking *to us* with your beautiful baritone voice *in our own languages*. While we're on the topic of the crowds, why not go out to us? Okay, but get ready: We will be the largest crowds in the history of the world. So you'll need a little car to drive you out to us, to take you into our midst — and you can call it a "Pope-mobile." Why not? And when you go out to us, don't just smile and wave. Reach out to us, touch us, bless us, speak to us, love us. That'll do it. That'll make the faith *real* for us.

Okay, second suggestion: *Canonize and beatify as many people as you possibly can.* I know, I know. The other Popes were more conservative on this point. Who cares? Remember how they told you in Kraków that you couldn't have a synod until the new code of canon law came out? Well, you made it happen anyway. So make it happen, John Paul. You're the Pope! And remember that the Second Vatican Council proclaimed a "universal call to holiness." How will people strive for holiness when it seems like the saints are all in Italy or Poland or places like that? Give us *concrete examples* of holiness. Give us our own saints! Saints who spoke our language. Saints who lived in our own time. Saints who came from our different walks of life. Saints who shared our specific burdens, struggles, and crosses. There already are many of these saints. You just need to officially recognize them. So, make saints, blesseds, and venerables by the hundreds — no, not by the hundreds, by the thousands! Why not? You can do it. You're the Pope! You remember all the hidden saints you yourself met during the dark days of the War. You remember those hidden martyrs and heroic men and women of faith. Well, don't hide them under a bushel basket. Let their light shine! Come on, John Paul. Let their light shine! The light of their faith will enrich the faith of the Church. It will make the faith real to us. It will bring it into our hearts. Holiness will have a face. Holiness will have a name. Each land will have its own patrons, its own intercessors to call on. This will bring the faith home to us. It will enrich our faith, and with our faith so enriched, we ourselves will be inspired to become saints. Lift up one saint, and a thousand follow in their wake. Saints breed saints — so get to it!

Third, *teach us how to pray*. We can't be saints, our faith can't be enriched, we can't be transformed in Christ *unless we pray*. And we can't pray unless someone teaches us. So teach us how to pray. But you don't have to reinvent the wheel, because there's already a perfect prayer, the Rosary. Teach us to pray it. Remind us to pray it.

Look, Mary has already acted in extraordinary ways to strengthen the faith of her children here on earth. She's undeniably appeared to people in our modern time. She's made herself very concrete. For instance, she appeared to St. Juan Diego in Mexico on a tilma that lasts to this day. She spoke in Lourdes, France, to St. Bernadette and gave a miraculous spring where people are healed by the hundreds even to this day! She spoke to three simple shepherd children in Fatima, Portugal, and gave evidence of her visits to more than 70,000 people through a massive miracle of the sun, and the secular newspaper accounts — with photos — remain to this day! Also, that Lady of Fatima will save your life on her feast. (You'll see.) Don't forget to be grateful, and remember what she said, "Pray the Rosary."

So, John Paul, teach us to pray the Rosary better. It's such a beautiful prayer. It helps make the faith concrete and real. It shows us that Jesus isn't just an idea. He's alive in his mysteries! Teach us to reflect on these mysteries. Actually, why not give us some more mysteries? This will encourage us to pray the Rosary and will enrich our faith. We've got Joyful, Sorrowful, and Glorious Mysteries already. Give us the Luminous Mysteries! Help us to see the light of Christ. Help us to reflect on his Baptism in the Jordan, to see the glory of his turning water into wine, to hear him preaching the good news of the kingdom, to bathe in the light of his radiance on Tabor, and to reflect on his concrete, bodily gift of love in the Eucharist. Come on, John Paul, you can do it!

And while we're on the topic of Mary, speak about her all the time. She helps make the faith concrete. In fact, inspire us to entrust ourselves to Mary, to consecrate ourselves to her motherly care. As you know, in the words of our beloved St. Louis de Montfort, this is one of the "quickest, easiest, surest and most perfect" ways to grow in holiness. Joined with faith and a sacramental life, it's the best way to be transformed in Christ! So be completely a "*totus tuus*" Pope. In other words, make Marian consecration your motto. And let us know, let us feel, let us experience that we have a spiritual mother, a real heavenly mother. Make this real for us. Do everything you can, so we'll realize that we have a mother in the order of grace who loves us tenderly. Help us to have a relationship with her, to entrust ourselves to her motherly care, and she will do the rest. She will lead us to her Son, to a deep, personal relationship with him. Then, with her spouse, the Holy Spirit, we'll be transformed in Christ so quickly and effectively.

Fourth, *help us to live a sacramental life, centered on the Eucharist.* Remind us of our Baptism, which brought us into Christ. Remind us that the Mass, the Eucharist, is the "source and summit" of the Christian life. Remind us that we need to approach the Eucharist through regular reception of the

Sacrament of Mercy (Confession). Also, renew devotion to the Eucharist outside of Mass. After the Second Vatican Council, Poland is doing well, but it hasn't been the same story nearly everywhere else. There's been so much confusion, especially in those places where people thought the Council called on us to get rid of devotions like the Rosary and Adoration of the Eucharist. Tell them, "No, no, no!" Help them see that these tried and tested devotions, and many others, actually lead to the celebration of the Eucharist and deepen our faith. How can we have a concrete and living faith without concrete devotions? What can be more concrete than visiting Jesus himself in the Most Blessed Sacrament, who waits for us with love? So, encourage people to love the Mass, fully participate in the Mass, live the Mass, and to adore Jesus truly present in the Blessed Sacrament. Give your own testimony to the power of this prayer.

Fifth, *invite young people to join you in prayer*. Help them discover the gift of *communio* and Christian fellowship. They are hungering for it more and more as modern life becomes increasingly individualistic, isolated, and lonely. When they see and experience hundreds of thousands of their fellow Catholics united in faith and prayer, their faith will deepen. They will say no to the "cultural-Catholic-with-no-commitment" mentality. You will make *communio* real for them, and they will long for a deeper *communio* with Christ in prayer, in the Sacraments, and in continued fellowship. And since these gatherings will be for the youth of the whole world, why not call them "World Youth Days"?

Sixth, *proclaim the dignity of the human person*. Open our eyes and hearts to the wonder of what it means to be a human person. Help us to see that it is "only in the mystery of the Word made flesh that the mystery of man truly becomes clear." Teach us that faith doesn't take us away from being truly human but that the glory of God is man fully alive! Also, call out the great attacks against human dignity. Have the courage to call things by their proper names, teaching the hard truth that euthanasia and abortion are *murder*. And teach us how to build a concrete culture of life in which the elderly are cherished, the unborn are loved, and those in crisis pregnancies and those who have been wounded by abortion are cared for and supported. Against the lies of the culture of death — for instance, that happiness is found in selfishness — proclaim the Gospel of Life, which declares that life finds its meaning not in selfishness but in self-giving love. And on this theme of self-giving, make it super concrete, so we'll see that it's as close to us as our very bodies, which we often forget are temples of the Holy Spirit and members of the Body of Christ. Yes, teach us this. Remind us of this. Give us a *theology of the body*!

Finally, *help us to rediscover who God is*. If we don't know the true face of God, that he is our Father who is rich in mercy (Eph 2:4), then we won't fully enter into a relationship with him. Everything hangs on this. Help us to know that God is mercy. Saint Faustina Kowalska will help you. Be a witness to the infinite mercy of God and totally trust in him.

John Paul, if you do all of this, then you will enrich the faith of the whole world. We will discover the faith as something concrete, real, and a relevant part of our lives. There will be the beginning of a new springtime in the Church during which the split between faith and life will be overcome, and ardent, on-fire Catholics will lead a new evangelization that will bring the whole world to God in Christ Jesus our Lord.

Of course, Pope John Paul II, the 265th Pontiff of the Roman Catholic Church, did all of this and more. Have we paid attention? Did it enrich our faith? Are we being transformed in Christ? To help us pay attention, I now want to direct our focus to what is perhaps the most important part of John Paul's whole pastoral program: Divine Mercy, which helps us rediscover the true face of God.

(c) The Message of Divine Mercy. If you're not familiar with the message of Divine Mercy, you may want to read Appendix Two first, which gives a kind of introductory course on the Divine Mercy message and devotion — think of it as "Divine Mercy 101." In what follows, I'm just going to cover the Divine Mercy basics and how those basics provide what I

earlier called the "golden-key-example" of John Paul's efforts to enrich our faith.

Now, we've all heard that God is merciful. In fact, we've probably heard a thousand times that God loves us, forgives us our sins, and so on. But simply hearing it only gives us a *notional* knowledge of Divine Mercy. So, how do we make it *real*? How do we come to a real, concrete, experiential knowledge of God's mercy? That's the challenge of the enrichment of faith, and here we're dealing with one of its biggest challenges.

Coming to know God's mercy in a "real" way is a big challenge because of original sin. Recall that we learned earlier that, after the fall, humanity now has a distorted image of God. In other words, we now tend to see God as someone from whom we want to run and hide (see Gen 3:8-10), as someone who is anything but merciful. And this original wound runs deep. For even the most faithful Christians are at times tempted to doubt God's love and mercy. For instance, on this point, St. Mother Teresa herself stated, "This is a danger for all of us."[109]

Okay, so Divine Mercy is a hard truth to get into our hearts. Well, why not skip it? Why not go for one of the easier truths, like the fact that we'll all die. Yeah, we can simply picture ourselves on our deathbeds, or something like that, and then be on our way. Morbid? Yes. But hey, it's an easy one. I mean, it doesn't take much for that truth to sink in if we just stop and think about it. It's as easy as a reflective visit to a cemetery. Of course, we don't like to think such thoughts, but my point is that the idea "human mortality" (notional knowledge) is relatively easy to convert to "I'm going to die someday" (real knowledge). On the other hand, converting the truth "God is merciful" (notional knowledge) to "God loves me ... he really loves *me*! ... and he loves me not because I'm so good but because I need his love and because he is Mercy itself" (real knowledge) can be a tough one to really let sink in.

So again, why not skip the lesson on Divine Mercy and stick with the simpler truths? Unfortunately, we can't. The truth of God's mercy is one of the most important lessons — if not *the* most important. After all, it's connected to the great commandment, "Love God with your whole heart, soul, mind, and strength" (see Mk 12:30). Right? It's like this: We're commanded to love God, but we cannot love what we do not know. And to know God is to know his mercy. Specifically, I say *mercy* and not just love. Why? Because of who God is and who we are. Bear with me ...

God is love. That's true. But when it comes to God's love for us, it always takes the form of *merciful love*. Why? Because of who we are. And who are we? Sinners. We're weak, broken, suffering sinners — that's right, every last one of us (see Rom 3:10-12). And what do we call love when it meets sin, weakness, and suffering? This kind of love is called *mercy*. So, this side of eternity, God's love for us is always *merciful* love.

Alright, so now it should be clear that, for us, to know God is to know his mercy. It's to know that he is infinite mercy, to know that he is Divine Mercy. And the more we come to know God's mercy, experience it, and make it real in our lives, then the more we will love God in return. That, in a nutshell, is what life is all about: receiving God's mercy and loving him in return. (We'll talk about loving our neighbor in Part Three.) So, basically, everything comes down to having a real knowledge of God as Divine Mercy.

And now, finally, after having sorted all this out, we're back to the million-dollar question: *How do we make it real? How do we come to a real knowledge of God's mercy?* We've just learned that it's difficult. We've just learned that it's super important. Alright then, so how do we get it? How do we make it real? Before giving John Paul's answer, I'd like to briefly look at Newman's, simply because it's so beautiful, not only in content but expression.

Newman says, "Survey your life and you will find it a mass of mercies."[110] In other words, if we simply take the time to review and reflect on our lives, we'll see so many instances of God's mercy, so many instances where he has helped us in moments of difficulty or distress. Newman further says, "One's whole life is a long experience" of God's mercy. In fact, for him, it really amounts to a kind of "proof" of mercy, as he explains to a friend:

[T]he proof which comes home to my own mind
that God is good, is His dealings with myself. This
proof any man may have — for it is a personal proof.
Nothing can get rid of it, and it grows the more it is
cultivated.[111]

So, Newman's answer as to how we can come to a real
knowledge of God's mercy is *to reflect on our lives*. He would
even advise us to prayerfully review each day at the end of the
day to recognize God's many gifts to us, which cultivates a real
knowledge of God's goodness and mercy.

Like Newman, Pope John Paul II also recommends that
we reflect on our lives and recognize God's mercy, but he goes
on to encourage us to embrace the Divine Mercy message and
devotion. Why? Because it's a powerful tool to help bring about
an enrichment of our faith regarding God's mercy. Here's the
background as to why.

Having grown up in such a rich Catholic culture as Poland,
John Paul knew that the enrichment of faith *usually comes
through a convergence of various avenues, channels, and influences.* We might understand this idea through a water analogy:
A little country brook meandering through a meadow isn't so
impressive. But when a thousand little brooks converge and
pour into a mighty river, well, then, we're dealing with something
substantial! Or, to use one of Newman's own descriptions, an
accumulation of influences are "like a bundle of sticks, each of
which … you could snap in two, if taken separately from the
rest,"[112] but as a bundle, they're virtually unbreakable.

In light of these illustrations, John Paul would say something like, "Yes, let's follow Newman's practice of reflecting
on our lives and recognizing God's mercy, *but there are also
many other influences that can help us come to realize his Mercy.*"
Again, some of these "other influences" that he vigorously and
consistently promoted are those found in the Divine Mercy
message and devotion that comes to us through St. Maria
Faustina Kowalska (1905-1938).

Instead of explaining the details of this message and devotion here, I'm going to limit myself to just generally pointing out the various aspects of the devotion, which approach the mystery of mercy from different *angles of influence*. This requires great restraint on my part, because I love the Divine Mercy message and devotion so much that I would like nothing more than to describe all the glorious details to you. To get those details, again, I encourage you to read Appendix Two. Until then, here's a barebones description of the different aspects of the devotion and how each aspect covers an important angle of influence in our experience of Divine Mercy.

First, there's the *angle of the personal*. For John Henry Newman, you can't get much more concrete than what's personal. For me, you can't get more personal than a diary. Well, the modern Divine Mercy message and devotion is incredibly concrete and personal, because its main source is the *Diary of St. Maria Faustina Kowalska*, which contains the thoughts, prayers, and mystical experiences of the one that Pope John Paul II called "the great Apostle of Divine Mercy in our time."[113] The testimony to God's mercy found in her *Diary* is deeply moving. In fact, many times, I've heard people say, "After the Bible, nothing has touched my heart more than the *Diary of St. Faustina*." I've also heard people say things such as, "It healed my image of God," and, "I now truly see God as my loving and merciful Father." In sum, the most concrete is often the most personal; often what's most personal is a diary; and the *Diary of St. Faustina* is a most deeply moving testimony to God's mercy. Indeed, the *Diary* makes Divine Mercy something concrete, personal, and real.

Second, there's the *angle of artwork* with the Image of Divine Mercy. Jesus asked St. Faustina to have an image painted according to the way he appeared to her, namely, as the merciful Savior. In the image, Jesus is taking a step toward the viewer. His right hand is slightly raised in a gesture of blessing, and his left hand points to an opening at the breast of his garment, revealing two rays of light that issue from his heart — a red ray and a pale ray, representing the blood and water that gushed forth from his pierced side as he hung upon the Cross (see Jn 19:34). At the bottom of the image appear the words, "Jesus, I trust in you."

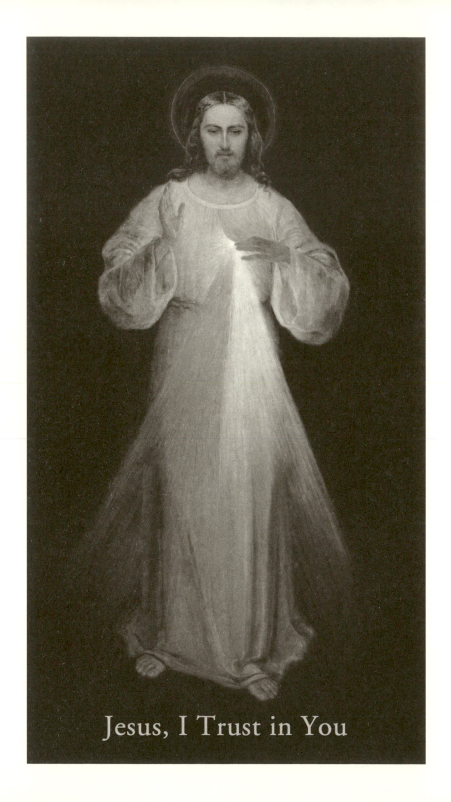

Jesus, I Trust in You

All the elements of this dramatic image combine to draw the viewer into a concrete experience of mercy. It doesn't speak so much to the mind as to the heart as in "heart speaks to heart," for the Merciful Heart of Jesus gently calls to us, "Receive My mercy." And our heart responds, "Jesus, I trust in you." At the Shrine of Divine Mercy in Kraków, Poland, Pope John Paul II commented on this dialogue that Jesus has with us through the Divine Mercy Image:

> Anyone can come here, look at this picture of the Merciful Jesus, his Heart radiating grace, and hear in the depths of his own soul what [St.] Faustina heard: "Fear nothing. I am with you always" (*Diary*, n. 586). And if this person responds with a sincere heart: "Jesus, I trust in you!", he will find comfort in all his anxieties and fears. In this dialogue of abandonment, there is established between man and Christ a special bond that sets love free. And "there is no fear in love, but perfect love casts out fear" (1 Jn 4:18).[114]

Third, there's the *angle of concrete prayer*, both personal-devotional and communal-liturgical. Regarding the personal, devotional prayer, there's the Chaplet of Divine Mercy, which is recited on ordinary rosary beads. It brings the one who prays it into a rhythmic invocation of the mercy of God in view of Christ's suffering. We see this in the prayer that's repeated on the "Hail Mary" beads, "For the sake of His sorrowful Passion, have mercy on us and on the whole world."

The prayer of the chaplet also echoes the liturgy, particularly during one of its holiest moments, namely, when the priest at the altar, holding the Body and Blood of Christ in his hands, says, "Through him, and with him, and in him, O God, almighty Father, in the unity of the Holy Spirit, all glory and honor is yours, forever and ever." The chaplet echoes this moment because, on the "Our Father" beads, one prays, "Eternal Father, I offer You the Body and Blood, Soul and Divinity of Your dearly beloved Son, our Lord, Jesus Christ, in atonement for our sins and those of the whole world." The Chaplet of Divine

Mercy, therefore, serves to bring about a powerful, personal experience of the mercy of God that also echoes the prayer of the Eucharistic Liturgy.

Regarding the communal-liturgical angle of influence, Pope John Paul II officially established the solemnity of Divine Mercy Sunday, which falls on the Second Sunday of Easter. Thus, the faithful can now gather every year to solemnly celebrate the liturgical feast of Divine Mercy, where Divine Mercy, which is at the heart of every liturgy, finds even more explicit expression. Indeed, nothing makes Divine Mercy more "real" than the liturgy, where God's mercy becomes incarnate in the Eucharist, the real bodily presence of Christ that we have the opportunity to receive. And because Jesus promised to pour out extraordinary gifts of grace on Divine Mercy Sunday, especially to those who receive the Eucharist, the experience of Divine Mercy on the Feast of Mercy becomes even more intense. (I encourage everyone to read about these extraordinary gifts of grace in Appendix Two.)

Next, there's the *angle of time*. The liturgical feast of Divine Mercy, Divine Mercy Sunday, which we just covered, obviously carries over into this category, because the feast is an *entire day* devoted to mercy. Yet there's an aspect of the devotion that's not just once a year but *every day*, kind of like a mini-Mercy Sunday each day. It's called the "Hour of Great Mercy." Jesus told St. Faustina that every day between 3:00 p.m. and 4:00 p.m. is the Hour of Great Mercy, a time of special grace during which Jesus wants people to reflect on the gift of his mercy, especially as it's poured out through his Passion and death. He promised to give many graces and blessings during this hour, and therefore, it's a privileged time to experience mercy. He also taught Faustina a Novena to Divine Mercy, which begins on Good Friday and ends the day before Divine Mercy Sunday, but it can be prayed at any other time as well. As nine days of prayer, this novena provides a prolonged reflection on and experience of God's mercy. Both this prayer and the Hour of Great Mercy are ways of creating daily contact with mercy that make it real for each one of us.

Finally, there's the *angle of action*. The Divine Mercy message and devotion culminates in a call to put mercy into action, a call to live mercy in deed, word, and prayer. While acts of mercy certainly flow from an enriched faith, performing them further strengthens our faith. In other words, putting mercy into action makes mercy real, concrete, and incarnate in our lives.

According to Pope John Paul II, the Divine Mercy message and devotion that I've been describing "has always been near and dear" to him and helped "form the image" of his pontificate.[115] In fact, not only did he write his second encyclical letter on Divine Mercy, *Dives in Misericordia* (*Rich in Mercy*), but he declared that from the beginning of his papacy, he saw the message of Divine Mercy as a "special task" assigned to him by God for our troubled times.[116] Pope Benedict XVI stated that the message of Divine Mercy was at "the center" of his predecessor's pontificate and a "synthesis of his magisterium," which goes to show that devotion to Divine Mercy "is not a secondary devotion, but an integral dimension of Christian faith and prayer."[117]

Why was the Divine Mercy message and devotion so important to John Paul? Again, because it helps people go from having a mere notional knowledge to a real knowledge of one of the most central truths of our faith: the truth that God is Love and Mercy itself. Like a wise general, the Pope enlisted the different aspects of the devotion, with their varied angles of influence as the perfect weapons for a multi-pronged rescue assault on the fortress of our hardened hearts. In other words, he knew that the devotion would help us fearful creatures to stop hiding from God, open our hearts, and experience his tender love and mercy. Summing up, those rescue weapons are as follows: *Diary of St. Faustina* (personal testimony), the Image of Divine Mercy (artistic expression), the Chaplet and the Novena of Divine Mercy (personal prayer), Divine Mercy Sunday (liturgical prayer), and the Hour of Great Mercy (sanctified time of prayer).[118]

Before closing this section, one question: What happens when someone is deeply influenced by a mystery such as Divine

Mercy? What happens when a truth of the faith goes from our heads to our hearts? *Christian attitudes* are what happen. In other words, according to John Paul II, a change takes place in those for whom the truths of the faith become "real." What change? Their overall outlook and basic spiritual attitude becomes a response to the given truth or mystery. In the case of the mystery of mercy, this attitude is the most fundamental of all Christian attitudes, namely, *faith*, which in the language of the Divine Mercy devotion is beautifully expressed by the prayer, "Jesus, I trust in you." So, for instance, we see this attitude in someone who has realized the truth of God's mercy deeply in his heart, who does not get discouraged by his weaknesses and falls, who does not live in fear about the future but rather has faith in God's mercy as he strives for holiness and enjoys the fruit of such an attitude of trust, namely, the peace of Christ.

In the next, final section of Part Two, we'll explore just how fundamental and timely this attitude of faith and trust is for ourselves and for the world.

5. Faith and the End of the World

There's a passage in the *Diary of St. Faustina* that used to trouble me during my seminary days. In it, St. Faustina relates that while she was praying for her country, she heard the Lord speak to her in the depths of her soul:

> **I bear a special love for Poland, and if she will be obedient to My will, I will exalt her in might and holiness. From her will come forth the spark that will prepare the world for My final coming.**[119]

This passage troubled me because I don't particularly like apocalyptic messages. For one, we don't know the day or the hour of the Lord's coming (see Mt 24:36), and speculation about it can be a distraction. Second, the end of the world isn't exactly a pleasant idea. Third, I thought this passage might scare off some of the clergy.

What I mean by that last point is that while I was in the seminary and before the Divine Mercy message and devotion became more widely known in the Church, I often heard and was saddened by statements made by some clergy that basically dismissed the whole thing as "just another 'unnecessary' devotion." In fact, a few of them wondered aloud whether devotions involving mystics might border on the "fanatical."[120] I thought to myself, "Gosh, if these guys were ever to read this 'spark' passage about the final coming of the Lord, they'd surely dismiss the whole thing." So, when I would come across that passage, I'd quickly move on and hope that those critical clergymen would never see it.

In the summer of 2002, I was shocked to read a homily by Pope John Paul II in which he not only quoted the passage about "the spark" but actually placed it at the heart of his message! You'll have to read it for yourself below to see what I mean. I'll just preface his words by saying that the occasion for him giving these words was the dedication of the Shrine of Divine Mercy in Kraków, Poland, during which he entrusted the entire world to Divine Mercy.

> Today, therefore, in this Shrine, I wish *solemnly to entrust the world to Divine Mercy*. I do so with the burning desire that the message of God's merciful love, proclaimed here through Saint Faustina, *may be made known to all the peoples of the earth* and fill their hearts with hope. May this message radiate from this place to our beloved homeland and throughout the world. May the binding promise of the Lord Jesus be fulfilled: from here there must go forth "the spark which will prepare the world for his final coming" (cf. *Diary*, n. 1732). This spark needs to be lighted by the grace of God. This fire of mercy needs to be passed on to the world. *In the mercy of God the world will find peace and mankind will find happiness!*[121]

Perhaps you're as surprised as I was when I first read those words. Here, we see that John Paul not only cites the "spark" passage but even strengthens its meaning by talking about it as a "binding promise" from the Lord! Then, he identifies the spark that will prepare the world for the Lord's final coming as the message of Divine Mercy, the true hope for the world. That's pretty amazing — but what exactly does this "preparing the world for the Lord's final coming" actually mean?

I realized the answer to this question shortly after John Paul died. Before I get to it, though, I should first say some things about the circumstances of his death, the most important of which was the timing.

Pope John Paul II died on April 2, 2005. In itself, that date isn't particularly special. What is particularly special is that April 2nd that year was *the day before Divine Mercy Sunday*. In other words, he was so close! I mean, he *just missed* dying on Divine Mercy Sunday. If only he could have held out for one more day! Actually, there's more to it than that.

John Paul's longtime personal secretary, then Archbishop Stanislaus Dziwisz, relates that at one point not long before the Pope died, he felt a strong tug in his soul, basically telling him to celebrate Mass in the room right away. Because it was past evening, Dziwisz offered the Vigil Mass for Divine Mercy Sunday. Although John Paul was going in and out of consciousness at the time of the Mass, he was able to receive a droplet of the Precious Blood of Christ and then died less than an hour later. In the words of Pope Benedict XVI, John Paul died "in the arms of mercy" on the very vigil of the feast day he had established![122] So, the Great Mercy Pope *did* go on Mercy Sunday, because vigils can be celebrated on the evening or night before the actual feast. To give an idea of how powerful this timing was, I'd like to relate a brief anecdote.

Pope John Paul II established Divine Mercy Sunday as an official feast of the Church on April 30 (Divine Mercy Sunday) during the Great Jubilee Year 2000. He announced the establishment of the feast, which took everyone by surprise, during his homily for the Mass of canonization of Faustina Kowalska. A banquet followed the Mass for those who had been involved with Faustina's process for canonization, and John Paul attended. One of the priests in my community, Fr. Seraphim Michalenko, MIC, who had done a lot of behind-the-scenes work for the canonization process, also attended the banquet. He relates that during the banquet, the Pope made a stunning revelation to Dr. Valentin Fuster, the cardiologist who investigated the canonization miracle. With deep emotion, John Paul told him, *"Today is the happiest day of my life."*

Wow. Surely John Paul had had a lot of happy moments in his life. Why was this day the happiest? I suggest that it was because he felt he was accomplishing his mission. Recall that he believed the message of Divine Mercy to be a "special task" assigned to him by God. Well, on that April 30, 2000, not only did he canonize Faustina, but he also declared Divine Mercy Sunday an official feast in the Church — a double-whammy of grace! How fitting it is, then, that the Great Mercy Pope would be called home to his eternal reward on the very feast that had brought him so much joy. But there's even more to the story.

The day after he died, on Divine Mercy Sunday, a message from Pope John Paul was read to the pilgrims gathered for Mass in St. Peter's Square. The Pope had prepared the message before he died and had intended to deliver it himself for the great feast day. Of course, he himself couldn't give it because he had passed away, so one of the archbishops of the Vatican read it. The message concluded with these words:

> How much the world needs to understand and accept Divine Mercy! Lord, who reveal the Father's love by your death and Resurrection, we believe in you and confidently repeat to you today: Jesus, I trust in you, have mercy upon us and upon the whole world.[123]

When I read this final message from the Great Mercy Pope, I was stunned — and enlightened. Here was the answer to the question I had had about Divine Mercy as the "spark" that will prepare the world for the Lord's final coming. Let me explain.

Of course, we don't know the day or the hour of the Lord's coming (see Mt 25:13). Nevertheless, keeping in mind his statement about the "spark" being Divine Mercy, John Paul's last words tell us that *the way we're to prepare for the Lord's coming is not with fear and trembling but with trust in Divine Mercy.* "Jesus, I trust in you." These words summarize the spiritual attitude we should have as we await the Lord's coming, whenever it may be.

"Jesus, I trust in you." I reflected on how this prayer at the end of John Paul's pontificate echoes its very beginning. For, during his very first homily as Pope, John Paul expressed the words that would become a hallmark of his entire pontificate: "Be not afraid!" Actually, the words "Jesus, I trust in you" are more than an echo of "Be not afraid!" They're the response. It's like this: John Paul begins by telling us what to do ("Be not afraid!") and ends by reminding us how to do it ("Jesus, I trust in you").

The interpretation I've just given to "Jesus, I trust in you" and the "spark" passage from the *Diary of St. Faustina* — that we prepare for the Lord's final coming not with fear but with trust in Divine Mercy — coincides with a statement of Pope Benedict XVI during an interview in 2010. The reporter asked him the following:

> About eighty years ago, Faustina Kowalska, the Polish nun canonized by John Paul II, heard Jesus say in a vision "You will prepare the world for my definitive return." Are we obliged to believe that?

The Pope responded as follows:

> If one took [Jesus' words to Faustina] in a chronological sense, as an injunction to get ready, as it were, immediately for the Second Coming, it would be false. But it is correct if one understands it in the spiritual sense ... as meaning that the Lord is always the One who comes and that we are always also preparing ourselves for his definitive coming, precisely when we go out to meet his mercy and allow ourselves to be formed by him. By letting ourselves be formed by God's gift of mercy as a force to counteract the mercilessness of the world, then we prepare, as it were, for his own coming in person and for his mercy.[124]

I think the key lines in the Pope's answer are "allow ourselves to be formed by him" and "letting ourselves be formed by God's gift of mercy." But what does it mean to "allow" someone to form us? More concretely, what does it mean to "allow" Jesus to form us by his "gift of mercy"? It means that we're to trust him, to have faith in him. So, when we trust in Jesus, when we say, "Jesus, I trust in you," when we are not afraid to let Jesus form us, then what does he do? How does he form us? More specifically, how does he *transform* us?

As we've been learning throughout this chapter, Jesus transforms us, through the power of the Spirit, *into himself*, making us into members of his very Body. We've learned that this transformation is a process, beginning in Baptism, nourished by the other Sacraments — especially the Eucharist — and deepened through living a life of faith. In my summary description of the pontificate of John Paul II (pages 113-119), we learned that the life of faith is also nourished by personal prayer and devotion, deepened by entrusting ourselves to the care of the Mother of God, and that it all aims at a love of God and neighbor.

So, in short, we prepare for the coming of the Lord by trusting in Jesus, by allowing him to transform us into himself, by living a sacramental life of faith. Alright, but now here's an amazing thought: In a sense, *our transformation in Christ IS the coming of the Lord*. Let's close by reflecting on what this means.

Recall that our final end is communion with the Trinity. That's the goal, the destination of our journey. We all go back with Christ, to the Father, in the Spirit by being transformed in Christ. Alright, in a sense, this is how the Lord comes again: *when his Body goes to him*, when we "form that perfect man who is Christ come to full stature" (Eph 4:13), when God will bring "all things in the heavens and on earth into one under Christ's headship" (Eph 1:10), when God becomes "all in all" (1 Cor 15:28).

To help us understand this coming of the Lord as including *our going to him*, let's read a passage from the beginning of the Acts of the Apostles, right after Jesus ascended into heaven:

[Jesus] was lifted up, and a cloud took him out of their sight. And while they were gazing into heaven as he went, behold, two men stood by them in white robes, and said, "Men of Galilee, why do you stand looking into heaven? This Jesus, who was taken up from you into heaven, will come in the same way as you saw him go into heaven" (1:9-11).

That last line is most telling. Jesus "will come in the same way as you saw him go into heaven." On it's surface, that's kind of a strange thought. Jesus will *come* again in the same way they saw him *go* to heaven. I think what this is saying is that part of how Jesus *comes* again is when his Body *goes* to him. Specifically, it's when his Body goes to him in the same way that he went, namely, by being "lifted up." I suggest that our being "lifted up" is not only the resurrection of our bodies at the end of time, but also our ongoing transformation in Christ and that all this is included in the mystery of how the Lord will come. At least one theologian expresses a similar idea:

> Instead of imagining [the Lord's] coming in glory as a kind of space travel, the reversal of what happened at the Ascension, we rather understand it as our transformation. The change will take place in us, not in him. The disproportion between our state and his will disappear, when the Spirit transforms this lowly body of ours into the likeness of his glorified body (Phil 3:21). Then we will become his members in the full sense of the word, the extension of his glorified personal body. As a result, we will then see Christ as he is in his glory, dwelling in him and he in us; and through Christ, with Christ, and in Christ, we will see the Father face to face and will recognize him as our Father.[125]

Like so much of our Christian life, we're dealing here with an "already but not yet" reality. We will be "lifted up" at the resurrection of our bodies. But, again, in a sense, we are *already being lifted up* as we're transformed into Christ in this life. Thus, we could say that the more we trust in Jesus and allow him to transform us, the more we already are being lifted up, which hastens and even helps bring about the "coming of Christ," which seems to include *our going to him.*[126]

Finally, at this point, I can now give the full answer to my question about the meaning of the "spark" that will prepare the world for the Lord's final coming. First, the spark is the message of Divine Mercy. Second, this message helps move us to trust completely in Jesus. Third, completely trusting in Jesus, allowing him to work in and through us, powerfully brings about our transformation in him. Fourth, our transformation in Christ is our "going to him." Fifth, this going to him is part of the mystery of his final coming insofar as it hastens it, prepares for it, and may even be a kind of cause of it.

Of course, if you're reading this book, the final coming hasn't happened yet. So, during this "not yet" time, this time of awaiting the Lord's final coming in hope — there's plenty of work to do. We're not just to sit idly by! In a sense, there are *two main works.* Throughout this Part Two, we've been talking about one of them, namely, the work of our own transformation in Christ through faith and the Sacraments. In Part Three, we'll be learning about the second work, namely, our mission to others and to the world, a mission of communion.

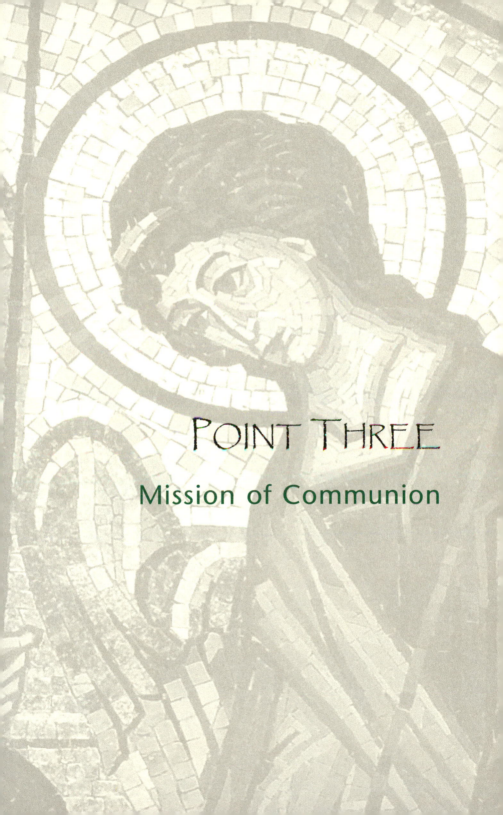

POINT THREE

Mission of Communion

I'd like to begin with a story.

*T*HE PASTA PREFACE. One of my seminary professors, a priest and prominent theologian, had an impressive mastery of the theology of St. Thomas Aquinas. Because I loved the structure, precision, and completeness of Thomas's thought, with Father's help, I earnestly strove to master it myself ... but maybe a bit *too* earnestly. For not only would I take up much of the class time with very detail-oriented questions, but after class, I would barrage the poor priest with this clarifying question and that. I figured that because St. Thomas himself had pondered how many angels could be in one place — "dance on the head of a pin," as some disparagingly put it — then I could and should do the same.

One day, after picking one picayune point too many, Father looked at me with uncharacteristic tenderness and asked, "Michael, what's your favorite food?" I was a bit taken aback by such an odd question, especially when we had such seemingly pressing theological questions to unravel. I replied, "Pasta," thinking that would put an end to the distraction. To my total surprise, he responded by saying, "*Michael, go eat some pasta.*" And with that, he silently packed up his papers and left the lecture hall.

So ended the best theology lesson I've ever had, one that I hope to impart now.

Theology truly is a science. It has its principles, conclusions, technical terms, and dominant theories. In fact, it's actually much more precise, organized, and difficult to master than most people think. Take me, for example. I remember going into the seminary, thinking I knew a thing or two about theology. But once the classes started, and I'd ask a question or write a paper, the "Pasta Priest" would tear it apart. It was a great blessing, because I quickly realized how much I didn't know and how theology demands that we be precise in our language and not wing it.

Through the "go eat some pasta" lesson, I realized that while theology is indeed a science, it's not so in a strict sense. Put differently, it requires not a rigid but a supple approach. Indeed, one needs to be flexible, because many of the teachings of theology don't fit into a tight, little box. Sure, in this book, I'm trying to neatly divide things into "three points of communion," but the reality is that the mysteries of salvation and of the Trinity spill over into each and every point. For instance, in a very real sense, our final end (Point One) has already begun. In fact, we began experiencing heaven at the moment of our Baptism, which brings about a true communion with the Trinity. Moreover, our mission of communion (Point Three) is actually part of our transformation in Christ (Point Two) such that, as we live out this mission, we're being more deeply transformed in Christ. Alright, but even after having said all this, I still think my three points of communion can be useful. I know they've helped me to organize my own thoughts and have deepened my grasp of a lot of theological topics.

So, as we begin Part Three (Point Three), know that there will be some carry over from the other parts, and that's okay. Remember, we're not approaching theology as rocket science but as the supple science that it is. So, go get a nice bowl of pasta (or whatever it is that you like), and enjoy the Third Part of our crash course in theology: Mission of Communion.

A RUBBER KEY WITH THREE TEETH. What is our mission of communion? It's great. It's glorious. But it's not so easy to explain. I began Part Three with the Pasta Preface because here, more than elsewhere, we need to be supple, flexible, and ready to go with the flow. This is because while I think I discovered just the right key to unlock the mystery of our mission of communion, the key itself is one that actually fits a lot of different locks. In other words, it's a flexible key — made not out of metal but of rubber. Moreover, how I go about applying it might at first seem like a stretch, but as we go through, I think you'll agree that it does indeed unlock the mystery of our mission of communion.

Okay, so our rubber key has three rubber teeth, three protrusions that tickle the tumblers of the lock, releasing deep insights into the mystery of our mission. These three teeth are the rich, biblical concepts of *priest*, *prophet*, and *king* — and the reason they're so flexible is because they're so rich. Anyway, the rest of Part Three is simply a reflection on our mission of communion from these three perspectives of priest (chapter one), prophet (chapter two), and king (chapter three). We'll go in reverse order, starting with "king," but before we take that royal road, by way of introduction, I should first say some things about the mission of communion itself.

*T*HE MISSION OF COMMUNION. In Part Two, we learned that a central goal of the Christian life is our transformation in Christ. Specifically, we learned that this transformation begins at our Baptism, which makes us into sons and daughters of the Father, in the Son.

Alright, so we're sons and daughters in the Son. But what does this mean? As we read earlier, it means that we're given a great many gifts. We're mercifully given the grace of the forgiveness of our sins. We're also given a share in the life of the Trinity: Father, Son, and Holy Spirit. But there's another gift we haven't yet covered. It's the gift of being called *to share in the mission of the Son*, the mission of Jesus Christ. And what is Christ's mission? It's a mission of communion. It's a mission to bring all of fallen humanity and the rest of creation, by the power of the Holy Spirit, back to the Father. As John Paul II puts it, "The ultimate purpose of mission is to enable people to share in the communion which exists between the Father and the Son" in their Spirit of Love.[127]

I clearly remember the time that the idea of this mission really came home to my mind and heart. It happened during my 30-day Ignatian retreat. While making such a retreat, a person has four to five meditations a day that successively follow the life of Christ. At the beginning of the meditations on Jesus' public life, St. Ignatius has the retreatants beg for the grace to know the Lord more intimately. Well, I begged for this grace, and then I'd reflect on a scene in the life of our Lord and think to myself, "Why is he here? What is he thinking? What does he want? What is he doing?" I recall that for each scene, the answer was the same. He's doing the will of the Father. He's bringing all back to the Father. He's trying to get everyone to know and love the Father. As Jesus says in the Gospel of John, his very "food" is to accomplish his Father's work (4:34). In fact, most of my meditations and spiritual reading during the retreat came from the Gospel of John — no surprise there — and I discovered that a huge theme of this Gospel is Jesus' identity. In passage after passage, Jesus speaks of himself as the one "sent by the Father."[128] For instance, we read:

> My food is to do the will of him *who sent me* ... (4:34).

> I seek not my own will but the will of him *who sent me* (5:30).

> I have not spoken on my own authority; the Father *who sent me* has himself given me commandment what to say and what to speak (12:49).

These passages tell us that the heart of Jesus' self-identity is the reality of *his being sent*. Specifically, it's the reality of his being sent by the Father into the world *on a mission*.

What is Jesus' mission? Again, it's a mission of communion. It's a mission to bring all of fallen humanity and the rest of creation, by the power of the Holy Spirit, back to the Father. It's the burning desire in the Heart of Jesus to accomplish the Father's work "that all may be one" in the communion of the Most Holy Trinity (see Jn 17). It's a mission that's fully expressed in what I earlier called "the greatest passage" in Sacred Scripture:

> Father, I desire that they also, whom thou hast given me, may be with me where I am, to behold my glory which thou has given me in thy love for me before the foundation of the world. O righteous Father, the world has not known thee, but I have known thee, and these know that thou hast sent me. I made known to them thy name, and I will make it known, that the love with which thou hast loved me may be in them, and I in them (Jn 17:24-26).

As we read earlier from Pope Benedict XVI, the "true center" of Jesus' personality is his communion with the Father, and if we don't realize this, "we cannot understand him at all." I would further add that without seeing Jesus as the one sent by the Father *on a mission of communion*, we cannot understand him at all. Moreover, without seeing Jesus as being "on mission," *we cannot understand ourselves either*. For, as Christians, as those who are being transformed into Christ, our identity is Christ's identity. We, too, must share in his mission of communion. We, too, must burn with the desire to accomplish this mission. We, too, must make it our very "food." Why? Because as Jesus himself says when he first sees the apostles after the Resurrection, "As the Father has sent me, even so *I send you*" (Jn 20:21). In other words, as an Easter gift, Jesus gives us his mission as our mission. He sends us into the world to make the Father known, so that the love with which the Father loves the Son may be in all (see Jn 17:18). In short, he sends us on a mission of communion.

Lest you think the mission of communion just comes from the Gospel of John, it doesn't. In fact, the Gospel of Matthew ends with the "great commission," whereby Jesus commands the apostles, "Go therefore and make disciples of all nations, baptizing them in the name of the Father and of the Son and of the Holy Spirit ..." (Mt 28:19). Moreover, the Gospels of Matthew, Mark, and Luke constantly describe Jesus' preaching of the kingdom of God, which has to do with the mission of communion, as we will now see.

CHAPTER ONE

The Kingly Mission of Communion

*W*HAT IS THE KINGDOM? The main theme of Jesus' preaching is the kingdom of God. But what is the kingdom? And who is the king?

Jesus Christ himself is the king. The kingdom is his reign over all things by his merciful love, and he accomplishes this reign *through his Church*. And what is the Church? The Church is Christ. The Church is the Body of Christ with Jesus himself as the Head and baptized believers as the members of his Body. So, the Church and the King and his kingdom are all intimately united.[129]

Again, the Church is the way that Jesus continues to carry out his mission of communion. After all, his mission didn't end when he ascended into heaven. Sure, Jesus did say from the Cross, "It is finished." And in a certain sense, at that moment, his mission was finished. For, by his suffering and death, Jesus won all the graces of salvation for the human race. Now, does this mean that everyone is suddenly saved? No. People need to accept God's offer of salvation in Jesus Christ. They need to accept it, live it in faith, receive it through the Sacraments, and enjoy it in the fellowship of the Church. In other words, fallen humanity has an urgent need to be brought into contact with Christ in the Church, and it's Christ's ongoing mission, through the members of his Body, to gather them into the Church and into the kingdom.

Because the Church is the Body of Christ, it's something visible. After all, as he walked the earth 2,000 years ago, Jesus was visible in his physical body. In fact, people not only saw him, they also heard him, touched him, and were touched by him — and so it is, too, with the Body of Christ, the Church. People see, hear, and touch the Church in its members, celebrations, good works, and especially its Sacraments.

In fact, the Church itself is a kind of sacrament. In other words, it's a visible thing that "effects what it signifies." And what does the Church signify? It signifies communion. For instance, when we walk into a Catholic parish during Sunday Mass and see people singing and praying and receiving the

Eucharist, we witness a visible communion of believers. This communion, though, is not only a sign of communion. It's actually a participation in the Trinitarian Communion. For, through Baptism and the Eucharist, Christians *are made into and sustained as* the Body of Christ. Also, through the Word that they hear proclaimed and that they put into practice in their lives, Christians become Word made flesh, are truly transformed into Christ, and are united with one another as one Body, sharing in the fellowship of Father, Son, and Holy Spirit. This is the Church, a manifestation of the kingdom. This is the sacrament of salvation, a sign of communion that actually causes the communion of God and man.

THE VISIBLE STRUCTURE OF THE KINGDOM. Before we turn our focus to our kingly role within the kingdom, we should briefly digress to reflect on the visible structure of the Church. This will help us develop what St. John Paul II called an "ecclesial consciousness."[130] In other words, it will help us realize in our hearts that we truly are members of the Church, the Body of Christ. For, when we spend time reflecting on the Church in her various parts, the idea of "the Church" can suddenly go from being something vague and abstract in our minds to something concrete and real in our hearts. Such deepened ecclesial consciousness makes us say, "I'm part of a communion of people made one in Christ and entrusted with an important mission for the building up of the Body."

This digression will also help us see how the remainder of Part Three will be structured. We already saw that the three chapters of Part Three will have to do with the three teeth of our rubber key: priest, prophet, and king. However, now we'll learn about some of the content of each chapter, namely, three groups within the Church.

Here's what I mean by the three groups in the Church: the hierarchy, laity, and those in the consecrated life. Each group is equal in dignity but has a different role, a unique sharing in Christ's priestly, prophetic, and kingly office, and yet all of them serve the one mission of communion. Let's look at each of the three groups now. (Forgive the technical language, but it's important that we have a solid and accurate foundation of what these three groups are.)

The *hierarchy of the Church* is made up of those who have received the Sacrament of Holy Orders, through which they are empowered to govern (kingly role), teach (prophetic role), and sanctify (priestly role) the members of the Church. There are three degrees of the Sacrament of Holy Orders. The first degree, which gives the fullness of the Sacrament of Holy Orders, is *Episcopal ordination* (the ordination of a bishop). The second degree is *priestly ordination*, by which a bishop entrusts a man, through the laying on of hands, with the office of his ministry. Ministerial priests are thus "co-workers of the bishops," and they exercise the bishops' ministry of governing, teaching, and sanctifying, though, in a subordinate degree: "Priests can exercise their ministry only in dependence on the bishop and in communion with him."[131] The third degree of the Sacrament of Holy Orders is the *ordination of deacons*, who do not share in the ministerial priesthood of Christ, as do bishops and priests, but rather are ordained "to help and serve them."[132]

The second of the three groups of people within the visible Church are the *lay faithful*. The Second Vatican Council describes them as

> ... all the faithful except those in Holy Orders and those who belong to a religious state approved by the Church. That is, the faithful, who by Baptism are incorporated into Christ and integrated into the People of God, are made sharers in their particular way in the priestly, prophetic, and kingly office of Christ, and have their own part to play in the mission of the whole Christian people in the Church and in the world.[133]

Chances are, you who are reading this book are one of the lay faithful. If so, then you're in for a treat, because Vatican II and subsequent Church documents have brought to the fore, like never before, the crucially important role of the laity in helping the Church fulfill her mission of communion. I'll be pointing out this key role in a later section.

Men and women in consecrated life are the third group within the visible Church. They are defined by the profession of the evangelical counsels of poverty, chastity, and obedience within a permanent state of life recognized by the Church. The Church has approved five forms of consecrated life: The eremitical life (hermits), consecrated virgins, religious life, secular institutes, and societies of apostolic life.[134] The most widely recognized form of consecrated life is "religious life," which includes such groups as the Benedictines, Franciscans, Dominicans, Carmelites, and Jesuits.

*T*O REIGN IS TO SERVE. Alright, now that we have the lay of the land regarding the three groups that make up the visible structure of the Church, we can get back to our subject of our kingly mission of communion.

All the members of the Church, by virtue of their Baptism, receive a share in Christ's kingly power, a power that is exercised especially *in service*. After all, Jesus Christ the King "did not come to be served but to serve and to give his life as a ransom" (Mk 10:45). Let's now briefly look at how this kingly service is exercised by the hierarchy (Pope, bishops, priests, and deacons), laity, and consecrated men and women.

We see perhaps the clearest example of the exercise of Christ's kingly service in *the Pope*, the Bishop of Rome, who a long tradition of the Church calls "the Servant of the Servants of God." His power truly is one of service, even while he does exercise a real authority over the Church — for he is, indeed, the successor of St. Peter, the "rock" upon which the Church was built, the one to whom Christ gave the "keys of the kingdom" (see Mt 16:19). As the pastor of the universal Church and successor of St. Peter, he has "full, supreme, and universal power over the whole Church, a power which he can always exercise unhindered."[135] This power, however, is to be used neither for personal gain nor for self-satisfaction but, rather, for the service of communion. In fact, the papacy itself brings about communion. For the Pope is "a visible, living, and dynamic principle of the unity between the Churches and thus of the universality of the one Church"[136] and "the perpetual and visible source and foundation of the unity both of the bishops and of the whole company of the faithful."[137]

In a lesser but comparable way to the Pope, *the other bishops*, especially in their dioceses, exercise a powerful authority. But again, it's an authority in the service of the communion of the Church. *Priests*, too, to a lesser degree, exercise a "kingly" authority of service in their parishes, which have been entrusted to them by their bishops for the building up of the Church. *Deacons*, then, assist the priests in exercising this authority.

The *lay faithful* also exercise a kingly authority according to their lay state. Although they have no diocese or parish entrusted to them, as do bishops and priests, they can still be involved in the governance of the local Church through their presence at particular councils, diocesan synods, pastoral councils, on finance committees, and in ecclesiastical tribunals. More directly related to their vocation of service to Christ in the world and in their families, they're called to order creation so it serves the good of humanity. Think, for instance, of so many parents who nurture, form, and educate their children in the faith. Also, there's the example of Catholic business leaders who bring Christian principles into the workplace through their personal witness.

The lay faithful have a special calling to use their kingly authority when others order creation against God's law. In such instances, they have the right and duty to unite forces with other lay faithful and people of good will to fight to remedy such situations or aspects of culture that are unjust or an inducement to sin.[138] Think, for instance, of the work of Lech Wałesa, co-founder of the Solidarity labor union that helped to peacefully bring down an atheistic communist regime in Poland. Also, there's the example of the pro-life efforts of someone like Nellie Grey, who founded and ran the annual March for Life in Washington, D.C., which brings together tens of thousands of people of good will in prayerful protest of the U.S. Supreme Court decision that legalized the killing of our unborn brothers and sisters.

Now, last but not least, we've come to the kingly role of *consecrated men and women*. Just keep in mind that what is most especially their role also applies to the rest of Christ's faithful — bishops, priests, deacons, and laity.

All Christ's faithful people, especially consecrated men and women, are called to exercise a kingly authority over themselves. In other words, they're to practice the discipline of holiness, prayer, and self-control, all of which increases the life of Christ within them. This way of exercising royal authority, like that exercised exclusively by the hierarchy, is at the service of communion. It serves communion because holiness builds up the Body of Christ — just as sin and corruption drag it down. Moreover, the holiness of the members who live out their vocations to the full *attract others* to the communion of Christ. So, when the faithful live out their kingly authority by overcoming the reign of sin in themselves, they fulfill an important part of their mission of communion.

Finally, all the Christian faithful, especially consecrated men and women, exercise their kingly role of service when they perform works of mercy, which the *Catechism* describes as follows:

> The works of mercy are charitable actions by which we come to the aid of our neighbor in his spiritual and bodily necessities. Instructing, advising, consoling, comforting are spiritual works of mercy as are forgiving and bearing wrongs patiently. The corporal works of mercy consist especially in feeding the hungry, sheltering the homeless, clothing the naked, visiting the sick and imprisoned, and burying the dead. Among all these, giving alms to the poor is one of the chief witnesses to fraternal charity: it is also a work of justice pleasing to God.[139]

Such works of mercy are a most important way by which Christ continues his mission of communion and love. By performing acts of mercy, Christians become worthy of and realize within themselves the dignity of their kingly call. And through such merciful actions, a person powerfully lives out the mission of communion. For who isn't drawn to the beauty of love that shines forth through authentic works of mercy? We need only call to mind the example of St. Mother Teresa of Kolkata and her work with the poor. Nearly every person of good will who sees photos or watches films about her work with the poor feels something within, drawing him to want to somehow be part of the beauty of such love. This is really what the mission of communion is all about, drawing everyone into the Communion of Love.

CHAPTER TWO

The Prophetic Mission of Communion

As we read in Part One, the Trinitarian communion of love, to which God calls each and every one of us, is *awesome*. Specifically, recall how we learned about salvation as redemption and glorification and how even the angels stand in awe of what God has done for us and in us. In the following passage, St. John captures this awe: "See what love the Father has given us, that we should be called children of God; and so we are" (1 Jn 3:1). Think of that, *and so we are!*

Do we truly appreciate this gift? I said earlier that when we do, we'll be shaking in our shoes with joy. But there's something else: The more we realize the gift, the more we'll want to share it with others. Out of gratitude to God for the gift of salvation, we'll want to labor in his vineyard. We'll want to set the world on fire with love for him. We'll want to bring others from the lonely darkness of sin and separation from God to the joy of communion with Christ and his Church. With St. Peter, we'll want to say to our neighbors who don't have a personal relationship with Christ, "That which we have seen and heard we proclaim also to you, so that you may have fellowship with us; and our fellowship is with the Father and with his Son Jesus Christ" (1 Jn 1:3).

How could we respond otherwise? We've been given so much, and yet there are literally billions of people out there who still haven't received the gift. How can we not burn to tell them about it? Not only this, we recently learned that Jesus himself sends us out on mission, "As the Father has sent me, even so I send you" (Jn 20:21), and he commands us, "Go therefore and make disciples of all nations, baptizing them in the name of the Father and of the Son and of the Holy Spirit ..." (Mt 28:19). This is our *prophetic mission of communion*, our mission of *evangelization*. Simply put, it's a mission to spread the good news that Jesus Christ is Lord and Savior, the one who offers to bring us out of the darkness of sin and death and into the light of life and the Communion of Love.

In this chapter, I'll be doing three things. First, I'll explain in greater depth what evangelization means for the Church. Second, I'll show how each of the three groups in the Church — hierarchy, laity, and consecrated men and women — is called to evangelize in its own manner. Third, I'll explain a way by which everyone can evangelize in our current cultural situation.

By the way, you'll soon find out that this chapter on our prophetic mission (evangelization) is much longer than the previous one. It deserves the extra treatment. This is because the mission of evangelization gets to the very heart of the Church, as I'll now explain, using the Church's own words.

1. Evangelization and the Church

By her very nature, the Church is missionary.[140] In fact, spreading the Gospel to all people is her "essential mission," her "deepest identity," and the very reason for her existence.[141] Moreover, "It is the *whole church* that receives the mission to evangelize, and the work of *each individual member* is important for the whole."[142] The whole Church, therefore, "has no rest so long as she has not done her best to proclaim the Good News of Jesus the Savior."[143] For she is "deeply aware of her duty to preach salvation to all."[144] And knowing that the Gospel message is for everyone, the Church "shares Christ's anguish at the sight of the wandering and exhausted crowds, 'like sheep without a shepherd' (Mt 9:36)."[145] In fact, she herself often repeats the Lord's words, "I feel sorry for all these people" (Mt 15:32).[146]

The Church doesn't simply feel sorry for the crowds of people who don't know Christ. *She does something about this situation.* She acts. She acts as Christ's co-worker, allowing him, with the Spirit, to continue the great work of evangelization through her. I call it the "great" work of evangelization because it truly is great: It goes out to the ends of the earth and involves billions of people.

To help us get a sense of what such a massive mission entails, let's consider the three situations into which Pope John Paul II divides the evangelizing work of the Church. They are as follows:

"specific missionary activity," "pastoral care of the faithful," and "the new evangelization."

Now, as we already learned from the "Pasta Preface," theology is a supple science. Therefore, it should come as no surprise that John Paul II gives the following disclaimer regarding these three divisions:

> The boundaries between *pastoral care of the faithful, new evangelization, and specific missionary activity* are not clearly definable, and it is unthinkable to create barriers between them or to put them into watertight compartments.[147]

Alright. Point taken. Let's go eat some pasta and then start with the first situation, "specific missionary activity."

'*SPECIFIC MISSIONARY ACTIVITY.*' This is also known as the Church's missionary activity "*ad gentes*" ("to the nations"). Such activity addresses "peoples, groups, and socio-cultural contexts in which Christ and his Gospel are not known or which lack Christian communities sufficiently mature to be able to incarnate the faith in their own environment and proclaim it to other groups."[148] It's the activity directed toward *all those who do not know Christ and his Gospel*, and who, for the most part, belong to other religions.

Regarding other religions, the Church encourages interreligious dialogue with them, which is part of the Church's evangelizing mission. Through such dialogue, the Church seeks to uncover what the Second Vatican Council referred to as "seeds of the Word"[149] and a "ray of that Truth which enlightens all men."[150] In other words, she looks for the action of the Holy Spirit who "blows where he wills" (Jn 3:8) and who is always mysteriously at work in the heart of every person, including in those who belong to other religions.

While the Church's dialogue with other religions should always be accompanied by a deep respect for the mysterious work of the Holy Spirit and even a conviction that "the Holy Spirit offers everyone the possibility of sharing in the Paschal Mystery in a manner known to God,"[151] this does *not* mean that the Church is dispensed from its obligation to proclaim the Gospel to all people:

> The fact that the followers of other religions can receive God's grace and be saved by Christ apart from the ordinary means which he has established does not thereby cancel the call to faith and Baptism which God wills for all people. ... [T]he Church is the ordinary means of salvation ... [and] she alone possesses the fullness of the means of salvation."[152]

Tragically, in our day, the Church's missionary activity *ad gentes* is just a small fraction of what it was before Vatican II. One major reason for the big drop off is that many Catholics have mistakenly believed that because Vatican II taught that the Spirit can work outside of the Church, therefore, non-Christians do not need to have the Gospel preached to them. And so, a surprising number of Catholics have become indifferent to mission work *ad gentes* and have even adopted attitudes of religious relativism such that they end up thinking to themselves, "Well, one religion is just as good as the next."

Such opinions are *totally wrong* and do great damage to the Church and to humanity. As Pope Paul VI said, our Catholic religion "effectively establishes with God an authentic and living relationship which the other religions do not succeed in doing, even though they have, as it were, their arms stretched towards heaven."[153] For, indeed, there is "no other name under heaven given among men by which we must be saved" than Jesus Christ (Acts 4:12). People have a right to know the name of Jesus. They have a right to hear the good news! They have a right to choose to accept the *fullness* of truth in the Savior of the world, in the one who is Truth itself (see Jn 14:16-17).

Unfortunately, Catholic Christians, the very ones who possess the earth-shaking message of salvation in its fullness, often don't seem to want to share it. We barely seem to care about the mission *ad gentes*. We've lost the old fire to proclaim the good news to the ends of the earth. And all this is largely because we've forgotten the absolute wonder, splendor, and uniqueness of Christianity. I think Chesterton was right: We've become too familiar with the facts of our faith, and this familiarity has led to fatigue. But like a bright red pagoda, at least one fact should jump out at us from the vast field of teachings of the world religions: *Jesus Christ claimed to be God*. That's a big deal. Yet, amazingly, this shocking fact is often ignored, brushed aside, and not taken seriously.

Jesus' claim to divinity is *not* something to be ignored. He can't be reduced, as is commonly done today, simply to some "great moral teacher." That was never his claim. So what did he claim to be? He claimed to be God himself — and that's a stunning idea everyone should face. C.S. Lewis has helped many to face it in a chapter of a book that has made more Christians than all his other books combined:

> I am trying here to prevent anyone saying the really foolish thing that people often say about Him: "I'm ready to accept Jesus as a great moral teacher, but I don't accept His claim to be God." That is the one thing we must not say. A man who was merely a man and said the sort of things Jesus said would not be a great moral teacher. He would either be a lunatic — on a level with the man who says he is a poached egg — or else he would be the Devil of Hell. You must make your choice. Either this man was, and is, the Son of God: or else a madman or something worse. You can shut Him up for a fool, you can spit at Him and kill Him as a demon; or you can fall at His feet and call Him Lord and God. But let us not come with any patronizing nonsense about His being a great human teacher. He has not left that open to us. He did not intend to.
>
> We are faced, then, with a frightening alternative. This man we are talking about either was (and is) just what He said, or else a lunatic, or something worse.

Now it seems to me obvious that He was neither a lunatic nor a fiend: and consequently, however strange or terrifying or unlikely it may seem, I have to accept the view that He was and is God. God has landed on this enemy-occupied world in human form.[154]

Three choices: Lord, liar, or lunatic. For Lewis, it's obvious that Jesus is neither a lunatic nor dishonest. And for those who are even faintly familiar with the Gospels, it's also obvious. Therefore, like Lewis, we "have to accept the view that He was and is God." And what a beautiful view this is — that Jesus Christ is Lord and Savior and that he has come to save us from sin and death and to raise us up to his own divine and eternal life, if only we will believe and follow him. This is the good news that must be proclaimed to all people. It's their right to hear it and the grave duty of every Christian to proclaim it, according to his state in life. Therefore, each one of us should say with St. Paul, "Woe to me if I do not preach the Gospel!" (1 Cor 9:16). Indeed, each one of us should fight the temptation to narrow our hearts and think only of ourselves, our families, and our communities. Each one of us should ask God to give us hearts like the Heart of the Good Shepherd, who is restless for the lost sheep that are suffering outside the fold:

We cannot be content when we consider the millions of our brothers and sisters, who like us have been redeemed by the blood of Christ, but who live in ignorance of the love of God. For each believer, as for the entire Church, the missionary task must remain foremost, for it concerns the eternal destiny of humanity.[155]

In such a sad time as ours, when the mission of the Church *ad gentes* is still in decline, we do well to end this section by reflecting on the stirring testimony of one of the greatest missionaries of all time, the patron saint of foreign missions, St. Francis Xavier. As we read his testimony, let's reflect on why the Church's missionary task should be at the forefront of our minds and hearts:

> We have visited the villages of the new converts who accepted the Christian religion a few years ago. No Portuguese live here; the country is so utterly barren and poor. The native Christians have no priests. They know only that they are Christians. There is nobody to say Mass for them; nobody to teach them the Creed, the Our Father, the Hail Mary and the Commandments of God's Law.
>
> I have not stopped since the day I arrived. I conscientiously made the rounds of the villages. I bathed in the sacred waters all the children who had not yet been baptized. This means that I have purified a very large number of children so young that, as the saying goes, they could not tell their right hand from their left. The older children would not let me say my Office or eat or sleep until I taught them one prayer or another. Then I began to understand: "The kingdom of heaven belongs to such as these."
>
> I could not refuse so devout a request without failing in devotion myself. I taught them, first the confession of faith in the Father, the Son and the Holy Spirit, then the Apostles' Creed, the Our Father and Hail Mary. I noticed among them persons of great intelligence. If only someone could educate them in the Christian way of life, I have no doubt that they would make excellent Christians.
>
> Many, many people hereabouts are not becoming Christians for one reason only: There is nobody to make them Christians. Again and again I have thought of going round the universities of Europe, especially Paris, and everywhere crying out like a madman, riveting the attention of those with more learning than charity: "What a tragedy: how many souls are being shut out of heaven and falling into hell, thanks to you!"

I wish they would work as hard at this as they do at their books, and so settle their account with God for their learning and the talents entrusted to them.

This thought would certainly stir most of them to meditate on spiritual realities, to listen actively to what God is saying to them. They would forget their own desires, their human affairs, and give themselves over entirely to God's will and his choice. They would cry out with all their heart: *Lord, I am here! What do you want me to do?* Send me anywhere you like — even to India.[156]

'P*ASTORAL CARE OF THE FAITHFUL.*' The Christian community about which St. Francis wrote was, to say the least, certainly fragile. We can imagine, however, that with time, if missionary priests could be sent, that seemingly insignificant community would grow and even blossom into a local Church with a bishop and its own native clergy. In such a situation, where adequate and solid ecclesial structures are established, where the people grow fervent in faith, follow the commandments, and witness to the Gospel, then at some point the mission *ad gentes* ends and the situation of "pastoral care of the faithful" begins.[157]

The pastoral care of the faithful simply means that the Church does what the Church does (preaches the Gospel, administers the Sacraments, and performs works of mercy) in a place where there are adequate and solid ecclesial structures and where the faithful are fervent. Geographic examples of this situation of "pastoral care" that come to my mind are places such as Poland or the Philippines, where the faith is strong and firmly established. This is not to say that everyone in these countries is a believer, but the faith has surely been set on solid ground. Another example of such a situation of "pastoral care" would be the Catholic communities of the United States — of the *1950s*. Of course, the Catholic Church in the United States today is spiritually in a much different place than it was some sixty years ago. For, while there are still many pockets and places where the faith is fervently lived, there are also many other places where people who were once strong in faith have now fallen into religious indifference and a secularist mentality. Such places need what Pope John Paul II calls a "re-evangelization" or, better yet, a "new evangelization."

'THE NEW EVANGELIZATION.' When John Paul spoke of the need for a new evangelization, I think he especially had Europe in mind. There, you have a place with ancient Catholic Christian roots where "entire groups of the baptized have lost a living sense of the faith, or even no longer consider themselves members of the Church, and live a life far removed from Christ and his Gospel."[158]

Many years ago, I spent a semester of college living in Europe, and I myself witnessed the situation that John Paul describes. I vividly remember visiting so many marvelous churches and cathedrals, museums packed with masterpieces of Christian art, and lovely roadside shrines. All the while, I can't recall meeting a single, native, Church-going Christian. It was a shocking experience: With the exception of Poland, what was once the bastion of the world's Christian faith had become a thoroughly secular society. I'm grateful that the Church, in promoting the new evangelization, is not letting the ancient faith be completely lost without a fight.

There's actually more to the new evangelization than simply bringing secularized Europeans, Canadians, and Americans back to a living Christian faith. The new evangelization is also about approaching evangelization with a freshness, new creativity, and dynamism born of a faith-infused engagement with our modern world. If that last sentence seemed to echo the style of the 1960s and Vatican II documents, I did it on purpose — and without any cynicism. For, even though the Council ended some 50 years ago, I think there's still reason to be optimistic. For Vatican II gave the Church a great idea that can lend a big hand to the work of the new evangelization. Of course, I'm referring to the great phrase of Cardinal Karol Wojtyła, the "enrichment of faith."

Yes, I already thoroughly covered this idea in Part Two, and I'm not going to rehash it. Here, I simply want to highlight how radically important the idea of the enrichment of faith remains for us today. I believe that in our day, people are searching for the concrete, the personal, and the real even more than before. Some of my friends who are seasoned teachers have told me that students today are noticeably different. They don't really trust the teachers, hardly listen to lectures, and can barely pay attention to anything for more than five minutes. Yet, they tell me, these same students are desperately seeking. They're looking for a concrete experience of God. Moreover, they're open to hearing the testimony of others, which is a great opportunity, because that's how evangelization is done. After all, as Pope Paul VI asked, "Is there any other way of handing on the Gospel than by transmitting to another person one's personal experience of faith?"[159]

Our separated brethren, especially the Evangelical Christians, have been on this path of the "personal" in matters of religion for years. (Yes, Blessed John Henry Newman would finally be pleased with them.) In Southern California where I'm from and where lots of Evangelicals live, I remember often being asked by them, "Have you been saved?" In other words, they wanted to know if I'd accepted Jesus Christ as my personal Lord and Savior. It's a good question! Of course, we work out our salvation with fear and trembling (see Phil 2:12), but we should also be striving for the perfect love that casts out fear (see 1 Jn 4:18), a love that comes from a deep, abiding personal relationship with Jesus Christ.

It's surprising that Catholics do not seem to emphasize this point of the personal as much as Evangelicals do. After all, how can you get more concrete and personal, as Blessed Newman observed, than by having Jesus Christ truly present, Body, Blood, Soul and Divinity in the Eucharist? Yet that's what Catholics have!

I wonder if some of the reasons why Evangelicals emphasize the personal so much is because, at least in America, their communities tend to be smaller and, therefore, closer knit than Catholic ones. (Even their "mega-churches" are still small compared to the great web of Catholic parishes.) Might Catholics learn something from the Protestants by establishing and participating in their own Catholic faith-sharing groups of prayer, Scripture study, and fellowship? Of course, such groups already exist in the Church and in some areas are flourishing, but doesn't it make sense to pursue this path even more? After all, if the aim of Vatican II was to help Catholics overcome the split between faith and life, then isn't it time to do more than just attend Sunday Mass? Isn't it time for Catholics to engage more deeply in personal prayer, Scripture reading, and fellowship? These are the kinds of things that have to do with the new evangelization, which involves being bold, leaving one's comfort zone, and going against the failing *status quo*. Indeed, the new evangelization is about doing such things as going to Eucharistic Adoration, striking up a conversation with a stranger after Mass, sharing the faith with the clerk at the grocery store, starting a family Rosary, and joining a Bible study or faith-sharing group. I'll close this section with this last point.

Of course, the super-concept I've been emphasizing throughout this book is *communio*, and we've already learned that we're made for communion and that we long for communion. Yet, when we look at our modern society, it seems to be becoming more and more fragmented, individualistic, and fraught with loneliness. For instance, so many of us are glued to our smartphones, too busy to spend time with others and too engrossed in ourselves and our attachments to do the work of building community. And yet, we're starving for communion all the more. So, we try to find it in such things as the virtual community of social networks, blogs, and other new media, but that's really not the deeper and authentic communion that we seek.

I believe that the new evangelization is all about communion — real communion. It's about building that personal communion with Jesus Christ, the real, living person and not just the idea. It's about letting Jesus, with the Holy Spirit, bring us into a deeper, personal relationship with our heavenly Father. It's about experiencing Christ in Christian fellowship, works of mercy, and in the mission of communion. It's really about fulfillment: receiving, sharing, building, and delighting in the communion that we all long for in our heart of hearts, the communion of the Church that's on a pilgrimage through Christ, with Christ, and in Christ, in the unity of the Holy Spirit, to the glory of God the Father.

*R*EVIEW. To conclude this section on evangelization and the Church, let's review. We read that the Church feels sorry for all the people who are "like sheep without a shepherd" (Mt 15:32; 9:36), and so, she labors to proclaim to them the good news of salvation in Jesus Christ. This proclamation goes out to all the world and is divided into three different situations. First, there's the situation of "*specific missionary activity*" (*ad gentes*), which is the Church's mission to peoples who do not know Christ and the Gospel. Second, there's the situation of "pastoral care of the faithful," which is the Church's mission in places where the Church is already firmly established and the faithful are fervent. Third, there's the situation of the "new evangelization," which is the Church's mission to those people who have rejected the faith or who have become lukewarm and indifferent to it.

So now, having gotten the "big picture" view of the Church's prophetic, evangelizing mission, we can more fruitfully turn our attention to the specific question of who is called to fulfill this mission and how.

2. Prophetic Mission of the Hierarchy, Laity, and Consecrated

Who has the mission of communion and evangelization? *Everyone.* Every single one of the baptized has it.[160] But while the great mission of the Church aims at one single goal — to bring all of creation back into the Trinitarian communion of God — Christians have a wide variety of roles to play in accomplishing this goal. St. Paul compares these roles to the different functioning parts of a single body:

> For as in one body we have many members, and all the members do not have the same function, so we, though many, are one body in Christ, and individually members one of another. Having gifts that differ according to the grace given to us, let us use them: if prophecy, in proportion to our faith; if service, in our serving; he who teaches, in his teaching; he who exhorts, in his exhortation; he who contributes, in liberality; he who gives aid, with zeal; he who does acts of mercy, with cheerfulness (Rom 12:4-8).

What's your role in the Body of Christ? You've certainly got one, and it's utterly unique! John Paul II calls it a "personal and unrepeatable life project"[161] that the Father entrusts to you as his gift to you — and as your gift back to him. Such a personal life project is not usually revealed all at once, but rather, it unfolds in and is discovered through a consistent life of prayer, discernment, and spiritual direction. Although I love the topic of discovering one's personal vocation, we don't have time to get into it here. So, instead, in the pages that follow, we'll look at a more general topic but one that's just as fascinating.

Earlier, we learned that there are three groups that make up the visible Church: hierarchy (the ordained), laity, and consecrated men and women. What we haven't yet learned is how each of these three groups plays its part in the Church's prophetic mission of communion, the work of evangelization. That's what we're going to do now. (And fortunately, learning about this will help us better develop an "ecclesial consciousness," which John Paul encouraged us to have.)

PROPHETIC MISSION OF THE HIERARCHY. Christ's command to preach the Gospel to every creature "primarily and immediately"[162] concerns *bishops,* who are the successors to the apostles. When acting in communion with the other bishops under the Bishop of Rome (the Pope), they have a special teaching authority by virtue of their ordination. *Ordained priests,* who cooperate with the bishops as instruments of their sacred ministry, also share (in a subordinate way) in the teaching authority of the bishops. Finally, *deacons* assist both the bishops and priests in fulfilling their prophetic mission.

Now, while it's true that everyone in the Church can and must give testimony to the Gospel, only the hierarchy of the Church does so with Christ's own teaching authority. In other words, God gives ordained ministers a special calling, mandate, mission, identity, and sacramental grace to proclaim the Gospel with authority and power. Does this mean that deacons, priests, and bishops will always give interesting homilies? No. Does it mean they will always be right in their judgments and conduct? No. (Although the Pope, as the successor of St. Peter, does receive a special grace of the Holy Spirit to be free from error when he makes official declarations on matters of faith and morals.[163]) Does this mean bishops who are in union with the Pope are to be "respected by all as witnesses to divine and Catholic truth"?[164] Yes. Does it mean that "in matters of faith and morals, the bishops speak in the name of Christ" and that "the faithful are to accept their teaching and adhere to it with a religious assent"?[165] Yes, again. Does the fact that bishops have been given this teaching authority mean that we are abundantly blessed? Absolutely. Let me explain.

Since the time that Martin Luther, the leader of the Protestant Reformation, first broke away from the Roman Catholic Church in the early 16th century, it's reported that there are now more than 30,000 different Protestant offshoots and splinter groups. What does this tell us? It tells us that when the Church's special teaching authority is rejected, unity breaks down, and Christians become increasingly fragmented and divided. Something else follows from this: Christ's teaching, when not linked to Christ-given authority, becomes confused, diluted, and compromised.

On this topic, I can't help but think back to when I was in high school and how different Protestant students would ask me if I was saved. I'd respond, "Well, what does that mean?" Each one of them seemed to have a different interpretation of what the Bible teaches about salvation and how one receives it. One of them said that you need to be baptized, but another said you don't. One said that all non-Christians certainly go to hell, but another said they don't. One said that you can lose salvation through serious sin, but another said, "Once saved always saved." Then, there seemed to be total confusion on controversial moral issues such as homosexuality, abortion, capital punishment, and artificial contraception. All this got me wondering, "By what authority are these guys saying what they're saying? Is it because their pastor, 'Pastor Bob,' said so? Well, who is Pastor Bob, and why should I follow his interpretation of the Bible? Why not follow Pastor Jeff, Joe, or Sally's interpretation instead?"

Thanks to my high school Protestant friends, I learned relatively early on what a gift it is to be Catholic. For, unlike them, I could point to an unbroken chain of teaching authority that goes back to Christ. In fact, I could even point to a particular moment in Sacred Scripture where that teaching authority was actually given to the Church by Christ himself. Our Lord did it during a conversation with the apostle Simon, whose name he changed to "Peter," meaning "rock":

> And I tell you, you are Peter, and on this rock I will build my church, and the powers of death shall not prevail against it. I will give you the keys of the kingdom of heaven, and whatever you bind on earth shall be bound in heaven, and whatever you loose on earth shall be loosed in heaven (Mt 16:18-19).

I never get tired of reading this passage. It reminds Catholics that our faith is firmly established on a rock-solid teaching authority given by Christ himself. For Catholics, this is a huge gift! We don't have to seek the truth by wading through a murky pool of Protestant personal opinions and differing private interpretations of Scripture. Rather, we can simply listen to the Church, which teaches with Christ's own voice not only on ancient, established truths but on contemporary issues as well. In fact, because of her strong, faithful voice in clearly proclaiming the Gospel today, it's not surprising that a growing number of Protestant leaders are taking notice and reuniting with her.[166]

Now, don't get me wrong. I'm not saying it's easy being Catholic. Belonging to the Church that Christ founded, the Church that is the "pillar and bulwark of truth" (1 Tim 3:15), is definitely not easy. In fact, sometimes the truth hurts. For example, here's a truth that probably hurts: Because Catholics have been given so much, much will be required of them (see Lk 12:48), a point that the Fathers of the Second Vatican Council didn't fail to emphasize:

> All the Church's children should remember that their exalted status is to be attributed not to their own merits but to the special grace of Christ. If they fail, moreover, to respond to that grace in thought, word, and deed, not only shall they not be saved but they will be the more severely judged.[167]

While this particular truth might make some of us fearful, we need not be afraid. For there are so many treasures in the Church that help us to be faithful to Christ, not the least of which are ordained preachers and teachers endowed with the grace and authority to rouse us to love Jesus and follow him more closely. This is a great gift for each one of us, and we should thank God every day for giving to his ordained ministers such a prophetic mission in Christ, for us. And if it sometimes seems that a bishop, priest, or deacon is not quite living up to the grace of his ordination, then our daily prayer of gratitude to God can turn into a daily prayer of intercession for him.

*P*ROPHETIC MISSION OF THE LAITY. I said earlier that if you're one of the laity, then you're in for a treat. Well, treat time has now arrived.

In the not so distant past, people used to think that the work of evangelization was just for bishops and priests. These same people often thought the job of the laity was simply to "pray, pay, and obey." Not so. Vatican II, Pope Paul VI, and Pope John Paul II all proclaimed the "universal call to mission,"[168] and now, like never before, the importance of the laity's mission is very clearly laid out — and what an important mission it is!

While the lay faithful do not speak with the same authority as the ordained, they've been entrusted with a mission to spread the Gospel in places and to people that the ordained can hardly hope to reach. In a sense, you might say that the job of the hierarchy is to be something like a rear-guard support team that prepares and readies the laity for action on the "front lines" of the new evangelization.[169]

Such action really is needed. I mean, many of my brother priests are so overwhelmed and overworked with administrative and pastoral responsibilities in their parishes that they can hardly hope to reach anyone outside the parish. But the lay faithful? Well, they're a completely different story. They can reach *billions* of people — literally. They're God's secret weapon, a huge sleeping giant in the Catholic Church. If they'll just wake up, they'll set the world ablaze with a fire so great that even bishops and priests will stand in awe and be warmed by its beautiful flames. *If* they'll wake up. Vatican II preached a message to rouse them, a heartfelt cry from the Council itself:

> The Council, then, makes an earnest plea in the Lord's name that all lay people give a glad, generous, and prompt response to the impulse of the Holy Spirit and to the voice of Christ, who is giving them an especially urgent invitation at this moment.[170]

Like Vatican II, John Paul II tried to wake the giant. For instance, after many days of discussions with the bishops of the world on the topic of the role of the laity in the Church and the world, the Pope basically summed it all up by saying that the laity *must* go out and work in the vineyard of the Lord. No excuses. He wrote, "*It is not permissible for anyone to remain idle.*" Why not? Because the work at hand is "so great." Therefore, he said, the Church calls out to the laity with a "particular urgency." In fact, with "even greater urgency," the Lord himself, the owner of the vineyard, continually repeats his invitation to each one of the lay faithful, "*You, too, go out in my vineyard.*"[171]

Are the laypeople listening? I think so. Well, at least, I really hope so. The success of the new evangelization and so much of the Church's mission of communion depends on their whole-hearted response to the Lord's repeated invitations and pleas. Alright, so how are they supposed to respond? What does it mean to "go out into the vineyard"? Well, let's begin by seeing what the vineyard (the part reserved for laypeople) looks like. Pope Paul VI describes it as follows:

> Their own field of evangelizing activity is the vast and complicated world of politics, society and eco-nomics, but also the world of culture, of the sciences and the arts, of international life, of the mass media. It also includes other realities which are open to evangelization, such as human love, the family, the education of children and adolescents, professional work, suffering.[172]

In short, the field open to the laity is everything that makes up human life in the world! (what Vatican II called "temporal affairs"). Now, think of this for a moment. In Part Two, we learned about the huge modern problem that Vatican II was responding to. What was it again? That's right: the split between what modern Catholics *profess* and *how they live in the modern world*. Well, which particular group of Catholics lives in the world? Of course, the laity. So, the laity have a huge part to play in realizing the goal of the Council. In fact, in many ways, the Council was most especially about the laity and for the laity. Its goal was basically to teach the lay faithful their mission and vocation in and to the modern world.

So what is it? What's their mission? Essentially, *it's to make God visible*. And how do they do this? One of my favorite passages from the documents of Vatican II explains it:

> This result [of making God visible] is achieved chiefly by the witness of a living and mature faith, namely, one trained to see difficulties clearly and to master them. Many martyrs have given witness to this faith

and continue to do so. This faith needs to prove its fruitfulness by penetrating the believer's entire life, including its worldly dimensions, and by activating him toward justice and love, especially regarding the needy. What does the most to reveal God's presence, however, is the brotherly charity of the faithful who are united in spirit as they work together for the faith of the Gospel (cf. Phil 1:27) and who prove themselves a sign of unity.[173]

This passage can be summed up in two ideas: "the enrichment of faith" and "communion." Let's unpack these ideas now, starting with the enrichment of faith.

First of all, don't worry. Although I keep bringing this topic up, I'm not going to rehash everything we covered in Part Two. I just want to point out that the enrichment of faith is exactly what the above passage is talking about. For an enriched faith is a "living and mature faith," a faith that's "trained to see difficulties clearly and master them." But what exactly does this mean? The next sentence gives us a clue. It speaks of martyrdom. Huh? When I first read that sentence, it seemed to have come out of left field. Why bring up martyrdom? As I thought about it more, it suddenly made perfect sense.

Martyrs are those whose faith and life are perfectly united, because they sacrifice their natural lives for the life of faith, thereby witnessing to the primacy of the *supernatural life of faith* over our *natural life in the world*. The problem with Christians living in the modern world is that too often they've got it reversed. They sacrifice the supernatural life of faith for the natural life of the world, but this is nuts! "For what does it profit a man to gain the whole world and forfeit his soul?" (Mark 8:36). Christians selling out the faith for the world is the wrong witness. It's an anti-witness. It's an anti-gospel.

Now, here's where the enrichment of faith comes to the rescue. Again, the enrichment of faith refers to "the witness of a living and mature faith" that faces the challenges of the modern world and doesn't back down. In fact, it "masters" those challenges by putting faith first. What does it mean to put faith first? It means choosing being over having, the person over things, a life of self-giving love over selfishness. This is what it means for the faith to "penetrate the believer's entire life." It means letting God's Word rule over all one's decisions. It means not limiting prayer to Sunday Mass. It means living the life of Christ, abiding in him, and being a contemplative in action. In sum, it means doing everything through Christ, with Christ, and in Christ, from riding the subway to folding the laundry. When the laity have such an enriched faith, God is made visible to the world through what they do and say and how they act and are. This is the witness of true holiness to which all the laity are called, as Pope John Paul II makes clear:

> True holiness does not mean a flight from the world; rather, it lies in the effort to incarnate the Gospel in everyday life, in the family, at school and at work, and in social and political involvement.[174]

Alright, then. So that covers the enrichment of faith, which makes God visible through the witness of a living and mature faith. Now to the next point, "communion."

According to the text from Vatican II that we've been reflecting on, what makes God most "visible"? Charity. Love. More specifically, it's the communion of "brotherly charity" between Christians. And why does this reveal God? Because God himself is a communion of love, Father, Son, and Holy Spirit, and where there is love, there is God.

Okay, so at this point, keeping what I just said about the communion of love in mind, let's take a step back and revisit the imagery of the vineyard. (Bear with me.)

The lay faithful are called to labor in the Lord's vineyard, and their specific plot of land is the world and temporal affairs. Their mission there is to make God visible. How? Well, we just learned that they do it through love, through the communion of love. Alright, but now let's look more closely at the imagery of the vineyard that came up toward the beginning of this section.

What grows in a vineyard? Vines. And where do we read about vines in Scripture? Actually, vines are mentioned throughout the Bible. But for me, the most moving place that talks about vines is — you guessed it — a chapter in the Gospel of John. In the Gospel of John, Jesus says, "I am the true vine and my Father is the vinedresser … . *Abide in me and I in you*" (Jn 15:1, 4). What does this mean? Well, I'm going to let Pope John Paul II answer this one. But just one warning: While the passage I'm about to cite is amazingly beautiful, it's also very difficult. So, how about this. I'll do my best to unpack it for you afterwards, and you do your best to prayerfully read and understand it now:

> "*Abide in me and I in you*" (Jn 15:1, 4). These simple words reveal the mystery of communion that serves as the unifying bond between the Lord and his disciples, between Christ and the baptized: a living and life-giving communion through which Christians no longer belong to themselves but are the Lord's very own, as the branches are one with the vine.
>
> The communion of Christians with Jesus has the communion of God as Trinity, namely, the unity of the Son to the Father in the gift of the Holy Spirit, as its model and source, and is itself the means to achieve this communion: united to the Son in the Spirit's bond of love, Christians are united to the Father.
>
> Jesus continues: "*I am the vine, you are the branches*" (Jn 15:5). From the communion that Christians experience in Christ there immediately flows the communion which they experience with one another: all are branches of a single vine, namely, Christ. In this communion is the wonderful reflection and participation in the mystery of the intimate life of love in God as Trinity, Father, Son and Holy Spirit as revealed by the Lord Jesus. For this *communion* Jesus prays: "that they may all be one; even as you, Father, are in me, and I in you, that they also may

be in us, so that the world may believe that you have
sent me" (Jn 17:21).

Such communion is the very mystery of the Church,
as the Second Vatican Council recalls in the celebrated
words of St. Cyprian: "The Church shines forth as 'a
people made one with the unity of the Father, Son
and Holy Spirit.'" We are accustomed to recall this
mystery of Church *communion* at the beginning of the
celebration of the Eucharist when the priest welcomes
all with the greeting of the Apostle Paul: "The grace
of the Lord Jesus, the love of God and the fellowship
of the Holy Spirit be with you all" (2 Cor 13:13).[175]

Okay, now that's a lot. John Paul II has just unfolded some
of the most beautiful passages in all of Scripture. In doing so,
he's taken us from our union with Christ to our union with the
Trinity to our union with each other in Christ and everywhere
in between. Now let me try to boil all this down to the barebones
while reviewing what came before it.

The lay faithful are called to make God visible to the world,
which for them, takes place in the vineyard of the modern world.
They make God visible by the witness of a living and mature
faith, which comes from *abiding* with Jesus in a real, personal
relationship of love. But from this communion that they experience with Christ, there immediately flows their communion
with others, because we are all branches on a single vine,
which is Christ — or, to use St. Paul's imagery, we are all
members of a single Body with Jesus Christ himself as the
Head of the Body. So, the Christian life is a life of communion
with Christ and communion with fellow Christians. But this
mystery of communion is also *already* a participation in the
communion of love of the Father, Son, and Holy Spirit. Jesus
himself summarizes this wonderful mystery in his prayer to the
Father, "that they may all be one even as thou, Father, are in
me, and I in thee, that they also may be in us, so that the world
may believe that thou hast sent me" (Jn 17:21). In this sublime
prayer, Jesus is praying to his Father that the communion of

Christians with one another in him may also be in communion with him as he is in communion with the Father, *that all may be one*.

Now, the "all" that Jesus wants to be one with the Trinity is not just Christians but the whole world. And how does the world of unbelievers enter into this unity? *By seeing the unity Christians have with one another and with Christ*, "that the world may believe."

Notice the great responsibility the lay faithful have: They are to make God visible! They are to make Father, Son, and Holy Spirit visible through their love for Christ and for one another. They are to make him visible through their personal witness of a living faith in Christ and through the witness of their fellowship, so unbelievers will say: "See their peace. See their joy. See how they love one another." And then, they will believe.

Now, what is it that the unbelievers see that moves them to believe? Communion. They see what their hearts long for, the communion of love, and then they believe. So, the witness of the communion of believers brings others into communion. This is a super important point that leads to one of the deepest theological ideas of the entire Second Vatican Council. I already mentioned this idea earlier, but it deserves to be brought up again. So, take a deep breath, and bear with me. I know I'm pouring on a lot of theology here, but if we stick with it, I think it will bear the fruit of great wisdom. It will help us understand the incredible vocation of the lay faithful living in the world. Alright, so here we go ...

One of the great, mega-teachings of the Second Vatican Council is that the Church herself is "the sacrament of salvation." More specifically, it says that the Church is "a kind of sacrament, that is, a sign and instrument of intimate union with God and of the unity of all the human race."[176] In other words, the Church is not only a sign of communion, it's an *instrument* of communion, meaning that it *brings about communion*. Let me further explain and underline this hugely important point by trying to answer the question, "How does the Church bring about communion?"

First, as we learned in Part Two, the Church brings about communion through *the Sacraments*, especially Baptism and the Eucharist. And what's the communion that Baptism brings us to? It's a communion with the Church, the Body of Christ. It brings us into communion with Christ, the Head of the Body, and with the members of his Body. And because Christ is also in union with the Father in the Spirit, Baptism also brings about our communion with the Trinity. Okay, so that's the first way the Church brings about communion, namely, through the grace of the Sacraments.

The second way the Church brings about communion is by being *a sign of communion*. For, when people see the Church (those who love and follow Christ), it draws them and is a compelling force, leading to faith. Indeed, seeing communion leads to faith, and *faith is communion with Christ*. So, Christians who radiate a deep, personal communion with Christ are not just signs of communion. They create it. Remember our lesson on the Sacraments: They're not just signs; they *do* something. And laypeople in the world who manifest authentic communion with Christ become living sacraments in the world. As such, they're not only signs of communion but they *cause* communion, because their witness draws people to faith. Let me try to make this as concrete as possible because it's so important.

You're a secretary. Your boss is an unbeliever named Pagano. Every day, he sees you diligently working at your desk. He values you as an employee. You're punctual, reliable, honest, and hardworking. He often says, "I wish I could find more employees like you." One day at the office, when others aren't around, he speaks to you in an unusual way: "Tell me something. You're always on time. You don't leave early. I've never caught you in a lie. You don't gossip, and you're always so hardworking. You know, when I'm away from the office, it certainly would be easy for you to leave early and slack off, but I've been told that you never do this, whereas, the others do. People just aren't like that these days. Why are you so different?"

You respond, "It's because I'm a Christian."

Okay. That's that. End of conversation.

A few weeks later, Pagano stops by your desk again after almost everyone else has left the office. "Tell me something," he says. "I know you've been through a lot this year with your mother dying, your own health issues, and the struggles your kids are having. Truth be told, if I were in your shoes, I'd have lost it — I'd have been in despair for months. But there's something about you. Even when you clearly have a weight on your shoulders, you're still so peaceful, kind, and even joyful. Why is that?" You respond, "Well, Pagano, I'm a Christian. Jesus is my Lord and Savior. He died for my sins and has given me the gift of eternal life. So, no matter how bad things get, I always have eternal life to look forward to, and he's even with me now as my strength, peace, and consolation."

I think you get the point, and I don't think you would be all that surprised if Pagano eventually changed his name to Christiano. You wouldn't be surprised because communion draws people to faith, whether that be the personal communion with Christ given in this example, the witness of the communion of believers gathered together in prayer and fellowship, or whatever. The point is this: Communion begets communion, because communion begets faith, and faith is already communion with Christ, and communion with Christ is communion with all believers and the Trinity.

There are many ways that the laity are called to evangelize, but all of them really come down to communion. For instance, family life is a key part of evangelization. For, when a family is what it's meant to be, a communion of love, then it becomes a force that draws and attracts others to faith. As Pope John Paul II's Theology of the Body teaches, the Christian family makes visible the invisible love of the Most Holy Trinity.

Another powerful example of how the laity evangelize is by their groups and associations. When centered on Christ, such groups strengthen the communion of the Church and draw others in. In the following passage, John Paul encourages the laity to form themselves into groups:

Church communion, already present and at work in the activities of the individual, finds its specific expression in the lay faithful's working together in groups, that is, in activities done with others in the course of their responsible participation in the life and mission of the Church.

In recent days the phenomenon of lay people associating among themselves has taken on a character of particular variety and vitality. In some way lay associations have always been present throughout the Church's history as various confraternities, third orders and sodalities testify even today. However, in modern times such lay groups have received a special stimulus, resulting in the birth and spread of a multiplicity of group forms: associations, groups, communities, movements. We can speak of *a new era of group endeavors* of the lay faithful.[177]

As I mentioned in an earlier section, prayer groups and gatherings of the faithful play a key role in the work of evangelization. Such groups break the downward slide of Western culture into individualism and the shallow counterfeits of true communion that leave people even more alone. Christian fellowship is authentic communion. As such, it takes people out of their loneliness and makes them happy. I know. I've seen it. For the last year, I've been working on a new initiative called Hearts Afire: Parish-based Programs from the Marian Fathers of the Immaculate Conception (HAPP®), which is one of many ways that laypeople can join together in groups for prayer, study, and an experience of the Lord with his people. At the risk of sounding like a commercial, I encourage you to look into the HAPP® program (see information pages at the end of the book) or into any faith-based small-group program if you're not already involved. Great things can come from joining a small group. Try it. You'll like it! — I almost said, "I guarantee it!" But then I'd really sound like a salesman.

While I'm not a salesman, I am a "religious priest," meaning I belong to the consecrated life, which is what we're about to cover. But just one important point before we get to it.

"That they may all be one" (Jn 17:21). I've mentioned Protestants several times in the previous pages, and at this point, it should be clear that working toward the unity of all Christians (ecumenism) is an important part of the work of evangelization. Why? Because, as we've learned, communion (unity) is a witness that actually begets communion by drawing people to faith. At the same time, we have to acknowledge that lack of Christian unity gives an anti-witness that drives people away from Christ. Therefore, in our modern times, when the forces of unbelief and secularism seem to be growing in strength, it's even more important to work for the unity of all Christians, "that the world may believe" (Jn 17:21).

I have a growing hope that more and more of our Protestant brothers and sisters, whose own Christian witness has inspired me in so many ways, will no longer feel the need to protest the Catholic Church and will return home to her. I say this because it looks to me that the main reasons for the initial protest are crumbling away. For instance, the heart of Martin Luther's protest, I believe, was not so much about the abuses and corruption that plagued the Church at the time of the Reformation, but rather, it seemed to have to do *with his own personal need to know the mercy of God.*

While Luther was still a Catholic, he fell into a torturous bout of scruples and lived with a paralyzing fear of God. Fortunately, he found relief in reading St. Paul's Letter to the Romans, which talks about the saving power of faith and the mercy of God. This was a moment of grace for Luther, and it freed him from his scruples and fear.

In his enthusiasm at finding freedom in faith, I believe Luther went too far by proclaiming an unbiblical doctrine of "faith alone." (I say "unbiblical" because in James 2:24, the Bible says it is "not by faith alone" that we are saved.) Having said this, I should point out that the Catholic Church and Lutheran Church have more recently come to a mutual understanding on this very issue, such that it's now clear that we more or less believe the same thing on this point.[178] The heart of it for both sides is that, in the end, it isn't so much a question of "faith alone" or "faith and works," but rather, "*grace alone*." In other words, as St. Thérèse of Lisieux puts it, "Everything is grace." And even though I believe that Luther was wrong to leave the Catholic Church and teach "faith alone," I think he was right in genuinely seeking to know the mercy of God, and he was right to found his whole life on faith in Jesus and trust in his grace and mercy.

But here's why I think the heart of the Protestant protest is crumbling away: *Catholics are starting to get it.* What I mean by this is that the teaching of saints such as Thérèse of Lisieux, Faustina Kowalska, and John Paul II have infused the general Catholic consciousness with a deeper — and sometimes much needed — sense of the mercy of God. Thus, many Catholics today are being healed of undue fear and a false image of God and are discovering the true face of the Father as a God of infinite mercy. Believe me, I know. I'm seeing it happen.

As I mentioned earlier, I live and work at the National Shrine of The Divine Mercy in Stockbridge, Massachusetts, and I read the conversion stories of those who write to us, hear the testimonies of the pilgrims, and witness their new-found freedom and joy in Christ and his mercy. God really is on the move! Indeed, in what may be the largest grassroots movement in the history of the Catholic Church, the faithful are turning to the mercy of God for everything and living an attitude of trust in Jesus. Of course, authentic trust in our Merciful Savior also requires conversion and turning away from sin, but I really mean it when I say that Catholics are getting it. They're getting the very heart of Sacred Scripture, the message of God's superabundant mercy for sinners.[179]

So, if Catholics begin to witness more powerfully to a personal relationship with Jesus and to having a deep, childlike, and joyful trust in the mercy of God, then where are the grounds for Protestant protest? And now that Christianity is no longer unified but rather divided into tens of thousands of Protestant groups and sects — something Luther never intended — might it be a good time to revisit the issue of authority? After all, the claim to having a special teaching authority has preserved the unity of the largest and most ancient Christian body in the world, the Roman Catholic Church. Might this authority be right after all even if, admittedly and obviously, the Church is still full of sinners? And what about the Eucharist? If the Catholics are right and it *truly is* the Body and Blood, Soul and Divinity of Jesus, then isn't this a big deal and a reason to reconsider coming home to enjoy such a sacred banquet? And getting back to mercy, isn't this miracle of the altar, where bread and wine truly become Body and Blood, *an even greater mercy* than mere symbols? And what about Mary? Well, surely she's the stumbling block, right? Quick story on this point.

The Hearts Afire program that I mentioned earlier begins with a six-week group retreat that's based on a book about Mary, *33 Days to Morning Glory.* Anyway, I'd heard there are these two guys in Southern California who have been amazing apostles of the program, putting fliers everywhere and organizing retreats at some 30 parishes and counting. Well, during a visit to California, I met them for the first time, and over some burgers and fries, they told me something I could hardly believe.

They said that at one of the largest Evangelical Protestant churches in the area, a woman from one of the Bible study groups had asked her pastor about Mary. The pastor responded by saying, "Well, you'll have to ask the Catholics about that." So, this woman took his advice and visited a neighboring Catholic parish. Nobody was around at the time, but she saw one of the fliers for the group retreat on Mary and called the number on the flier, which belonged to one of the guys. She asked him if she and her group could start one of the group retreats on Mary, even though they were Protestant. He said, "Of course!"

So, a Protestant Bible study group of 17 people went through the whole six-week retreat, consecrated themselves to Jesus through Mary on a Marian Feast day, and now, all 17 of them are taking RCIA classes in preparation for entering the Catholic Church.

So, is Mary a problem? Not if you're looking for an even deeper, more personal relationship with Jesus. I say this because some of the most common feedback I've received from the thousands of people who have made the Marian retreat is that Mary has brought them into an even deeper personal relationship with Jesus. So what's the problem?

I encourage all Catholics to witness to their Protestant friends and invite them to come home. We need them! The zeal and energy of former Protestants who have become Catholic has really fired up the Church in recent years. In fact, I can think of many prominent Catholic evangelists who once were Protestant and who are now helping Catholics rediscover the beauty of their Catholic faith. What would happen if Protestants began to enter the Church by the tens of thousands or even hundreds of thousands? They'd help set the world on fire. Let's pray for it and do what we can to make it happen at least by the witness of a deep, personal relationship with Christ our Lord and an ardent love for his Church.

*P*ROPHETIC MISSION OF CONSECRATED MEN AND WOMEN. While everyone is called to a deep, personal relationship with Jesus Christ, there's one group in the Church that's been chosen to witness to that relationship even more so than others: consecrated men and women. Like the laity, their task is primarily to live out their prophetic mission of evangelization *by making God visible*, and they do this above all in two ways: (a) through faithfulness to their calling to a more radical life of holiness and (b) through their community life. Let's now look at both of these ways in turn.

(a) A more radical holiness. Earlier, we saw that martyrs are those who speak most eloquently to the true unity of faith and life that's, unfortunately, not found in so many modern Christians. In the face of the scandalous split between faith and life, where many believers sell out the faith to worldly desires and aspirations, the blood of the martyrs reminds us that nothing in this world is as important as faith, not even life itself. The witness of consecrated men and women also reminds us of this fact.

Church historians generally agree that the consecrated life really began to take off when the "age of the martyrs" of the early Church ended. In other words, when the Roman emperors stopped persecuting Christians, the world still needed to see a radical witness to faith. The Holy Spirit provided that witness by inspiring certain generous souls to renounce the power, pleasure, and riches of the world and to live the three evangelical vows of poverty, chastity, and obedience. While these vows are certainly not the same as blood martyrdom, they're a martyrdom nonetheless. As such, through the ages, they provide a powerful witness to the world of the primacy of Christ. They remind us that "here we have no lasting city" (Heb 13:14), that "the form of this world is passing away" (1 Cor 7:31), and that in the fullness of the kingdom of heaven, the children of God will take neither wife nor husband but will be like the angels of God (see Mt 22:30). Thus, through living out their evangelical vows, consecrated men and women "remind their other brothers and sisters to keep their eyes fixed on the peace which is to come, and to strive for the definitive happiness found in God."[180]

The key words in that last sentence are "peace" and "happiness." For the special note of the martyrs is a deep peace and even joy in the face of impending death because of the promise of the life to come. The key mark of consecrated men and women is also peace and joy. This is not directly because they are poor, chaste, and obedient but because their three vows unite them more closely to Christ, who also lived a life of poverty, chastity, and obedience. In other words, consecrated men and women are a witness to the world of the peace and joy that come from intimate communion with Christ through sacrificial love.

I myself get to see this witness every day. There's a small community of older sisters who support the priests and brothers of my community with domestic help. Every day, as I pass by the kitchen and see them diligently preparing a meal or cleaning up (yes, I do my best to lend a hand), I'm lifted up by their peace and joy. They seem to be constantly happy, even in the midst of illness and suffering. Why are they so happy? I believe it's because they're deeply aware that, as consecrated women, they're wed to Christ, and the joy that comes from so intimately belonging to him can't help but overflow to others — even to a busy priest who is also consecrated to God and who sometimes needs to be reminded of the joy of that fact! But their witness is not just for me. God gives the consecrated life to the whole world so that "this world may never be without a ray of divine beauty to lighten the path of human existence."[181]

In the great Church document on the consecrated life, *Vita Consecrata,* by Pope John Paul II, the key theme is *beauty.* For example, in one place, the Pope writes that the consecrated life is one of the "tangible seals" that the Trinity impresses on the world "so that people can sense with longing the attraction of divine beauty."[182] I love that phrase, "the attraction of divine beauty." Beauty does, indeed, attract. It draws people. More-over, *divine* beauty, in a sense, goes even further: It lifts people out of themselves and invites them into communion, and this communion itself is the beauty that attracts. For God himself is a splendid mystery of Communion, and he is gloriously beautiful in that communion. In a special way, this divine beauty is seen in the witness of the community life of consecrated men and women.

(b) Consecrated community life. Let's go back to those sisters I just mentioned. Individually, their peace and joy is beautiful. But what's even more beautiful is the way they work together, pray together, and really are "of one heart and one mind" (Acts 4:32). They constantly cooperate, care for each other, laugh together, and bear one another's burdens. This, for me, is the most beautiful part of their witness — as it should be. For consecrated men and women who live in community have a vocation to be witnesses to the beauty of communion. Again, this is lived out not only individually through the radiance of holiness that comes from intimate, personal communion with Christ but also through the splendor of authentic communal life, which is described by the Church as an "object of contemplation."[183]

When I first read that community life is an "object of contemplation," I just about fell out of my chair. I'd always heard it described in *other* terms. For example, I seem to recall a certain Latin phrase sometimes quoted by the seminarians: "*Vita communis est mea maxima penitentia*," meaning, "Life in community is my greatest penance." So, in reading that community life is an "object of contemplation," I thought to myself, "Sure thing … just like the Sorrowful Mysteries of the Rosary are objects of contemplation!" With this cynical thought still lingering in my mind, I reluctantly headed down from my room to what most of the seminarians called "mandatory fun." In other words, it was time for some regularly scheduled recreation with the community.

This particular day, like most days, I wasn't enthusiastic about attending community recreation. It almost always seemed like a waste of time, something to endure, something to get through — and this day was no different. Or was it? I couldn't put my finger on it. Perhaps it had to do with the idea that was still floating in my mind, the idea that community life is an "object of contemplation." Whatever the case, something was definitely different, and it made me approach this particular time of recreation with different eyes.

It was a summer afternoon, and all the seminarians, about twelve of them, had gathered together in the seminary courtyard for some watermelon. As I walked into the scene and took it all in, I started thinking to myself, "Here are these twelve guys who are all so very different: different ages, different temperaments, and from different cultures and countries. Yet they're all here on this sunny afternoon because Jesus called them to follow him."

I knew well that many of the guys, before entering the community, had had high-paying jobs, beautiful girlfriends, loving parents, and very dear brothers and sisters. And yet, here they all were, far away from their previous lives, obediently present for mandatory fun, eating watermelon, talking and laughing, and spending time simply being together — all because of Jesus. It was actually a beautiful moment, and I believe Jesus was deeply pleased with each one individually and with the group as a whole. I remember thinking to myself, "Man, if people in the world could see this, they'd be amazed." And that actually gets to the point of the consecrated life: It's meant to amaze our divided, broken world with a glorious sign of communion in Christ. In fact, Pope John Paul II calls on consecrated men and women to be "true experts of communion and to practice the spirituality of communion."[184] In the following passage, he explains what this means:

> The Church is essentially a mystery of communion "a people made one with the unity of the Father, the Son, and the Holy Spirit." The fraternal life [of consecrated men and women] seeks to reflect the depth and richness of this mystery, taking shape as a human community in which the Trinity dwells, in order to extend in history the gifts of communion proper to the three divine Persons. Many are the settings and the ways in which fraternal communion is expressed in the life of the Church. The consecrated life can certainly be credited with having effectively helped to keep alive in the Church the obligation of fraternity as a form of witness to the Trinity. By constantly promoting fraternal love, also in the form of common life, the consecrated life has shown that *sharing in the Trinitarian communion can change human relationships* and create a new type of solidarity. In this way it speaks to people both of the beauty of fraternal communion and of the ways which actually lead to it. Consecrated persons live "for" God and "from" God, and precisely for this reason they are able to bear witness to the reconciling power of grace which overcomes the divisive tendencies present in the human heart and in society.[185]

I'd like to start unpacking this incredibly rich quote by making a confession. I've lived consecrated communal life now for so long that I frequently forget how much the rest of the world hungers for the witness of it. I mean, while I'm grumbling to myself about my *"maxima penitentia,"* a lay guest, who happens to be visiting our community at the time, will suddenly surprise me by exclaiming, "How good it is to be here!" And then, he'll go on to express deep gratitude for having experienced the communal life.

One time, I clearly remember a particular guest saying to me, with a touch of sadness, "*It's not like this in the world.*" Hearing this made me realize that I'd taken for granted that community life "reflects the depths and richness" of the mystery of the Trinity and that it truly can be a place "where the Trinity dwells." Not only that, it reminded me that being in such a place where the Trinity dwells "can change human relationships and create a new type of solidarity." In other words, when people live life "for" God and "from" God, it's a thing of grace and healing as it "overcomes divisive tendencies present in the human heart and society."

Getting back to that summer afternoon of mandatory fun with my fellow seminarians, I now see how right the Pope was to write that "communities of consecrated life, where persons of different ages, languages and cultures meet as brothers and sisters, are *signs that dialogue is always possible* and that communion can bring differences into harmony."[186] Also, as I think back to the joyful surprise of lay guests who have visited my community, I see how right the Pope was to say that community life itself is something *missionary*, and therefore, it's a key way that consecrated men and women fulfill their prophetic mission of communion.

Let's conclude this section by reflecting on John Paul II's profound words as he describes the missionary force of fraternal life in communion:

> The life of communion in fact "becomes a *sign* for all the world and a compelling *force* that leads people to faith in Christ … . In this way communion leads to mission, and itself becomes mission"; indeed, "communion begets communion: in essence it is a communion that is missionary."[187]

3. Evangelization for Everyone: Building the Culture of Life

At this point in the chapter, we've looked generally at evangelization and the Church and then more specifically at evangelization according to the different states of life in the Church (hierarchy, laity, consecrated life). Now we're going to go back to a more general perspective, namely, a way that each and every member of the Church — bishops, priests, deacons, laity, and consecrated men and women alike — is called to evangelize. It has to do with building what Pope John Paul II calls "a culture of life." Because this way of spreading the Gospel is for every member of the Church and every person of good will, we're going to give it some extra time and attention.

A LIFE-CHANGING LETTER. In Part Two, I shared that when I was in college, one of my friends had given me a book — more specifically, an "encyclical letter" — called *The Gospel of Life* (*Evangelium Vitae*) by Pope John Paul II and that it had changed my life. The life-changing moment began as soon as I read the introduction, where the Pope describes the purpose of the encyclical. What struck me was not just what he said but how he said it. See for yourself:

> The present encyclical ... [is] meant to be a *precise and vigorous reaffirmation of the value of each human life and its inviolability*, and at the same time a pressing appeal addressed to each and every person, in the name of God: respect, protect, love and serve life, every human life! Only in this direction will you find justice, development, true freedom, peace and happiness!
>
> May these words reach all the sons and daughters of the Church! May they reach all people of good will who are concerned for the good of every man and woman and for the destiny of the whole of society! ...
>
> To all the members of the Church ... I make this most urgent appeal, that together we may offer this

world of ours new signs of hope, and work to ensure that justice and solidarity will increase and that a new culture of human life will be affirmed, for the building of an authentic civilization of truth and love.[188]

I can't adequately describe the impression these words made on me as a sophomore in college. Here was the Pope himself addressing an average guy like me with a "most urgent" and "pressing" appeal "in the name of God." Not only that, I didn't think Popes used so many exclamation points! And so, I said to myself, "Man, this must be really important." I mean, as a practicing Catholic, I was pro-life and everything, but I didn't fully realize the situation was so serious. The Pope was talking in a much more forceful way than I ever would've expected, and as I read on, I continued to be blown away by his message.

In the subsequent chapters of his encyclical, John Paul described a historic drama of incredible proportions that's unfolding in our time. I was surprised to find him speaking in terms of a "profound crisis of culture,"[189] a "war,"[190] a "dramatic struggle,"[191] and even a "conspiracy."[192] He warned that modern man is living in a period in which "a long historical process is reaching a turning-point" with "tragic consequences."[193] Indeed, he explained that we ought to be "fully aware" that we are facing "an enormous and dramatic clash between good and evil, death and life, the 'culture of death' and the 'culture of life.'"[194]

At the time I read the Pope's words, I was not "fully aware" of any problem. In fact, I was really quite *unaware*. I mean, life seemed great. I had my friends, my classes, a chapel right on campus, and a fully-loaded cafeteria for my meals. Back home, my family was healthy and doing well. What more could I ask for? Yet John Paul II was talking about this "enormous and dramatic clash." What? Where? Not only that, he was saying that we are "all involved and we all share in it" and each person has the "inescapable responsibility" of choosing between the "culture of death" and the "culture of life." In the words of Moses, he was exhorting us: "Choose life that you and your descendants may live" (Deut 30:19).[195] Yet he was also making it clear that simply choosing life isn't enough. Indeed, he was calling us to action, and his words left no doubt about what's at stake:

> [T]he challenge facing us is an arduous one: only the concerted efforts of all those who believe in the value of life can prevent a setback of unforeseeable consequences for civilization.[196]

This Pope was rocking my world. I'd never heard anything like this. I needed to speak with my friend about it, the one who gave me the encyclical. When I told him that the Pope's words were blowing me away, he replied with a laugh, "Ha! You think that's strong stuff? Listen to *this*." Then, from memory, he quoted a statement of Karol Wojtyła that Wojtyła had made while visiting the U.S. less than a year before becoming Pope:

> We are now standing in the face of the greatest historical confrontation humanity has gone through. I do not think that wide circles of American society or wide circles of the Christian community realize this fully. We are now facing the final confrontation between the Church and the anti-Church, of the Gospel versus the anti-Gospel."[197]

These words floored me. My friend went on, "Why do you think I gave you that book? People need to hear this stuff! And didn't you hear what the Pope said at the last World Youth Day in Denver?" I said I hadn't. My friend continued, "He said, 'Woe to you if you do not succeed in defending life,' and then he told us that he's counting on us young people to spread the Gospel of Life."

I couldn't believe what I was hearing. The Pope was counting on *me*? I had to see for myself. So, later, I found the full quote of the Pope's words to the youth of the world. Reading them lit a fire in my heart:

> At this stage of history, the liberating message of *the Gospel of Life* has been put into your hands. And the

mission of proclaiming it to the ends of the earth is now passing to your generation. Like the great Apostle Paul, you too must feel the full urgency of the task: "Woe to me if I do not evangelize" (1 Cor 9:16). *Woe to you if you do not succeed in defending life.* The Church needs your energies, your enthusiasm, your youthful ideals, in order to make the Gospel of Life penetrate the fabric of society, transforming people's hearts and the structures of society *in order to create a civilization of true justice and love.* Now more than ever, in a world that is often without light and without the courage of noble ideals, *people need the fresh, vital spirituality of the Gospel.*

Do not be afraid to go out on the streets and into public places, like the first Apostles who preached Christ and the Good News of salvation in the squares of cities, towns and villages. This is no time to be ashamed of the Gospel (see Rom 1:16). It is the time to preach it from the rooftops (see Mt 10:27). Do not be afraid to break out of comfortable and routine modes of living, in order to take up the challenge of making Christ known in the modern "metropolis." It is you who must "go out into the byroads" (Mt 22:9) and invite everyone you meet to the banquet which God has prepared for his people. The Gospel must not be kept hidden because of fear or indifference. It was never meant to be hidden away in private. It has to be put on a stand so that people may see its light and give praise to our heavenly Father.[198]

After reading *The Gospel of Life* several times and after prayerfully reflecting on these words to the youth gathered in Denver, I decided to dedicate my life to building the culture of life, starting with trying to make people aware of the difficult situation we're in. So, that summer, about 10 of my college friends and I walked across the country, coast-to-coast, witnessing to the Gospel of Life. Literally. We spoke at parishes, to youth groups, and with anyone who would listen. We raised money for women in crisis pregnancies. We prayed silently at abortion clinics. We took to the roads with rosaries in our hands and white shirts on our backs that said in big, blue letters, "PRO-LIFE." It was awesome, and the whole experience deepened my commitment to dedicate everything to building the culture of life. But how exactly does one build a culture of life?

It took me a while to figure that one out. In fact, it took many years of hard study and persistent asking in prayer. I'd like to share the answer to this question now, because it, too, can be life-changing, and it brings us to the heart of why I titled this section "Evangelization for Everyone." But before we can talk about building the culture of life, we first need to be clear about what we're up against: the culture of death. And before we can look at the culture of death, I should first say something about culture in general.

WHAT IS CULTURE? Culture is one of those things that's so close to us, we often don't think about it. As some say, "It's the air we breathe." And who thinks about air? For this reason, culture is an extremely difficult thing to explain and define. Here, I'm going to attempt an explanation and definition that's related to an idea that has kept coming up since Part Two: the enrichment of faith. Also, as we get into all this, we're going to have to delve a bit into some philosophy. But don't worry. It won't take too long, and our efforts in this section will pay off later by making subsequent sections easier to understand.

Recall that the enrichment of faith has to do with moving from a mere "notional knowledge" of the truths of the faith to a "real knowledge," meaning a knowledge that is concrete, personal, experiential, and taken to heart. Now, this kind of enrichment that moves from notional to real knowledge *is not limited to people of Christian faith.* In other words, the movement from notional to real is the task not only of Christians *but of every human being.* This is because each one of us is created with a thirst to know the truth (notional knowledge) and not only to know the truth but also to experience it, enter into it, and make it our own (real knowledge). This desire to seek the truth, to reflect on it, and to make it one's own is uniquely human. Animals don't have it. They don't philosophize, ponder their existence, and ask "the great questions." We do.

Where did I come from? Why am I here? What is man? What is there after death? Does God exist? If God exists, what does he want me to do? What is the meaning of life? These are some of the great questions that arise in the heart of every reflective human being.

But again, we humans don't just ask the great questions. We don't just seek the truth. For, once we find it, we have the task of putting it into practice. Stated differently, when we find the truth, we're suddenly confronted with the command, "*Live this truth.*" This command comes from what's most noble in us. Indeed, it comes as a movement of our hearts, exhorting us to conform our lives to the truth that we know, to take the truth into our very being so it forms our attitudes and outlook. One could say that this is the great task of human life, namely, to make our very lives reflect the truths we discover, the truths we've been taught, the truths that have been revealed to us.

Each one of us has experienced the interior, noble command to live the truth that we know. Moreover, each one of us has also heard the seductive voice of our lower nature, which coaxes us away from living the truth: "*Take it easy. Enjoy yourself. No one will ever know. Come on, you deserve it.*" And when we've given in to this voice, when we've settled for mediocrity, when we've sold out the truth for our own petty desires, wants, and drives, then we've all felt our higher nature, our consciences, convicting us. This goes not only for Christians but for every human being. For there is, indeed, a universal human sensitivity to the badness of hypocrisy, the badness of living the opposite of what we know to be the truth, the badness of living a lie. And the nobler part of us says, "Shame on you for giving in to what is beneath you!" We've all heard this voice, even if we haven't wanted to. Actually, if we really don't want to hear it, we may eventually get our wish. For the more we act against this inner voice of conscience, the more it quiets down, and then our lower nature takes over. (More on this later.)

Alright. So what does all this have to do with culture? Don't worry. I'm getting there. I just need to give one more very brief philosophy lesson.

According to Aristotle, man is a "*rational* animal." This simply means that, as we just learned, we seek the truth, can know the truth, and feel moved to live the truth. Man is also what he calls a "*social* animal." In other words, it's part of our very nature to live in unity with others, to enjoy social life, to share in the communion of family and society. And as for the person who cannot live in such community or who doesn't need it, he is, according to Aristotle, "either a beast or a god." Of course, we're neither beasts nor gods — so, yes, we're all social animals.

Now, having completed our philosophy lessons, we come to the heart of our topic. Let's put together the points we've just covered: (1) By nature, we seek the truth; (2) by nature, we're moved to live the truth that we know; (3) by nature, we live in community with others. Alright, well, guess what. This is the formula for culture! It goes like this: (1) seeking and finding the truth + (2) living the truth + (3) being in community with others = *culture*. Let me explain what I mean.

Because it's our nature to seek the truth and because we're social animals, we naturally seek the truth *together*. We philosophize with one another. We ask each other about the big questions. We discuss, debate, and decide. Yes, we *decide*. Contrary to popular belief today, life is not meant to be a perpetual seeking. Seeking is made for finding, and people do find the truth or at least settle on answers to the great questions. They do this both individually and communally, and *a culture is basically a particular community's answers to the great questions*, the answers to questions such as, "What is man? Why are we here? Who is God? What good ought we to do?"

Great. So we have our definition of culture: It's a given community's answers to the great questions. But it's more than that. For, remember, life isn't just about knowing the truth (notional), it's also about making the truth our own, incarnating it in our lives (real). Indeed, life is about giving flesh to the truth. And because each individual feels the movement to make the truth incarnate in his life, when there's a whole group of people living as a community, then they'll feel moved from within to make the truths they've discovered part of the life of the community. In other words, the individual consciences that say, "*Live the truth*," join together within the community to say, "*Let's live this truth!*" And so, the community strives to incarnate the truth, to give it flesh, and to make it real. This, then, is an even fuller definition of culture: *It's a particular community's* incarnated *answers to the great questions.*

And how are these answers made flesh by a given culture? In a whole multitude of ways. First of all, they're made flesh in the people themselves who have made the answers of their culture their own. They're also made flesh by the great artists of the community who become great because their artwork best expresses (or challenges or refines) the answers of the community. In fact, it's often the artists, writers, filmmakers, and musicians who, in a certain sense, "give back" to the community the answers that they themselves received from it. Thus, the members of the community point to their great art, literature, cinema, and music and say, "Yes, that's what we mean. That's our answer. That's who we are!" And so, art becomes the expression of the community's answers to the great questions.

The answers of the community to the great questions are also reflected in how the community works, buys and sells, recreates, celebrates, worships, and mourns. They're found in the communal history, politics, laws, and language. They're found in just about every way the community expresses itself.

Now, here's something interesting about culture: It's both parent and child. As we've just seen, culture is the *child* of the community, because it's born from and formed by the people of the community. On the other hand, it's also the *parent* of the people of the community, because it nurtures and forms them. In other words, it *educates* them, and education, according to Pope John Paul II, is the "primary and essential task" of culture.[199] Let's look at this idea more closely.

At first glance, it might seem that culture isn't such an important part of education — at least not for us Westerners. I say this because our own culture tends toward a radical individualism that can give the impression that education is primarily the task of the individual. For instance, we've all heard of the "self-made" or "self-taught" man, which is supposedly a distinction of honor. But it's really an illusion. For while every person truly has a responsibility for his growth and maturity, the reality is that all education is *communal*. This becomes clear when we simply reflect on the idea of language. Who of us invented the language that we use? Of course, none of us have. Others handed it on to us. And yet the language that we've received from our culture is itself the primary tool that we use to learn. Moreover, even the self-taught man learns from teachers, from books, and from watching others. Even he has picked up much of what he knows from his family and immediate environment.

All this is a good thing. For, as we learned in Part Two, the enrichment of faith (or the enrichment of a person in the truth) takes place through a confluence of many streams. In other words, we become a mighty river of mature and enriched knowledge only after a thousand tributaries of influences have been poured into us. We attain a richly formed mind, heart, and consciousness only after receiving the personal influence of virtuous family members, teachers, and friends. We mature as persons only after being influenced by such excellent things as good books, fine art, and participation in communal efforts. In sum, we're formed, enriched, and educated (in the fullest sense of the word) by our culture.

At this point in this section on culture, some nagging questions need to be addressed. Am I saying that every culture has got it all right? Am I saying that cultures are perfect? Am I saying that cultures reflect the fullness of truth? Of course not. There are surely errors in all cultures, including Christian ones. There are surely wrong answers given by the people who form a culture. For we remain fallen human beings. Still, every authentically human culture does express the wisdom of God in some way. Every culture expresses certain truths about human existence and the meaning of life, and it's these truths that open a culture to its deepest fulfillment in the revelation of God in Jesus Christ, our Lord. Now, some of the most important of these truths are the moral teachings of a culture, what John Paul II calls the "first and fundamental dimension of a culture."[200]

Why are the moral teachings of a culture so important? Because it's the moral teachings that, above all, shape each human person. The way we morally (or immorally) act forms us. So, for instance, when we give in to a life of sin, we become a particular kind of human being. Gossiping makes us gossips. Stealing makes us thieves. Lying makes us liars. Fornicating makes us fornicators. Murdering makes us murderers. Now, if a culture is fulfilling its true task, it should help us to avoid these things. It should equip us to resist the temptation to be less than our calling. It should reinforce in us the "natural law," which is the moral law that's been written on our hearts. It should lead us to the true freedom and happiness that comes from virtuous living and that prepares the way to fully embracing the message of the Gospel.

Before concluding this section, let's briefly look at the idea that's just come up and that's so important for understanding and assessing culture: the natural law.

God loves us so much that he has inscribed the basic instruction manual for human happiness within our hearts. This instruction manual is the natural law, which tells us what we should and should not do. For instance, we all know that we should not eat glass. We all know that we should show gratitude to those who do good to us. We all know that we should not murder. Or do we? Unfortunately, after the fall of Adam and Eve, the natural law that's written on our hearts is often difficult to read. Knowing this, in his mercy, God revealed the Ten Commandments, which basically spell out the main points of the natural law, the way of life and happiness for human beings.[201]

Okay, well, now that we know the Ten Commandments, we follow them perfectly, right? Wrong. Unfortunately, we can know something is true but not live it. Because God understands this, in his great mercy, he sent his Son to teach us the law more perfectly, which is to live the "new commandment" of love, and he gives us the grace to live it. Yet, even with Christ's teaching, example, and grace, we still don't always live the way that leads to life. Because God knows this, in his great mercy, he gives us a multitude of aids to help us better know and live his life, one of which is *a culture of life*, a culture that reinforces in us "the way, the truth, and the life" (Jn 14:6). Because Satan also knows about the many helps God gives us, he fights against them by forming a *culture of death*. We'll now look at both of these kinds of culture in turn, starting with the culture of death, and what it means for a culture to be "bad" or "good."

*T*HE CULTURE OF DEATH. Just as people are not morally equal — some are good and some are bad; some are very good and some are very bad — neither are cultures morally equal. For cultures are simply the reflection and expression of the people who create them. Now, if the people of a community know the truth and live it, they will have a good culture. If the people of a community know the truth but do not live it, they will have a bad culture. If the people of a community do not know the truth, then they cannot live it, and they'll fall back on their lower nature, live like animals, and have no culture to speak of. If the people of a community believe lies and live those lies, they will have a very bad culture, an anti-culture. Good cultures lead to morally good people, to peace, life, and happiness. Bad cultures lead to morally bad people, to war, death, and misery.

Of course, life is not so simple. Just as we ourselves are a mix of light and darkness, so are our cultures. Take the present situation of Western culture. In many ways, our modern Western culture manifests profoundly true answers to the great questions. This is due to its foundation in the relatively virtuous pagan cultures of Greece and Rome and its long Judeo-Christian history. At the same time, our modern Western culture currently manifests blatant lies in response to the great questions. This is especially due to the influence of the so-called "enlightened" ideas of the 17th century and to so many modern philosophies such as pragmatism, social Darwinism, and atheistic humanism.[202]

Therefore, as John Paul II pointed out in *The Gospel of Life*, we really are in the midst of a kind of war between cultures, between two conflicting sets of answers to the great questions. We're in a historic battle between a culture of life and a culture of death.

In the remainder of this section, we'll look at what answers to the great questions lie behind the culture of death. We'll do this by conducting an interview with the culture itself. In the section that follows this interview, we'll begin looking at the culture of life. Alright, now to the interview …

Reporter: Hello, Culture of Death. I have some questions for you. Right up front, you should know that I'll be asking you some deep, philosophical questions — the big questions, the great questions. So get ready …

Culture of Death: I'm sorry. I cannot answer such questions.

R: Why not?

C of D: Because you are seeking the truth. I mean, you think there is such a thing as truth. But to the great question, "*What is truth?*" I answer, "There is no truth — at least, there's no objective truth." You see, my teaching is that the truth is relative. For instance, I tell people that what they think is the truth is really just the truth *for them*. What you think is the truth is really just the truth *for you*. So it's all just opinion. I say there is no objective truth.

R: I see. So you say there is no truth. Is it true that there is no truth?

C of D: Point taken. So, I contradict myself. Look. I'll just cut to the chase. I'll tell you what I'm up to. I know there is truth — but I hate it. Rather, I hate *him*. I'm a liar and the Father of Lies, and I hate the one who came to bear witness to the truth. I hate the one who is Truth. I hate the one who came to set people free by the truth. I don't want people to experience this freedom. I want them enslaved to their passions. So, I tell people there is no truth, that truth is relative. That's my message.

And here's how it works. Here's how my message enslaves. If I tell people there is no truth, then there's nothing to challenge them to be chaste, honest, temperate, faithful, and self-sacrificing. If there's no objective truth, then each person can do whatever he pleases. Each one can come up with his own "truth" that justifies his lifestyle and selfish desires. Each person can say to himself, "Oh, I really don't think there's anything wrong with being unchaste or intemperate. So, as long as I'm a nice person, that's all that really matters." It's amazing how often people, when told there is no objective truth, will conveniently believe exactly what justifies their own lifestyles. They'll say, "Well, I just feel that such and such can't be wrong. It may be wrong *for you* but it's right *for me*."

So, by convincing people that there's no such thing as objective truth, I open the door for them to choose their own truth. And when they choose their own truth, they inevitably become enslaved to their passions. For, if reason doesn't rule a person, the passions will. Cut off the head, and the belly is king. Kill the truth, and the appetites dominate. That's my game. I want to take out the truth so people will do whatever their lower desires dictate. In short, I want to turn men into animals, and the quickest route to the zoo is to do away with objective truth.

R: Well, for the Father of Lies, you sure are being honest. But your strategy can't work. I mean, the idea that there is no truth and that we can do what we want may work for a while, but if there's no truth, then there's no meaning. And people can't live without meaning. So, they'll turn back to the truth at least to find meaning for their lives.

C of D: What you say is not true. Just because I tell people there is no truth does not mean that they have to go without meaning. They'll still ask the great question, "*What is the meaning of life?*" And I have an answer for them. I tell them, "You get to pick! Just as you get to pick your own truth, you also get to pick your own meaning for life." I try to make it seem bold and exciting, "Hey, create your own meaning!" And what do people do? They do the very same thing as when I tell them to pick their own truth: They go for what is convenient, what justifies their lifestyles. They pick a "meaning of life" that caters to their egos. In other words, nine times out of ten, they choose *selfishness* as their meaning of life, even if they don't come right out and call it that. And to find this "meaning," people hardly need any goading from me. I simply present to them the allure of power, pleasure, and pride — and they fall right in. They feed themselves on these things, and they quickly become addicts, slaves to themselves and to me.

R: So it's all a trap. You tell people they're free to choose, but then they end up choosing slavery?

C of D: Yes, and so you have my answer to another one of the great questions, "*What is freedom?*" I'll tell you what I say freedom is: I say *it's to do whatever you want.* And yes, you're right to see the trap. This is obviously *not* true freedom, because it leads to slavery. It's the so-called freedom that chooses chains and prison. It's a false freedom that chooses bondage to one's lower nature.

Look, my job couldn't be easier. I simply tell people, "Hey, you're an adult. You're free to choose. So do whatever you want! Choose your own meaning!" And when it's all up to them, they almost always choose slavery. It's like giving a child a choice between a feast of steak, mashed potatoes, and vegetables on one table and a pile of candy, ice-cream sundaes, and pitchers of soda on the other. The kid is free to choose, but he's not free. He'll choose the sweets. He doesn't know any better. Of course, he'll feel sick after only eating sweets, and he'll become addicted to them. The key idea is that he doesn't *know* any better. So long as there's no truth to challenge people, their lower natures will rule them. The one I hate said, "The truth will set you free." He was right. So, I keep people far from the truth. They ask, "What's the truth?" I say, "It's all relative."

R: You just quoted Jesus, who said, "The truth will set you free" (Jn 8:32). And Jesus is God. So what about God? Doesn't the love of God put a stop to your scheme? Or doesn't at least a healthy dose of the fear of God and the punishment of hell keep people from abandoning the truth?

C of D: I try my best to keep God out of it. Sure, people ask themselves, "*Is there a God?*" It's one of your so-called "great questions." But here's how I respond: "God? Where is God? Has God ever come down with thunderbolts when you've told a fib? No. Did he come down to stop that massacre you heard about on the news? No. So where is God?" I tell them, "Look. Have you ever seen God? No. So trust your senses. There is no God."

Unfortunately, most people are wise to me. The religious sense in them runs so deep that they don't usually flat out reject the existence of God. Fine. But then, my next move is to ask them, "Well, where is this God whom you believe in? I'll tell you where he is. He's up in heaven, the great clockmaker in the sky. He set everything in motion but stays far away. He's very respectful, you know. He leaves you alone." The scientifically minded often go for this one, but not the others who really want a God who is close to them. Well, to them I say, "Oh, yes, there is a God. He's a great power that moves through the universe. He's awesome. He's in everything, and he's especially *in you*. He's that inner light within you. You really are divine, you know." Lots of people fall for this one. I tell them, "Yeah, be spiritual but not religious. You don't need any of that institutional religion. You don't need other people. You can just commune with God in nature and in that inner light that is you."

I can't tell you how many people eat this stuff up. The great part of it is that this idea of God as an abstract power, an impersonal Great Spirit doesn't put any demands on anyone. There's no commitment. This kind of God is as imposing as Jell-O and demanding as a sunset. He doesn't challenge any lifestyle. And because he's just a silent, impotent energy, guess who gets to be the real God in this scenario. That's right. People do. They're the ones who get to play God as they conveniently choose their own truth and meaning.

R: I have no doubt that lots of people fall for this idea of God, as you said. But I also know there are plenty of other people who want a relationship with a personal God, and they won't accept these answers.

C of D: You're right. There are many, many people who hunger for a personal God and see through my smoke. After all, God is a person, and he calls everyone to relationship with him. But I really can't allow such a personal relationship. It ruins everything. So here's what I do. One option is that I tell people, "Sure, there's a personal God. And he is love and all that. Yeah. In fact, he's a great, big Grandpa God who gives you whatever you want. He's so kind and nice that he will never, *never* condemn or correct what you do."

Many people accept this idea. It's a God who reminds them of so many parents who never rock the boat, parents who say to their kids, "I'm not going to impose anything on you. Do whatever makes you happy. I just want you to be happy." So, echoing this, I tell people, "Hey, God just wants you to be happy!" Of course, they don't take this as the true happiness that comes from living the truth (a truth that often challenges). Rather, they take it as the "happiness" that's really just a catering to whatever their passions, appetites, and egos dictate, which, again, leads to slavery. And so, the jolly old Grandpa God happily sanctions and approves whatever they do. Of course, he sends *everyone* to heaven. And *nobody* goes to hell — except maybe those mean, intolerant people who say there's such a thing as objective truth.

R: Alright, I have no doubt some people fall for this idea of a Grandpa God, too. But I'm sure there are many who don't accept it.

C of D: Right again. And so, because many people don't accept it, I've got another option. It's what I call "the Ogre God approach." This is where I present the idea that God is really just a mean ogre who's always ready to smash people for the slightest infraction of his oppressive rules. He's the God who says *everything* is a sin, who is impossible to please, and who dangles people just above the fires of hell, ready to cut the rope.

With this God, love must be earned, and it's only earned through a miserable obstacle course of penances and deprivations that eventually leave people feeling exhausted, discouraged, and depressed. With this ogre God, love is really an illusion, and all you're left with is fear and eventually a secret hatred of God. People finally flee from this ogre God right into my arms, and they become my apostles, telling everyone about the "freedom" they've found in making their own rules, meaning, and truth. They don't realize they've never really known God, and the liberation they feel is just liberation from a false god. Of course, in the big picture, this is not true liberation. For, as usual, in choosing their own rules, truth, and meaning, they quickly become enslaved to their own selfish desires.

R: I have to admit that you're covering a lot of ground. You've got a false idea of God for almost everyone, and they all lead to the slavery that is your goal. But what do you do about those who, even after hearing all your lies, still persist in believing in a personal God who truly loves them?

C of D: Well, the hardest ones for me to pick off are the Evangelicals with their deep, personal relationship with God and the Catholics who have been given the fullness of the truth and who are nourished on the Eucharist. With the Evangelicals, because their pastors can preach more or less as they please, I tempt them to avoid the hard truths. But if they do teach these truths, then I tempt their listeners to go down the street to the other preacher who is more "up to date" — in other words, the one who won't challenge their lifestyle. So, if I can't take out the truth, I can at least try to water it down.

With the Catholics, my strategy is a bit different. I do everything I can to keep them from knowing the fullness of truth that they have. I tell them that being Catholic simply means going to Mass on Sundays — if you're in the mood for it, of course. Yet, if they do begin to discover the harder truths that threaten to free them from my grip, I simply say, "Well, you don't have to change your life. You can just be a cafeteria Catholic, like so many others, picking and choosing only what seems true *to you*, what works best *for you*." I tell them, "What does the Pope know? He's just a sinner and a man like any other." And so, I undermine the teaching authority given to the leaders of the Church by your Christ. In fact, I hammer Church leaders, pointing out their sins and imperfections. I say, "Well, they're just a bunch of out-of-touch old men. How can the Spirit work through them?" I do everything I can to hide the divine nature of the Church behind the sinful, human nature of its members. I keep the flock from finding the treasure of truth in earthen vessels by pointing out the cracks in the pots. That's my strategy.

R: Clever. Very clever. If you can't do away with God, then you distort the image people have of him and of his Church. But now, let's go back to how you distort people's image of God.

That part of your strategy, I must admit, is actually more than clever. It's brilliant. And when it works, when people fall for your lies about God, you're actually killing two birds with one stone. For when one's sense of God disappears, so also does his sense of man, the sense of his being made in the image of God. In one bold move, you basically destroy the great commandments to love God and love neighbor! For who can truly love some aloof clock-maker God in the sky, or an impersonal Great Spirit, or an Ogre God, or even the hollow, old Grandpa God? And if we can't love such images of God, then how can we love the creature made in God's own image?

C of D: Congratulations. You're really getting it. Now try to understand why I'm doing all this: I hate God, and I hate his image in man. Because I can't directly attack God, I attack the creature made in his image. I try to destroy God's image in man. I do this by trying to get man to live not as God intended (by reason, heart, and truth), but rather, I try to get men to live like beasts, who are dominated by passions, instincts, and animalistic desire.

At the same time, I try to destroy the image of God in man by convincing man not that he's made in the image of God but that he *is* god. I tell him, "Hey, you. Yes, *you*. You, my friend, are the center of the universe." The implication of this is the following: "Since you're the center of the universe, everyone else revolves around you. Everyone else is just *an object* for your gain, pleasure, and use."

There's a real irony in all this: When man makes himself a god, the center of the universe, the other things in the universe actually become his gods. For, as he uses them simply as objects for his pleasure and pride, he becomes addicted to them, and so they end up ruling him.

R: Well, now you've answered the last of the "great questions" I had for you, namely, "*What is man?*" Of course, you know that man is made in the image of God and that people are called to be his sons and daughters in Christ. But what you're actually telling people is not that they're made in the image of God but that they're really just animals ... and gods. They're animals, you tell them, because they can't help but follow their drives and appetites. They're gods, you tell them, because each one is the center of the universe.

Alright, but if people are gods, then are you saying they have great dignity? After all, who has more dignity than a god?

C of D: No, I'm not saying that at all. Think about it. If each individual is his own little god and he sees everyone else as an object, then *nobody* has dignity. If each person sees himself as the center of the universe, then everyone else is just an orbiting planet. If each person sees himself as the almighty "I," then everyone else is just an "it." But you can't love an "it." An "it" has no dignity and deserves nothing except the honor of serving the "I." In my scenario, in a world of selfish "I's," the "I's" don't see one another as "I's" but rather as "it's." Effectively, then, the reign of the "I's" makes everyone into an *it*, creating a world of "it's." And in this world, "it's" only have worth insofar as they bring the "I's" profit, praise, and pleasure. This is a subjective, assigned, extrinsic worth but not an intrinsic, inherent, inalienable worth. Therefore, apart from the whim and will of the "I's," "it's" can be trampled, discarded, ignored ...

R: ... and killed?

C of D: Sure. Why not? If some "it" stands in the way of the "I's" profit, plans, and pleasure, then sure. No problem.

R: Is that why you're called the Culture of Death?

C of D: Alright, I see where you're going. You want to talk abortion and euthanasia. Well, that's just a part of it, my friend. Yes, I'm deeply gratified by more than a billion abortions in the last 30 years, and I look forward to ramping up the killing of the sick and the elderly. But you have to understand that physical murder is not my greatest achievement. *Spiritual murder* is what I'm truly aiming at. That's the death I'm really all about. Now, don't get me wrong. While I do rejoice at the murder of the innocent, I'm *overwhelmed* with delight at the eternal death of the soul. Above all, that's my goal, and when people listen to my lies and put them into practice, then they quickly die a spiritual death. That's my desire. I lure them with pleasure, riches, and praise till they're puffed up little "I's" with hearts as cold and hard as ice. And when their hearts die, their souls die, and then they're mine. And unless the One I hate steals them from me by his mercy, their physical death simply seals the deal. This death of souls is the full flower and fruit of my lies, and it's my great glory.

Ah, but the masterpiece, the absolute masterpiece, is when I can bring entire families and communities to this spiritual death. This is when my lies become a culture, rather an anti-culture, a culture of death.

R: I see. Ideas truly have consequences. And so your master plan is really to bring spiritual death not only to individuals but to families. For as the family goes, so goes the society, so goes the culture.

C of D: Yes, but there's another reason why I focus on the family. Again, it's because I hate God. And again, because I can't directly attack him, I attack his image, which is man, *but especially man as family*. You know that God is a family of love: Father, Son, and Holy Spirit. Well, human families are meant to make the love and communion of the Trinity visible on earth. So, just as the Father gives himself to the Son and the Son to the Father and there's the procession of the Holy Spirit, so God's plan for the family is for the husband to selflessly give himself to his wife and for the wife to give herself to her husband, and from this love there is the procession of children.[203] Well, I hate that. I want to destroy that image of God, that communion of love. And I do destroy it through my lies.

R: So you destroy the family through your anti-Gospel of selfishness, and once that poison is taken, the family falls apart. Okay, yes, that's clear. Marital infidelity, sterilization, artificial contraception, divorce, abortion, and domestic abuse — these all flow from selfishness and work to destroy the love, life, and communion of the family. You've certainly been busy lately.

C of D: Very busy — and there's even more. You should know that I've recently opened up a second front against the family. As a mockery of marriage and the natural law, I've introduced the logical results of my message that there is no truth. For when there is no truth, when everything is relative, when the idea of truth gives way to "my truth" and "your truth," then it's easy to reshape even the basic foundations of society. For instance, marriage can be redefined as "my marriage" and "your marriage" and whatever I have in mind for marriage. It doesn't have to be between man and woman. It can be between man and man, or woman and woman, or man and woman and woman and woman. Or why not man and animal? You see, without objective truth and without God, everything and anything goes. Arguments suddenly are not based on truth but on feelings. And when men act on feelings and throw out the natural law, they behave as less than animals. I mean, even the animals know that the organ of life is not made for the organ of excrement. Yet when there is no truth, anything goes if it "feels right," and those who claim that there is truth become the enemies. Moreover, when we relativists hold the power and the means of mass communication, we can crush those who believe in objective truth. I think your Pope called it "the dictatorship of relativism." He was right, and the first things dictators do is silence voices that speak the truth.

R: Well, Culture of Death, you've just about left me speechless — but not completely. For the time being, those of us who hold that there is truth are still allowed some free speech. And while we still have it, I'm going to conclude with that last point you made about the means of mass communication.

It seems that the various means of mass communication are the base camp for building your culture. After all, you own Hollywood and Broadway, television and newspapers, and many politicians and artists. All these can be an effective army for building a culture, for getting out your answers to the great questions. But yours aren't the only answers out there. And while you can send out a message that fills the earth from a thousand talking heads, one voice that speaks the truth can cut through all the lies and win the war.

C of D: I know that. And that's what has me worried.

*B*LUEPRINTS FOR *B*UILDING THE *C*ULTURE OF *L*IFE. I already told the story of how the culture of death began to lose its grip on me because of one voice that spoke the truth. Specifically, it was Pope John Paul II's life-changing letter, *The Gospel of Life*. The voice of truth in its pages cut through many years of the culture of death's lies and opened my eyes to the truth of the Gospel.

In this section, I want to share the heart of John Paul's message. In particular, I want to look at the Church's answers to the greatest of the great questions. To get these answers, we're not going to conduct an interview with the culture of life, at least not in the same way we did with the culture of death. Rather, my goal here is to summarize the whole of John Paul's teaching, a teaching that provides the key answers to the great questions and, thereby, presents the blueprints for building the culture of life.

Now, wait a minute. Did I just say I'm going to summarize the teachings of John Paul's entire pontificate? Yes, I did. Don't worry, though, it won't take a hundred pages. Thanks to the Holy Spirit, I can do it right here in one section. For, just as the Holy Spirit gave us the super-concept of *communio* that helps summarize the Church's wisdom, so also, he provides us with some key concepts that help us get to the core of John Paul's great wisdom and that lay out the blueprints for building the culture of life.

So let's begin.

The first key concept that brings us to the Pope's wisdom is the one we've seen several times already. Recall that John Paul believed that after Vatican II, the whole pastoral program of the Church centers on bringing about the enrichment of faith. (Yes, here it is again.) In other words, he believed that all the Church's efforts should be directed toward helping the faithful to make the truths of the faith their own. Thus, he wanted to help believers realize the truths of the faith, to move those truths from head to heart.

Alright, so which truths?

Well, all of them. But, of course, John Paul had his priorities. He always had in mind certain key truths that he believed are most important, especially for our time.

Alright, so what are those key truths?

Well, two of them stand out from all the rest. Two of them get to the heart of John Paul's whole pastoral program. Two of them provide answers to the greatest of the "great questions." I know, I know. You're probably saying, "So tell us already!" Unfortunately, I can't just come right out and say them. These two key truths need to be unfolded properly, and they'll begin to unfold after we identify the two great questions that they answer. Those questions are these: "*Who is God?*" and "*What is man?*"

When answering these questions, John Paul II almost always would begin by quoting what's probably his favorite passage from the Second Vatican Council. In fact, the following passage is one of the most frequent citations from the Council to appear in his writings:

> It is only in the mystery of the Word made flesh that the mystery of man truly becomes clear. For Adam, the first man, was a figure of him who was to come,

namely Christ the Lord. Christ, the final Adam, by the revelation of the mystery of the Father and his love, fully reveals man to himself and makes his supreme calling clear.[204]

Simply put, *Jesus Christ* is the answer. He's the one who fully reveals *who God is* and *who we are.* He solves the mystery of God and of man. Okay, so in the deepest sense, the great answer to our two questions (to all of our deepest questions) is really one answer, one truth. It's Jesus Christ, who is the Truth (see Jn 14:6). Most fundamentally, he is the Truth that needs to go from our heads to our hearts, the Truth that we must fully enter into if we want to be set free.

Alright, so Jesus Christ is the answer. He answers the two great questions about God and man — but he answers them *by revealing two other truths.* It's these two truths that John Paul himself highlights right at the beginning of his pontificate in his very first encyclical letter, *The Redeemer of Man* (*Redemptoris Hominis*). In the first chapter after the introduction, John Paul puts these two truths about God and man in the context of what he calls "*the divine dimension of the mystery of Redemption*" and "*the human dimension of the mystery of Redemption.*" Let's look at each one of these in turn. (Here, "redemption" = "salvation.")

What is the divine dimension of the mystery of redemption? It has to do with the question, "*Who is God?*" It has to do with God's work in Jesus Christ in reconciling us with the Father. It is Jesus Christ, through his Paschal mystery, bringing about the forgiveness of our sins, joining us to himself, and making us sons and daughters of the Father. As a truth for our hearts, it's a revelation of love, "a revelation of the mystery of the Father and his love," a revelation that can be summed up in one word: "*mercy.*"[205]

Recall that we treated God's mercy at length in the last two sections of Part Two. There, I showed that John Paul II helps the faithful to bring this most important truth about God home to our hearts and into our conscious life by his promotion of the Divine Mercy message and devotion. There, I also showed that as the truth that God is mercy penetrates our minds and hearts, we develop the *attitude* or *outlook* of trust in God's mercy, of trust in Divine Mercy Incarnate, who is Jesus Christ: "Jesus, I trust in you."

Because we covered the topic of God's mercy in Part Two, we don't need to revisit it here. Suffice it to say that it's the first of the two great truths that is so crucial to John Paul's whole pastoral plan.

Okay, so now let's move on to the second of the two great truths revealed by Christ, the one that is the real key to building the culture of life: It's the truth that answers the great question, "*What is man?*" Since we haven't yet spoken about this truth in detail, we'll give it its own section.

*T*HE *HUMAN* *DIMENSION* OF *REDEMPTION*. What is "the human dimension of the mystery of redemption"? It has to do with what Jesus Christ reveals about man. It has to do with some of John Paul II's favorite words from Vatican II, "It is only in the mystery of the Word made flesh that the mystery of man truly becomes clear." So, what does Christ make clear about the mystery of man? What is the human dimension of the redemption? It's the revelation of human dignity. According to John Paul, Jesus Christ reveals to man "the greatness, dignity and value that belong to his humanity."[206]

In Part One, we already spent some time reflecting on man's dignity in Christ. There, I said that when we truly realize what God has done for us in Christ, it will make us shake in our shoes with joy. I also pointed out that because the angels fully realize what God has done for us, they are filled with awe (and the demons burn with envy). Well, that earlier treatment wasn't enough. The truth about human dignity is so important that we need to dedicate even more time to it. For it's the truth that, along with Divine Mercy, is most important for us to grasp as the key to building the culture of life. It's a most important truth for us to bring from our heads to our hearts.

How important is it that we grasp the truth of human dignity in Christ? How important is it that we develop a sense of wonder for the dignity of each human person? How important is it for us to be able to say to ourselves, "How precious must man be in the eyes of the Creator, if he 'gained so great a Redeemer,' and if God 'gave his only Son,' in order that man 'should not perish but have eternal life'"?[207] How important is it for us to say with awe, "How precious must each human person be if the Son of God has taken up human nature in himself, if the Son of God died on the Cross for man, if the Son of God has made man into sons and daughters of God in him"? Here's how important it is. In an astonishing passage from *Redemptoris Hominis*, John Paul II gives the answer:

> In reality, the name for that deep amazement at man's worth and dignity is the Gospel, that is to say: the Good News. It is also called Christianity. This amazement determines the Church's mission in the world and, perhaps even more so, "in the modern world."[208]

So, this deep amazement at man's dignity is the Gospel? It's the Good News? It's Christianity? It's what determines the Church's mission in the modern world? These are strong statements — and it's a strong truth. Also, it makes perfect sense if we consider another one of John Paul's ideas: "Man is the primary route that the Church must travel in fulfilling her mission: *he is the primary and fundamental way for the Church.*"[209] Actually, this isn't just one of the Pope's ideas. It's something that goes back to the preaching of the Apostles, who had "a deep esteem for man." In fact, John Paul himself points out that "the human person's dignity itself" was part of the very content of the Apostle's preaching but "not necessarily in words but by an attitude towards it."[210] In short, human dignity is such a key truth for John Paul that our amazement toward it *is* the Gospel and *is* Christianity.

The key point is *amazement*. In other words, it's not enough to simply know the truth that we have an inestimable dignity in Christ. We have to *know* it. We have to experience it, make it our own, take it to heart. As John Paul wrote before becoming Pope,

"*The value of the person must be not merely understood by the cold light of reason but felt.* An abstract understanding of the person does not necessarily beget a feeling for the value of the person."[211] It's only when we have a real, felt knowledge of the truths of the faith that they form our attitudes and outlook. In the case of a person who deeply *knows* the truth of God's mercy, the attitude and outlook is trust in God's mercy, as we've seen. In the case of a person who truly *knows* human dignity, the Pope calls it "amazement" or "the contemplative outlook."

In my favorite passage from all of John Paul's writings, he describes what the "contemplative outlook" consists in. We'd do well to ponder it deeply.

> Our proclamation [of the Gospel of life] must also become *a genuine celebration of the Gospel of life.* ... For this to happen, we need first of all to foster, in ourselves and in others, *a contemplative outlook.* Such an outlook arises from faith in the God of life, who has created every individual as a "wonder" (see Ps 139:14). It is the outlook of those who see life in its deeper meaning, who grasp its utter gratuitousness, its beauty and its invitation to freedom and responsibility. It is the outlook of those who do not presume to take possession of reality but instead accept it as a gift, discovering in all things the reflection of the Creator and seeing in every person his living image (see Gen 1:27; Ps 8:5). This outlook does not give in to discouragement when confronted by those who are sick, suffering, outcast or at death's door. Instead, in all these situations it feels challenged to find meaning, and precisely in these circumstances it is open to perceiving in the face of every person a call to encounter, dialogue, and solidarity.
>
> It is time for all of us to adopt this outlook, and with deep religious awe to rediscover the ability to *revere and honor every person*, as Paul VI invited us to do in one of his first Christmas messages. Inspired by

this contemplative outlook, the new people of the redeemed cannot but respond with *songs of joy, praise and thanksgiving for the priceless gift of life*, for the mystery of each individual's call to share through Christ in the life of grace and in an existence of unending communion with God our Creator and Father.[212]

Why is this outlook so important? Why should we foster it in ourselves? What's so special about having a sense of "wonder" for others? Why should we see life in its deeper meaning? Why should we see the image of God in everyone? And do we really need to respond with songs of joy, praise, and thanksgiving? Isn't all this a bit much? Isn't it a bit too mystical, emotional, and idealistic? Can't we just be nice and tolerant of people and do our duty?

In short, *no*. Why not? Because we're made for love. And while love is an act of the will, it's also supposed to well up from the heart. It's supposed to be felt. My favorite definition of love is that it's an attitude that says, "I delight that you exist." Are we really supposed to feel this delight? According to John Paul II, *yes*.[213] Why? Because love is a value response. It's a response of the heart to seeing the intrinsic value, worth, preciousness, and dignity of another. So, to love from the heart requires that we *see* the dignity of others. As a young priest, Karol Wojtyła once wrote to a friend of his, "The great achievement is always to *see* values that others don't see and to *affirm* them. The even greater achievement is to *bring out* of people the values that would perish without us."[214] The way we affirm the value of another person and bring it out of him is *through love*.

Let's examine more closely this idea of seeing "values" and, more specifically, seeing the dignity of the human person. For, seeing human dignity has everything to do with helping all the faithful to live out their *prophetic mission of communion*. It has everything to do with building the culture of life or, as John Paul also called it, "the civilization of love." It has everything to do with giving the response of love and affirming the dignity of each human person. For, remember, love is a response to *seeing* the dignity of the human person. So how do we come to see it?

A TRUTH, BEAUTY, AND GOODNESS BATH. Ideally, we naturally develop the ability to see human dignity and experience amazement, wonder, and awe for the human person (the contemplative outlook) simply by growing up in a culture of life. Now, recall that culture educates people. Through its various forms and expressions, it teaches us its answers to the great questions as if by a kind of osmosis — and what seeps in is more than just head knowledge. Culture provides the kind of deep education that makes the truth go from head *to heart*, the kind of formation that creates an abiding consciousness, outlook, and attitude. In short, culture imparts *real knowledge*.

Now, here's a problem. Many of us haven't been taught by a good culture or a culture of life. Instead, most of us were brought up with and now live in a pervasive culture of death (which has grown considerably since John Paul II wrote *The Gospel of Life*). In fact, most of us have absorbed, to one degree or another, certain answers of the culture of death to the great questions. Probably without even realizing it, this has subtly affected our attitudes and outlook. For how many of us live most of our lives forgetful of God? How many of us think of freedom as the ability to do whatever we want? How many of us have fallen into relativistic ways of thinking regarding the truth? How many of us tend to see other people as objects? How many of us act as if the meaning of life were all about selfishness? How many of us are totally free from the influence of consumerism and materialism? How many of us have lost touch with such things as awe, wonder, humility, silence, solitude, simplicity, reverence, gratitude, community, honesty, detachment, self-control, loyalty, honor, tradition, and respect for the elderly?

Since all of us have been children of the culture of death, since we've been shaped by it, at least in subtle ways, how can Pope John Paul II call us to be the *parents* of a culture of life? How can he call us to build a culture of life when we don't even have the tools? How can we start a culture of life when we ourselves haven't fully adopted its attitudes and outlook? Is it even possible?

Absolutely. It's totally possible. But it takes some work. It requires some washing. It means giving ourselves a bath. Specifically, it means giving ourselves a great big truth, beauty, and goodness bath that washes off the lies of the culture of death. In other words, it means surrounding ourselves with things that are true, good, and beautiful. It means following St. Paul's advice, "Finally, brethren, whatever is true, whatever is honorable, whatever is just, whatever is pure, whatever is lovely, whatever is gracious, if there is any excellence, if there is anything worthy of praise, think about these things" (Phil 4:8). It means turning off the TV and reading good books, especially the Bible. It means reflecting on what we read. It means seeking out cultural forms that express truth, goodness, and beauty. For instance, it means finding movies, music, museums, art, and novels that lift our spirits. But it does *not* mean we have to be like my born-again friends.

I have some friends who recently had a born-again experience and returned to the Lord after being away from him for many years. This is great news, and I'm very happy for them. In their zeal, however, I wonder if they've thrown out the baby with the bathwater. Some things needed to go. Other things, I'm not so sure. Now they only listen to explicitly Christian music, only watch explicitly Christian movies, and only have explicitly Christian friends. If it's not *explicitly* Christian, they want nothing to do with it. It's like a never-ending preach-fest! God love them. But this is not what I mean by a truth, goodness, and beauty bath. I'm talking about the Catholic version.

One of the great gifts of being Catholic is that, if we let it, our faith rewards us with a "sacramental outlook." In other words, it creates in us a tendency to seek and find the presence of God *in things*. And this is because of the Sacraments. Recall that the Sacraments involve visible things communicating invisible grace. Well, when we live a sacramental life, especially by regularly receiving the Eucharist (the invisible God in visible, tangible form), we develop a sacramental outlook, a habit not only of seeking and finding the invisible God in things but also of making the invisible God visible in things, of making culture.

The Catholic sacramental outlook I'm talking about accounts for the long tradition in the Catholic Church of great artists, poets, and writers who make God visible through their work. For instance, J.R.R. Tolkien, the Catholic author of the world's bestselling books of fiction, *The Hobbit* and *The Lord of the Rings*, stated that his Catholicism massively influenced all of his work. Regarding *The Lord of the Rings*, he said that it is "a fundamentally religious and Catholic work."[215] Yet, when you read his famous trilogy, you find no mention of the Church or the Sacraments or the Pope. Why is this? Because, he says, "The religious element is absorbed into the story and the symbolism."[216] In other words, the faith is there, but it's not in your face. It's subtle. It's like the Sacraments. The Sacraments are not portraits of God. Rather, they're pointers to God that actually give us God. So it is with great art, literature, and film: They point to what is true, good, and beautiful and actually give these gifts to us. Such cultural expressions need not be explicitly Christian, and when they're not, that's often even better — for subtlety speaks to the heart.

One of my favorite professors in the seminary, Peter Kreeft, often explained the power of great art, literature, and film for healing and forming hearts, especially those hearts that have become ravaged by the images and ideas of the culture of death. He would say that the culture of death often doesn't preach its anti-Gospel in a direct way. Rather, through its images and stories, it comes "under the radar" of reason and poisons our hearts from within. Kreeft would then say that we have to fight the culture of death with good, true, and beautiful images and stories that also subtly speak to our hearts and "baptize the imagination." In fact, he'd say that when the true, the good, and the beautiful are discreetly and organically packaged in stories and art, they have a deep, transformative power. He elaborates on these ideas in the following interview with the *Mars Hill Review* (MHR):

MHR: You have stated that you see some mysteries or truths better in concrete stories rather than in abstract concepts — in novels rather than in philosophy. How has that been true for you?

PK: It has been true for me in my reading of C.S. Lewis, Chesterton, Tolkien, Charles Williams, Dorothy Sayers. These writers have plugged into the depths of the Christian tradition. Their images and stories have influenced me from below.

MHR: What do you mean by "below"?

PK: Let's use the image of water. A city is surrounded by walls and it is fighting a war. The enemy is trying to knock down the walls, but they can't do it because the walls are too strong. Then a great rainstorm comes. As the rain suddenly gets underneath the walls and softens the ground, the walls fall down and the city is conquered.

Rational arguments are like bullets. They're useful, but if we're going to conquer the city that is the world, we need rain and not just bullets. Images and attractive symbols are like the rain. They soften the ground as they seep into the unconscious. Lewis called it "baptizing the imagination."

MHR: Is the study of literature important for the church?

PK: It is crucial — absolutely crucial. We are still deeply influenced by stories. We learn morality more from stories than from anything else. If we're not good storytellers, and if we're not sensitive to good storytellers, we'll miss out on the most powerful means of enlightening ourselves and transforming our world apart from a living, personal example.

Christianity has always produced great writers. But, unfortunately, I cannot name a single great one who is alive today. Walker Percy and Flannery O'Connor may be the two last great Christian writers. I'm sure there will be more, because it is in our tradition.[217]

In this interview, Kreeft speaks about specifically Christian writers. But he would also say in class that our ally in "the culture war" is *any* writer or artist who loves and expresses the true, the good, and the beautiful.

Any writer? Any artist? But don't we have to be careful about speaking with non-Catholics and especially with non-Christians about the truth? Aren't they excluded from helping us with our "truth, beauty, and goodness bath"?

No. Not at all. All the great world religions have some measure of the truth, as the Second Vatican Council taught.[218] Moreover, we can and should learn from all people of good will.

What? But don't Catholics have the fullness of truth?

Yes, we do, and what a gift (and responsibility) it is.

But what can non-Catholics teach us?

A lot. Let me explain what I mean.

Okay, I'm going to do it yet again. I'm going to bring up the idea of "the enrichment of faith." You've probably noticed by now that it's a hugely important idea. It answers a lot of questions, particularly the one I just raised about learning from non-Catholics.

So, here's the key distinction, the key point: There are two kinds of knowledge, notional and real. Or, as Karol Wojtyła puts it, there are two kinds of truth, "ontological" and "existential."[219] Because there are these two kinds of knowledge (or truth), we don't have to worry about falling into relativism when we learn from non-Catholics about the truth. In other words, we can still hold that there is an objective, ontological, notional truth and that we Catholics have the fullness of it, but we can also recognize that others may *live* certain truths more deeply than we do. Specifically, we may have to admit that some

Protestants, Jews, Mormons, or Muslims *realize* and *existentially live* certain truths better than particular Catholics. On this level of "existential truth" (real knowledge), we can have fruitful dialogue and do not have to settle for mere toleration of others, which, for Wojtyła, has a negative sense.

In a difficult but marvelous passage, philosopher Rocco Buttiglione comments on the thought of Karol Wojtyła and explains more thoroughly what I've just introduced:

> Toleration has a negative value: error is considered and is permitted in order to avoid a greater evil. Or, worse, different errors are tolerated for lack of confidence in the possibility of achieving the truth. It is necessary instead to give attention to the human effort to reach the truth and to the different attempts which people make to achieve it, and to respect this effort in the dynamism which is proper to it. In the acknowledgement of religious freedom the right of error is not sanctioned but rather that of truth to be sought and achieved. The strict connection with Wojtyła's anthropological view is also evident here: the truth is an objective fact but at the same time a subjective experience, a true perfection of man through his free adherence to objective truth. From the objective point of view, Christian truth is protected whole and uncorrupted in the deposit of faith entrusted to the Catholic Church. From the existential point of view, it is necessary, however, that it become experience. In this respect the Catholic will have to learn much from the Separated Brethren [Protestants] as well as from all men who manifest many truths with an existential weight much greater than Catholics have been able to realize because of their personal and cultural limitations. This recognition permits a dialogue which is respectful and attentive to the truth of the other but that does not imply anything like systematic doubt about one's own faith.[220]

So, we don't have to settle for merely tolerating others. We can actually share the truth with one another in its "existential" aspect. Indeed, true dialogue and friendship is possible even with non-Christians. We can learn from them, and they can learn from us. It's worth repeating the central point: While Catholics do have the truth "whole and uncorrupted" as an "objective fact" (notional knowledge), such truth is also a "subjective experience" (real knowledge). Moreover, from our point of view, it's necessary that this objective truth become our subjective, existential experience. This is our responsibility, and on this point, non-Catholics "who manifest many truths with an existential weight" can help make the truth *real* for us. Let me try to make this important point as clear as possible with an example.

When I was in high school, one of my best friends was a Mormon. After school, I'd frequently go to his house, and I was deeply edified by his family life. In fact, I'd never met a Catholic family that manifested the Church's teaching on marriage and family as much as this Mormon family did. Anyway, my experience with them greatly contributed to my "reversion" to the Catholic faith during my senior year of high school. I remember thinking to myself, "Wow, authentic family life is totally beautiful … and my own Church has an even more robust teaching on it than the Mormon religion. Yet these Mormons are actually living it better than the Catholics I know." Sadly, I'd never gotten to know a Catholic family that fully lived what the Church taught on marriage and family. So, I remember thinking to myself, "Well, I'm going to fully live this as a Catholic."

Though I didn't get married and became a priest instead, I'll never forget the positive effect of the example those Mormons had on me and on my faith. Today, the example of many Catholic families (as well as the example of some Jewish, Protestant, and even pagan families) inspires me as a priest. Indeed, the witness of their love and sacrifice is a powerful truth, beauty, and goodness bath for the soul.

Now, obviously, the truth about marriage and family is crucially important for building the culture of life. But remember, there's one particular truth that's especially important for building a culture of life: the truth of human dignity or what John Paul II calls "the human dimension of the mystery of redemption." While this idea is included in everything we've been looking at in this section, we still need to go even deeper into this idea. For this is not only one of the most important truths that needs to form our hearts for the building of a culture of life, it's also one of the truths that's most viciously attacked and undermined by the culture of death.

HOMING IN ON HUMAN DIGNITY. As we saw during our interview with the culture of death, one of its aims is to make us look at others merely as objects for our use — as "it's." Seen as "it's," other people only have value insofar as they bring us profit, praise, and pleasure. They can be manipulated, exploited, and used for selfish purposes such as making money, gratifying sexual desire, and satisfying the ego. They can be trampled on, discarded, ignored, and even killed.

In response to this, Pope John Paul II says we need to look at people not from "the outside" as objects but from "the inside" as persons. But what does this mean? We'll find an answer as we now reflect on the difference between a crowd and a multitude.

John Paul once stated that he did not like the word "crowd," which seemed too anonymous and impersonal. Instead, he preferred the word "multitude" (in Greek "*plēthos*"), which is used to describe the people who followed Jesus during his public ministry.[221] How did Jesus see the people who followed him? Well, he certainly did not see them as some anonymous mass. Rather, as the *Catechism* teaches, "Jesus knew and loved each of us and all" during his earthly life.[222] Now, it is estimated that, as of this writing, 108 billion human beings have lived. Undoubtedly, the Lord knows and loves each and every one of them, and not one of them becomes insignificant in the face of billions of others. Why not? Because each human person is, as John Henry Newman puts it, "as whole and independent a being in himself, as if there were no one else in the whole world but he."[223] In a beautiful sermon, Newman thoroughly develops this point, this truth about the uniqueness and individuality of each human person. He begins by showing how difficult it is to bring this truth home to our hearts, to "realize" it:

> [D]o you think that a commander of an army realizes [this truth], when he sends a body of men on some dangerous service? I am not speaking as if he were wrong in so sending them; I only ask in matter of fact, does he, think you, commonly understand that each of those poor men has a soul, a soul as dear to himself, as precious in its nature, as his own? Or does he not rather look on the body of men collectively, as one mass, as parts of a whole, as but the wheels or springs of some great machine, to which he assigns the individuality, not to each soul that goes to make it up?[224]

Like the army commander in this example, we also work with people in our daily lives. Of course, it's unlikely that we'll have to order them around and send them off on dangerous missions, but we do interact with them. When we do, do we see each individual person as having a soul "as precious in its nature" as our own? Or do we look on people "collectively" and merely against the background of our desires and plans? Do we take time to see them from the inside or just from the outside? This is an important question.

Newman uses another example of how we might think of human beings in a "collective" way as if from the outside, a way that is not necessarily a bad thing but one that does not yet reflect the full truth of the human person:

> Or again, survey some populous town: crowds are pouring through the streets; some on foot, some in carriages; while the shops are full, and the houses too, could we see into them. Every part of it is full of life. Hence we gain a general idea of splendor, magnificence, opulence, and energy.[225]

We've all probably experienced something similar to this at some exciting event where there's a huge number of people. Maybe it was a Fourth of July fireworks show or a college football game. At such events, there's an energy that comes from the crowd, from so many people gathered into one place for a thrilling spectacle. At such events, do we ever stop to reflect on the full truth about the crowd, that it is, in fact, a "multitude," a gathering of independent and unrepeatable individuals? Newman gets us to stop and reflect as he continues with his illustration:

> But what is the truth? why, that every being in that great concourse is his own centre, and all things about him are but shades, but a "vain shadow," in which he "walketh and disquieteth himself in vain." He has his own hopes and fears, desires, judgments, and aims; he is everything to himself, and no one else is really any thing. No one outside of him can really touch him, can touch his soul. … He has a depth within him unfathomable, an infinite abyss of existence; and the scene in which he bears part for the moment is but like a gleam of sunshine upon its surface.[226]

In a remarkable move, Newman shifts our perspective. In the previous quote, we were looking at a crowd buzzing with life — *from the outside*. Now, here, we've suddenly discovered the true depth of the crowd, marveling at the infinity found within a single person. The comparison drives home the point: Each person is a whole world unto himself, much greater and glorious than an anonymous crowd. The real marvel is that while a great crowd can itself be a thing of excitement and emotion, a single human person seen *from the inside* is infinitely more awe-inspiring and amazing.

Newman's words and especially his shift in perspective from outside to inside, remind me of a reflection of Pope John Paul II in his apostolic letter, *Novo Millennio Ineunte*, written for the close of the Great Jubilee Year 2000, during which time, millions of pilgrims made their way to Rome. The Pope writes:

I have been impressed this year by the crowds of
people which have filled Saint Peter's Square at the
many celebrations. I have often stopped to look at the
long queues of pilgrims waiting patiently to go
through the Holy Door. In each of them I tried to
imagine the story of a life, made up of joys, worries,
sufferings; the story of someone whom Christ had
met and who, in dialogue with him, was setting out
again on a journey of hope.

... We have only been able to observe the
outer face of this unique event. Who can measure
the marvels of grace wrought in human hearts? It
is better to be silent and to adore, trusting humbly
in the mysterious workings of God and singing his
love without end: "*Misericordias Domini in aeternum
cantabo!*"[227]

John Paul begins by stating the objective fact, remarking
on the crowds of people that he observed from the outside. But
then, he immediately takes us deeply to the inside. In other
words, he reflects on each person, taken as it were, from a kind
of inside *philosophical perspective*. Thus, he considers each one in
his joys, worries, and sufferings. He also considers the human
person from an inside *theological perspective*, as someone "whom
Christ had met" and in whose heart God mysteriously works
"marvels of grace." In what follows, we're going to reflect on
these two "inside perspectives" of the human person, the
philosophical and theological. By doing so, we'll come to better
appreciate the dignity of the human person and, thereby, develop
a contemplative outlook.

*P*ERSONALISM. I said that the first inside perspective is a philosophical one. Specifically, John Paul II calls it "personalism":

It is difficult to formulate a systematic theory on how
to relate to people, yet I was greatly helped in this by
the study of personalism during the years I devoted
to philosophy.[228]

What is personalism? It's a philosophical approach to the human person from the perspective of his uniqueness and dignity. In the words of one of my favorite philosophy professors, it involves a fascination

> ... with the fact that each person is unrepeatably and incommunicably himself or herself, that each is not only an objective but also a subjective being, that each lives out his or her interiority, that each is a being of surpassing, indeed infinite worth and dignity, that each can live and thrive only by existing with and for other persons.[229]

I wish we had time for a whole book-length crash course on personalism, since it's such a rich and wonderful study. Here, we'll have to settle for a much shorter summary. Our guide into it will be none other than Pope John Paul II (Karol Wojtyła).

The heart of John Paul's personalism is reflected in one of his favorite passages from the Second Vatican Council. Like his other favorite passage, "It is only in the mystery of the Word made flesh that the mystery of man truly becomes clear," this one also comes from *Gaudium et Spes*:

> Indeed, the Lord Jesus, when he prayed to the Father, "that all may be one ... as we are one" (Jn 17:21-22) opened up vistas closed to human reason, for he implied a certain likeness between the union of the divine Persons, and the unity of God's sons in truth and charity. This likeness reveals that man, who is the only creature on earth which God willed for its own sake, can fully discover his true self only in a sincere giving of himself (see Lk 17:33).[230]

Most everything that John Paul has to say about the human person, at least from a philosophical perspective, flows from this passage. Specifically, it's all in the last sentence, which contains two important points: (1) man is the "only creature on earth which God willed for its own sake" and (2) man "can fully discover his true self only in a sincere giving of himself." This polarity of what we'll call "self-possession" and "self-donation" tells us just about everything we need to know, philosophically speaking, about what it means to be a human person, about what it means to see man from the inside. We'll look at both these poles in turn, starting with self-possession.

(a) Self-possession. Think about it for a moment. Man is the only creature willed *for its own sake.* Chemicals, minerals, plants, and animals are not willed for their own sakes. In fact, they're willed *for man,* and man can use them as objects for his enjoyment, growth, and good. There's nothing wrong with this. On the other hand, the human person himself should never be used as a mere object by anyone. Wojtyła formulates this in what he calls "the personalistic norm," which he states both negatively and positively:

> The norm in its negative aspect, states that the person is the kind of good which does not admit of use and cannot be treated as an object of use and as such the means to an end. In its positive form, it confirms this: the person is a good towards which the only proper and adequate attitude is love.[231]

We'll consider the positive aspect of the norm in the second point, "self-donation." Here, we'll treat the negative aspect. Before we begin, however, it's interesting to note that Wojtyła goes on to say that this norm "defines and recommends a certain way of relating to God and to people, a certain attitude towards them."[232] Fostering in ourselves this "way of relating" and this "attitude" — what John Paul II calls the "contemplative outlook" — is the central goal of this chapter. And the way we're going about fostering this way of relating, this attitude and outlook, is by meditating on the specific truth that, when it goes from our heads to our hearts, can best form it in us. Of course, I'm talking about the truth of human dignity. Here, specifically, let's continue our philosophical reflection on human dignity by turning our attention to the negative aspect of the personalistic norm, namely, *that the human person cannot be treated as a mere object of use.*

Why shouldn't man be treated as a mere object? It's because while it's true that human beings are "objects" in the world — for instance, we can see them bodily, "from the outside" — they are also *subjects*, meaning they have a whole inner, conscious life. As Newman put it, man has "his own centre." He has that truly awe-evoking ability to say, "I." This is a wonder of wonders! Human beings, unlike animals, can be *present to themselves.* They are self-conscious. We all know this, but at the same time, self-consciousness is something so familiar to us, so close to us that we often don't *realize* it. Let me give an example to help us realize it now.

I'm typing these words on my computer. As I'm typing them, I'm also present to myself as the one typing. I can see my hands working away on the keyboard. I'm looking at those hands on the keyboard, and I can say to myself, "Those are *my* hands." I stop typing and can feel my heart beating. I can say to myself, "That is *my* heart I feel beating in *my* chest." Yet, even if I'm not actually saying, "Those are *my* hands, and that is *my* heart," the self-awareness is still there. Like someone looking over my shoulders as I act, it's always there, to a greater or lesser degree. Who is that someone? It's me! It's me watching myself, me being present to myself, me acting with awareness of myself. Again, this self-awareness is so familiar that it may not seem like much of a wonder. We're used to it. After all, it's been with us since we gradually awoke to it in childhood.

We can better appreciate the wonder of our self-awareness if we contrast it with something that doesn't have it: Animals. According to John Paul II, before God created Eve, Adam, the original man, felt "original solitude," even though he found himself in a garden bursting with life. He felt "alone," even though he was surrounded by animals.[233] Why did he feel this way? Because he couldn't fully relate to any of the animals. They were totally different from him in a most important respect. Father Norris Clarke explains:

> Although [animals] are aware through their senses of
> the outside world, they are locked into an extraverted
> focusing on the objects of their senses and cannot
> make that "full return of the soul to itself," as St.
> Thomas puts it, which would enable them to be
> *self-present* as well as present to others, in a word, to
> be self-conscious.[234]

This truly is a wonder. Unlike animals, we're not lost in our external environment. Unlike animals, we can make that "full return of the soul to itself," meaning that we can step back from our external environment and be present to ourselves as the ones knowing and acting. We can look at ourselves looking! We can say, "*I* am looking." This is such a wonder that St. Thomas Aquinas, and many thinkers after him, used it as powerful evidence to show that we are spiritual beings. For only spirit can be, as it were, in "two places" at the same time — in this case, both "outside" (me seeing) and "inside" (me being present to myself seeing).[235]

And the wonder grows. Not only are we self-present or aware, but we're also *responsible* beings. In fact, it's because we're self-present, because we can say, "I," that we are, therefore, responsible for our actions. Animals are not responsible for their actions. They don't act as "I's," but rather, they respond to their environments through blind instincts and urges. They aren't free. We are — insofar as we act as persons. Moreover, we realize that our lives are moral dramas, meaning that we can (and must) choose to live either as persons or as animals, as men or as devils. Indeed, we can choose the type of person we will be through our actions. In a sense, as Wojtyła says, we can "create ourselves." Or, as Clarke puts it, "By my actions, therefore, especially the repeated ones, I gradually construct an abiding moral portrait of myself, like an artist's self-portrait, proclaiming implicitly, 'This is the kind of person I am.'"[236]

Even God himself shows great respect for the moral drama that is the life of each human person. For instance, while he surely invites and calls us to follow him, he definitely doesn't force us. (He doesn't treat us as objects but as subjects.) Of course, he has in mind the kind of person he wants us to be, but it's ultimately our choice whether or not we'll cooperate. Moreover, the moral law we're called to follow is not some arbitrary law imposed on us from the outside. Rather, as we saw earlier, it is *written on our hearts*. So, God is not calling us to be something we're not. Rather, he's simply saying to us, as Fr. Clarke puts it, "*Be* fully what you in fact *are*," or, better yet, "*Become* fully what you already *are*, in the deepest, most authentic longing of your nature."[237] He's inviting us to use our freedom to come back home, which is what following the natural law is really all about. It's our road map back to our Creator and Father, showing us the way to complete the Great Circle of Being.

From a philosophical perspective, then, it's ultimately because of our moral responsibility, our ability to determine our course, to choose Goodness itself (himself), that we should never treat others as mere objects. For each of us has a solemn task to become what we were created to be. It's a sacred calling that, as we saw, even God respects. John F. Crosby elaborates:

> Persons are not just there, like rocks or plants; they are handed over to themselves, they are their own. As a result, they can make different things of themselves, they can accept or reject themselves. Above all, they can determine themselves in freedom, indeed, in a certain sense, they can create themselves. If you try to use a person as a mere instrument, then you deprive that person of the space he needs for the uniquely personal work of self-creation. If we are really going to respect persons, then we must step back from them, take our heavy hands off them, and let them be, that is, live as self-determining beings. In respecting them like this and in abstaining from all using, we treat persons as their own end.[238]

The key word here is "respect." We need to respect all human beings because of what they are: not mere objects but subjects, not mere means but ends, not "it's" but persons. As self-possessing beings, then, human persons have a dignity that we should recognize, honor, and regard with the deepest respect.

(b) Self-Donation. While the key to the last section was the personalistic norm, that a person should never be used as a mere object for use, the key to this section is that each person is utterly unrepeatable (incommunicability) and infinitely interior (subjectivity). Put differently, each person is a unique being of inexhaustible depth who should evoke our wonder and even love. For, as the personalistic norm says in its positive form, "The person is a good towards which the only proper and adequate attitude is love."

In the last section, we saw that the human person is able to be self-conscious or "self-present" (and for this reason, he can be "self-determining:" He can, in a sense, create himself). This truly is a wonder. But we can also marvel at the infinite depth that this *interiority* entails. Newman called it "a depth within him unfathomable, an infinite abyss of existence." Father Clarke calls the human person a "known-unknown," a "mysterious abyss" in which there's always more that's unknown than known, "like a tip of an iceberg emerging above water."[239]

What accounts for this inner mystery? Well, first of all, Fr. Clarke points out that there are "vast depths of our unconscious" that will always remain "either unknown or only partially and indirectly accessible to consciousness."[240] So, just below the surface of our conscious life, there's a vibrant, hidden life that, from time to time, bubbles up to our conscious awareness indirectly through things like dreams or artistic expression. Because this hidden life is subconscious, we can't simply turn our attention to it nor can we force it to show itself. So, it remains a mysterious part of ourselves that we only glimpse from time to time. Yet even more profound and mysterious than this subconscious life is the spiritual dynamism at the core of our being. Father Clarke describes it as follows:

[T]here is the natural depth of the self, stemming from the fact that as spiritual intellect and will we are naturally open to, and have a natural drive towards the whole of being as both intelligible and good. Since this includes implicitly Infinite Being itself, there is a kind of infinite or inexhaustible depth in our spirit, due to its openness to the Infinite, which cannot be plumbed by our explicit consciousness short of the direct vision of God himself, when we shall see ourselves totally as God sees us, i.e., as we really are. As the German mystical poet, Angelus Silesius, puts it, "The abyss in man cries out to the abyss in God. Tell me, which is deeper?"[241]

This most profound inner depth of our souls, this openness and drive for the infinite, this "deep calling out to deep" (Ps 42:8) is like a God-shaped hole in our hearts. For, as beings made in the image of God, only God can fill our souls. Saint Augustine expresses this idea in his famous prayer, "You made us for yourself, O God, and our hearts are restless until they rest in you."[242] And so, the human person, in his interiority, is an awe-inspiring wonder of infinite depth. Because Fr. Clarke meditated so deeply on this mystery, he felt such awe to an amazingly deep degree.

I mentioned in Part Two that Fr. Clarke had an incredible sense of childlike wonder, even as a man well into his 80s. One example of his sense of wonder sticks out vividly in my mind. It happened several years after I'd had his class in college. I was in the seminary at the time, and Father was scheduled to give a lecture at a local university, which I went to hear. On my way, as I neared the lecture hall, I noticed Fr. Clarke approaching with Peter Kreeft, who was one of my seminary professors that semester. I arrived at the main door before them and opened it to let them pass through first. I sort of hid behind the door, not wanting to disturb their conversation. As Fr. Clarke was passing through, he suddenly saw me, stopped, and cried out, "*Who are you*?!" A bit taken aback by his surprise, I said, "Well, Father, I had you for class several years ago, but you surely don't remember me. I sat at the back of the class and never said anything." He said, "Oh, yes, I clearly remember you. *How are you*?" He asked the question with so much interest that I was tempted to actually open up a bit. At the same time, I knew the lecture was scheduled to begin any minute, so I kept my answer short. But he kept asking me questions with sincere interest. So, here was this distinguished philosopher, professor, and past president of the American Catholic Philosophical Association, keeping a packed auditorium of professors and graduate students waiting, simply to speak with a lowly seminarian. Of course, I was uncomfortable — but also deeply moved.

The next day, I had class with Professor Kreeft, and I asked him about the incident. I said, "Dr. Kreeft, when I was in Fr. Clarke's class, I was just an undergraduate, and the class was for graduate students. I was intimidated by the other students and hardly said a word. How could he have remembered me?" Kreeft replied, "It's because he loves much. Father Clarke has a remarkable sense of wonder for each human person, and that's the source of his love. He doesn't forget the people he meets." I was blown away. The whole experience made me realize the incredible value of the philosophy of personalism, and so I studied it with even greater zeal, especially this connection between wonder and love. What follows is a summary of the fruit of those studies, which can be divided into two categories: reverence and empathy. (Keep in mind that we're still within the general category of "Self-donation" — also known as love.)

Reverence. Love begins with recognizing, seeing, and grasping what is lovable, and then responding to it with love. In other words, as I mentioned earlier, love is a value response. But how do we recognize, grasp, and see values? We begin by developing an attitude of *reverence.* Reverence is not exactly the same thing as what John Paul II means by the contemplative outlook. For, while the attitude of reverence includes the contemplative outlook, it also includes other things. It's a wider and broader attitude.

In his beautiful little book, *The Art of Living*, Catholic philosopher Dietrich von Hildebrand describes the attitude of reverence as the "the mother of all moral life" because, through reverence, "man first takes a position toward the world which opens his spiritual eyes and enables him to grasp values."[243] And what does he mean by values? He says values are "a ray of light, a reflection of the infinite glory of the living God; they are a message from God in all created goods and exist as an ultimate reality in God Himself, who is, after all, Justice itself, Goodness itself, Love itself."[244] Remember in Part Two how we looked at the question of why God created such a multitude of things? Recall that God created such a multitude so his goodness, truth, and beauty could be variously manifested in many things. That presence of God's goodness, truth, and beauty in things, giving them inherent worth, is what von Hildebrand means by value.

Again, reverence has to do with "opening our eyes" to grasp values, to grasp the goodness and beauty of persons, places, and things. Now, to understand the attitude of reverence properly, von Hildebrand believes it's important to contrast it with the attitude of *irreverence*, of which there are two types, exemplified by two kinds of men — the same kinds of men produced by the culture of death.

First, there's the man who is irreverent because of *pride*. Such a man is blind to values because he's always asking, "Will this make my own glory grow? Will it bring me praise? Will it make me increase in the eyes of others?" Because he always bends every situation to his ego, such a man never sees things "from within." In fact, in his pride, he "approaches everything with a presumptuous, sham superiority." He acts like the "know-it-all" who "believes that he penetrates everything at first sight." He stands as the man "for whom nothing could be greater than himself, who never sees beyond his horizon, from whom the world of being hides no secret."[245] His pride so blinds him that he

> ... suspects nothing of the breadth and depth of the world, of the mysterious depth and the immeasurable fullness of values which are bespoken by every ray of the sun and every plant, and which are revealed in the

innocent laughter of a child, as well as in the repentant tears of a sinner. The world is flattened before his impertinent and stupid gaze; it becomes limited to one dimension, shallow and mute. ... He passes through the world with a blighting incomprehension.[246]

So, again, the first irreverent man is blinded to the world of values by pride. He's the quintessential modern man who wrongly thinks scientific knowledge provides every answer and has drained the world of mystery. He knows nothing of the inherent worth of anything. In his eyes, the things of the world — and they're all *things* to him — only have worth to the extent that they bring him honor, praise, and glory.

Then, there's the second kind of irreverent man. He's blinded to the world of values by his *concupiscence* or *carnal desire*. He's the man who bends everything to his appetites and for whom the world is "only an occasion to serve his lust."[247] Such a man "can never remain inwardly silent."[248] And so, he never allows any person, place, or thing to speak to him from its inner depth. Why not? Because he's too busy looking and listening to himself, particularly to his appetites:

He limits his interest to one thing only: whether something is agreeable to him or not, whether it offers him satisfaction, whether or not it can be of any use to him. He sees in all things only that segment which is related to his accidental, immediate interest. Every being is, for him, but a means to his own selfish aim. He drags himself about eternally in the circle of his narrowness, and never succeeds in emerging from himself. ... [H]e overlooks all things and seeks only that which is momentarily useful and expedient to him. ... His look falls on all things flatly, "from the outside," without comprehension for the true meaning and value of an object. ... He fails to leave to any being the "space" which it needs to unfold itself fully and in its proper mode. This man also is

blind to values, and to him again the world refuses
to reveal its breadth, depth and height.[249]

So, this second irreverent man, like the first, is also blind.
He's not concerned with any answers to the world's mysteries,
scientific or otherwise. He doesn't care. He only cares about his
appetites. He's the addict whose vision is narrowed to what will
give him his fix, whether it be drugs, food, sex, or TV. He looks
on things lustily from the outside while never knowing or caring
about their inner depth. The commonality shared by both types
of irreverent men is that *the world is no mystery to them*. They give
it no opportunity to open up to them. Rather, they see it from
the outside, grab hold of it, and bend it toward themselves, to
their egos or appetites.

The *reverent* man approaches the world differently. Von
Hildebrand describes him as one who "does not fill the world
with his own ego, but leaves to being the space which it needs
in order to unfold itself."[250] He's one who has an appreciation
for *being itself* and marvels that things exist when they very well
might not have existed.

Regarding this reverence for being, Pope John Paul II once
wrote that, as a young man, his philosophical study of being
(called "metaphysics") was "a turning point in my life" and that
"a whole new world opened up before me."[251] Indeed, when we
realize that God is the great I AM, that he is Being, that he holds
all beings in existence, that being is given by him, and that
existence itself is a gift, then it gives us an appreciation for
everything that exists. Then, everything is a mystery, and we
begin to perceive its inherent worth. Thus, with the reverent
man, we can see that "there is a value inherent in every stone,
in a drop of water, in a blade of grass, precisely as being, as an
entity which possesses its own being, which is such and not
otherwise."[252]

Because the reverent man sees that being (existing) itself has
inherent value, he doesn't immediately presume to grab hold of
beings and bend them toward himself. Rather, with a sacramental
imagination, he is able to see God in things and situations. He's

able to listen to being and open his spiritual eyes "to see the deeper nature of every being."[253] Von Hildebrand asks,

> To whom will the sublime beauty of a sunset or a Ninth Symphony of Beethoven reveal itself, but to him who approaches it reverently and unlocks his heart to it? To whom will the mystery which lies in life and manifests itself in every plant reveal itself in its full splendor[?][254]

He then answers his own questions by saying that being reveals itself in all its beauty, splendor, and mystery "*to him who contemplates it reverently.*" He goes on to say that it does not reveal itself to one who sees in the world "only a means of subsistence or of earning money, i.e. something which can be used or employed." Now, of course, von Hildebrand recognizes that we need to use things. In fact, we are called to have dominion over the world (see Gen 1:28). However, at the same time, he's pointing out that we also need to keep our eyes reverently open, so we can "discover the meaning, structure and significance of the world in its beauty and hidden dignity."[255] And what's the most beautiful part of the whole world, the part that has the greatest dignity? It's not really a part but a person — it's every person. Personal being is the greatest wonder of the cosmos.[256]

So, the reverent man, because he gives space to being, knows how to allow human persons to open up to him in their mystery. And when they do, what does he discover? He discovers that each human person is *utterly unique*, which is itself a profound source of human dignity. Think of it. If we were to get to know and love someone deeply, and then that person were to die, we would rightfully be very sorrowful. Why? Because we would recognize that there's a hole in the cosmos that no one else can fill. Furthermore, we would clearly see the absurdity of someone saying, "Oh, don't be sorrowful. There are six billion other people in the world." This would be absurd because we would have known the deceased person as *unrepeatable* and incomparably unique. Well, the reverent man has the ability to see this unrepeatable uniqueness in others, because he gives space for the mystery of others to unfold. And when he beholds this mystery, it leads to the response of love, as John F. Crosby explains: "[W]e arrive at the center of a person, at the mystery of this individual person, at that which above all engenders love for the person, only when we encounter the person as unrepeatable."[257] Again, the way we encounter others as unrepeatable is by reverently allowing the depth of their being to unfold and open up before us.

Empathy. There's yet another way, besides reverence, by which we come to a deep awe and appreciation for the mystery of human persons — which leads to love — and that is through empathy. Empathy gives us an experience of another person *as a person* in his interiority and subjectivity. Empathy is, in a sense, to experience another person within ourselves *as the other person experiences himself.* Of course, I have to say "in a sense," because we can never actually experience another person as he experiences himself. After all, my own subjectivity, the way I experience myself internally as an "I" through self-presence and self-consciousness, is strictly *my own*. It's sacred ground and a garden enclosed, which, this side of eternity, no one else can enter.[258] Here's an example of how empathy works.

I'm typing away at my keyboard. You're looking on and, if you yourself have ever typed on a keyboard, you can easily imagine yourself in my place sitting here typing. You can feel in yourself the hard chair, cramped back (I've got to work on my typing posture), and play of the keys under racing fingers. Actually, even if you've never typed before, you can still recall when you've experienced making a typing-like motion — for instance, when you've struck the keys of a piano — and then, you can creatively merge that experience with what you see me doing. Thus, even if you've never typed, you can still enter into and empathically understand what it's like to be typing away at the keyboard. The main idea with empathy is that it's based on the memory of our own self-experience, whether it be the same kind of experience (typing on a keyboard) or one that's similar (striking keys on a piano).

Alright, so what I've just described is empathy. But my example hardly leads to love. Sure, there's a small chance you're feeling a *tad* of compassion for me because of the hard chair and cramped back, but more likely you're saying, "What a complainer!" Still, when we make efforts to empathically understand others, to walk in their shoes, it often does lead to love. (By "love," I mean the general idea of delighting in the existence of others and wishing them well.) I say that it leads to love because, when we empathize with others, we necessarily see them not from the outside as objects but from the inside as persons. For empathy is to experience another person, in a sense, as the other person experiences himself (subjectively). And when we truly experience others as persons, we cannot help but begin to be moved to delight in their existence, for each person is a wonder and gift. Let's now look at an example of this.

Recall the quote that immediately preceded this section, the one that described how John Paul II would look at the huge crowds of pilgrims in Rome during the Great Jubilee Year. On the outside, of course, they were simply a mass of humanity — surely an impressive spectacle but not really lovable as a group. John Paul, however, found a way to approach the crowds (or rather, multitudes) with an attitude of empathy that leads to love. Let's read part of that citation again:

> I have been impressed this year by the crowds of people which have filled Saint Peter's Square at the many celebrations. I have often stopped to look at the long queues of pilgrims waiting patiently to go through the Holy Door. In each of them I tried to imagine the story of a life, made up of joys, worries, sufferings; the story of someone whom Christ had met and who, in dialogue with him, was setting out again on a journey of hope.

Notice how the Pope actively puts himself into the shoes of each pilgrim, trying to imagine the story of his life and the most important relationship of all, his relationship with Christ. Surely, this moved his pastoral heart to love.

In the next section, we'll see how the light of Christ makes the human person appear as even more awe-inspiring and wonderful, which leads to an even greater response of love. Here, however, I'd like to end by pointing out that when we recognize the dignity of others, it doesn't just lead to love. It also leads to our own enrichment when we love them.

Recall the citation toward the beginning of the section on self-donation that said that man "can fully discover his true self only in a sincere giving of himself." This "Law of the Gift,"[259] as John Paul called it, means that by being reverent instead of irreverent, by going out of ourselves toward what has inherent worth rather than by bending everything toward ourselves, by turning our focus from ourselves and to the unrepeatable dignity of others, by empathically reaching out to understand others from the inside, *we thereby discover ourselves.* Indeed, through self-donation, we come to recognize our own inner depths more fully and can say, "I," more completely. We become more fully self-possessed and, thus, ready to go out of ourselves in an attitude of reverence and love. This is the great paradox of human life. The man who seeks to gain his life loses it, but the one who loses his life through reverence, empathy, and love gains it and is ready for even deeper acts of self-donation and love.

We'll learn more about this in the next section.

*T*HE *CONTEMPLATIVE OUTLOOK.* Thanks for hanging in there with me as I laid the foundation for our discussion. Now, we're ready to delve more deeply into the topic of the contemplative outlook, which you'll see was well worth the wait. But first, we need to consider an important theological principle, which is this: "Grace builds on nature." In other words, the supernatural doesn't destroy the natural, but rather, God lovingly takes the natural world and raises it up to himself by his power and love. Because of this principle, during the course of seminary studies, candidates for the priesthood always begin studying natural wisdom (philosophy) before studying supernatural wisdom (theology). In fact, for centuries, philosophy has been referred to as "the handmaid of theology" (*ancilla theologiae*), because of the way it prepares people for theology.

Well, all the philosophy that we've just covered (personalism) is now going to be raised up and perfected by grace, by theology. Because of the continuity between these two sections, I was going to call this one "Theological Personalism." However, because theology elevates what we've learned to such a higher level, I decided to call it "The Contemplative Outlook." For here is where the truth about "human dignity," which we covered only from a philosophical perspective in the last section, takes on its deepest meaning. And if we take this deeper meaning to heart, it will give us the contemplative outlook in the fullest sense.

Let's begin by briefly recalling what the contemplative outlook is: It's our attitude of deep amazement at man's worth and dignity that John Paul II calls "the Gospel" and "Christianity." It's an attitude of wonder and awe for each human person (which leads to love), an attitude that, in itself, proclaims the good news of what God has done for us in Christ. This amazement, this outlook, and this love "determines the Church's mission," especially in the modern world. It's incredibly important! And that's why this section, "Evangelization for Everyone: Building the Culture of Life," is the longest one in the book. For, as John Paul pointed out in *The Gospel of Life*, unless each of us develops this outlook and wholeheartedly responds to others with love, our civilization will see a setback of unforeseeable consequences.

Alright, so let's try to foster the contemplative outlook in ourselves by keeping in mind the philosophy we learned in the last section and by reflecting now on human dignity in light of divine revelation.

(a) Image of God. We begin our theological reflection on human dignity with its bedrock foundation: man as *image of God*. This idea goes all the way back to the first chapter of Genesis,

"Let us make man in our image, after our likeness" (Gen 1:26). But what does it mean to be made in the image of God? Well, most fundamentally, it has to do with the wondrous powers of our souls: We have minds capable of knowing the truth and are present to ourselves as the ones knowing (self-consciousness); we have wills capable of choosing the good in freedom and, in a sense, can create ourselves through our choices (self-determination); and finally, we have hearts capable of delighting in beauty and of loving God and neighbor. For these reasons, man is a wondrous being who should never to be treated as a mere object or means. Indeed, he is "the only creature on earth that God has willed for its own sake."[260]

So far, most everything I've just mentioned about man being the image of God was covered in the last section on personalism. What we didn't cover there, however, is how man is made in the image of God *as male and female*, "male and female he created them" (Gen 1:27). This is a *hugely* important aspect of our understanding of man as image of God. For God himself is a communion of love, and man is called to reflect the Trinitarian communion in both his soul *and* his body as man and woman in spousal love. Indeed, according to John Paul II, this is the very purpose of man and woman's existence, namely, *to make visible the invisible Triune God in their bodies* as a kind of "primordial sacrament":

> [A primordial sacrament is] a *sign that efficaciously transmits in the visible world the invisible mystery hidden in God from* eternity. And this is the mystery ... of divine life, in which man really participates. ... The sacrament, as a visible sign, is constituted with man, inasmuch as he is a "body," through his "visible" masculinity and femininity. The body in fact, and only the body, is capable of making visible what is invisible: the spiritual and the divine. It has been created to transfer into the visible reality of the world the mystery hidden from eternity in God, and thus to be a sign of it.[261]

What amazing dignity! What an amazing vocation! And what an important antidote to our sex-crazed culture. Here, the Pope seems to be saying that sex isn't just "fun" or "good" or even "great." He's saying that sex is *sacred*. It's glorious. It's sacramental. He's saying that the image of God, man (as male and female), is made to be "a sign" of the communion of Trinitarian love in his very body, a sign that also truly manifests that love. For, indeed, the human body as male and female is made "to transfer into the visible reality of the world the mystery hidden from eternity in God," which is the Trinity. Again, what an amazing vocation!

But with this glorious call comes great responsibility. For man can only fulfill his vocation *as a person* and not as an animal. In other words, in the communion of man and woman, he's called not to mere copulation like the animals but to spousal love. And while the bodies of male and female animals also complement one another, they don't have man's exalted vocation of reflecting the Trinity in their bodies. Why not? Because man is much higher in being than the animals. He has subjectivity and interiority. He is self-present and can say, "I." Man and woman can give themselves to each other in love and can *personalize* their sexual relations. Animals don't have interiority. They can't say, "I," and give themselves in love. So, again, while animals copulate and have sex, human persons make love, specifically, *spousal love*.

I emphasize spousal love, because sexual relationships between human persons are only legitimate and only truly personal within the context of the lifelong commitment of marriage. For marriage is necessary to give stability to the family, to safeguard the sacredness of spousal intimacy, and to open the spouses to the graces they need to fulfill their vocation of reflecting the life and love of the Trinitarian communion. Without this lifelong commitment of marriage, domestic life falls apart, sex becomes an impersonal using of another as an object, and divine help is harder to come by.

Now, within the context of marriage, spousal love is only possible when the man and woman have developed a contemplative outlook toward one another. In other words, for their love to be true, they must recognize each other's personal dignity and unrepeatability, be awed by it, and respond in love. Thus, they need to overcome any irreverent attitudes they have toward one another, whereby they see each other as mere objects for use. Above all, they need to see each other as persons. Does this mean that sexual values have no place? Of course not. In fact, sexual values should be recognized and enjoyed to the full.[262] But the sexual value of the other person (for instance, his or her ability to elicit sexual pleasure) must never eclipse the value of the other as a person of inestimable dignity. When it does, then it's not a situation of spousal love but of manipulation and using, which violates human dignity.

Regarding sexual value, I should say that true spousal love requires that the spouses recognize *the fullness of sexual value*, which is that sexual intercourse not only can bring pleasure and union but also *new life*. As common sense shows, the very nature of sexual intercourse is that it is unitive (it unites and bonds the spouses) *and procreative* (it can result in the creation of new life). Moreover, both aspects of sex, its union-making-aspect and its baby-making-aspect, are part of how spousal love makes visible the Trinitarian life, which is a union of fruitful love.

Now, does this mean that every sexual act of the spouses must result in children? Of course not. In fact, God himself has built into the woman's cycle times when she's infertile, and it's legitimate to postpone conjugal love to such times to avoid pregnancy for serious reasons (called "Natural Family Planning"). However, the procreative nature of sex *does* mean that if spousal love is to be truly personal, it must in principle always be *open to life*. In other words, in their interiority, the spouses must have *a readiness for and willingness to accept parenthood*. Thus, they cannot outright reject the idea that by this act, "I may be a mother" or "I may be a father." After all, it's the nature of the act — it goes with the territory! So, if, within himself, the man or woman is saying, "By this act, I'm not open to life at all," then his interiority does not match the language and nature of the act, and a kind of hypocrisy enters in, what John Paul II calls "a sexual lie."

Sexual lies can enter into the relations even of those couples who use the legitimate means of regulating birth, Natural Family Planning (NFP). For, if they have a "contraceptive attitude" of unwillingness to be a parent, then their act itself becomes a lie. So, even if they justifiably want to avoid pregnancy, they must still be open to life in their intentions. In other words, they must be willing and ready to accept new life if it is conceived. If they have this attitude, then NFP is a legitimate and morally responsible way of regulating birth.[263]

Now, regarding contraception, it is never lawful. In other words, it is intrinsically evil and always a sexual lie. For, by its very nature, contraception causes the man and woman to say, "By this act, I am not open to life at all." Moreover, contraception changes the nature of the act itself. Whether by means of a barrier, chemical, hormone, *coitus interruptus*, or whatever, contraception actively sabotages the act of sexual intercourse, so it cannot be what it was intended to be by the Creator. What makes matters even worse is that many forms of artificial contraception, including the pill, often result in micro-abortions.[264]

Unfortunately, the culture of death in which we live has made intrinsically evil acts seem not simply "not so bad" but even good! Indeed, it has opened up a whole Pandora's box of sexual perversions from contraception to masturbation to homosexual acts to things that I shouldn't even mention (see Eph 5:3). At the root of all these perversions is the lie that *the sexual act is not intrinsically made for the procreation of children*. But nothing could be more obvious! Of course, there is also the unitive aspect to sexual intercourse. But as soon as the unitive aspect is intentionally separated from the procreative, then anything goes, and people do the most disordered things with their bodies. And because sexuality gets to the core of who we are as human persons, and because we create (or destroy) ourselves by our actions, acts of sexual perversion deeply damage people in their thinking, feeling, acting, and outlook. In fact, such acts foster the opposite of a contemplative outlook, namely, an irreverent outlook that sees people as sexual objects rather than as persons. Moreover, those who perform such acts degrade themselves in their own eyes such that they begin to see themselves as not worth very much. So, if we want to develop in ourselves a contemplative outlook, it's especially important to strive for chastity according to our state in life.[265]

Speaking of the states in life, lest we think that married spouses get to have all the dignity (and responsibility), even those of us who are not married are called to live the spousal meaning of the body. And what is its meaning? That we are made for self-giving love. In the next section, we'll say more about this. Until then, suffice it to say that whatever we do to express true love for God and neighbor, whatever we do to build up the communion of love — which often comes with a price of fatigue, toil, and suffering — we make the love of God visible in our bodies. Moreover, the very renunciation of the good of marriage for the sake of such work is yet another expression of self-giving love (as is the loving acceptance of this sacrifice by those who cannot marry for whatever reason). So, whoever we are, we can be signs that transmit to the visible world the invisible mystery of God. As creatures made in the image of a God who is communion of love, what amazing dignity we have!

Alright, now let's look at our dignity in light of Christ.

(b) Human dignity gloriously elevated by Christ. Let's begin by re-reading some of John Paul's favorite words from Vatican II: "It is only in the mystery of the Word made flesh that the mystery of man truly becomes clear. ... [Christ] fully reveals man to himself." What does Jesus reveal about man? What becomes clear? Among other things, *our incredible dignity.* Two mysteries of the life of Christ reveal our dignity more than any others: the Incarnation and the Passion. We'll look at both of these mysteries in turn and see how they shed a superabundance of light on the truth of human dignity and, thus, help foster in us a contemplative outlook.

I said earlier that grace builds on nature. Well, perhaps the ultimate and greatest example of grace building on nature is *the Incarnation*. For, after the disobedience of our first parents, God did not destroy humanity and "start over" with creation — which he very well could have done. Instead, he began a work of salvation that culminated in "the fullness of time," when he mercifully united humanity to himself in a manner that truly boggles the mind: The divine person of the Son assumed a human nature — the Word became flesh — God became man.

The technical, theological phrase used to describe the Incarnation is "the hypostatic union," which means that the divine nature of the eternal Son became inseparably united to an assumed human nature in the divine person of the Son. In short: Jesus Christ is *one divine person* (the Son) *in two natures* (human and divine). Without getting too deeply into this most central and important topic of Christology, here's the key point: By taking on a human nature and uniting it to the divine nature, God has elevated human nature to a dignity that truly staggers the imagination. The Second Vatican Council describes it like this:

> To the sons of Adam, [God] restores the divine likeness which had been disfigured from the first sin onward. *Since human nature as he assumed it was not annulled, by that very fact it has been raised up to a divine dignity in our respect, too.* For by his Incarnation the Son of God has united himself in some fashion with every man. He worked with human hands, he thought with a human mind, acted by human choice and loved with a human heart. Born of the Virgin Mary, he has truly been made one of us, like us in all things except sin (see Heb 4:15).[266]

Okay, a couple of important points here. (1) The text says "human nature as he assumed it was not annulled." This reiterates the idea that grace does not destroy but rather builds on nature. For human nature was "*assumed*" (taken up) and "*not annulled*" (not destroyed) by the eternal Son at the Incarnation. In other words, Jesus really does have a human nature. He doesn't just look like a man. He truly is man. He's the God-man who "worked with human hands" and "thought with a human mind." Alright, now here's the kicker: (2) Because Jesus Christ is truly man, "by that very fact," our human nature "*has been raised up to a divine dignity.*" Let's reflect more deeply on this remarkable point.

In Part Two, a question came up about the Incarnation: "So what happens when the eternal God becomes incarnate and enters time as a man?" I answered by saying, "Well, it makes the events in the life of such a man utterly unique. They become 'God events' that happen in time but transcend all time." In other words, every action of Jesus during his earthly life had a huge significance. Whatever he did became a *divine event*, and it sanctified that specific human activity. For instance, when he worked, human work was raised to a divine dignity. When he rested, human rest was raised to a divine dignity. When he lived with Mary and Joseph in Nazareth, family life was raised to a divine dignity. But there was one event that's the foundation for all of these actions: the very fact of his becoming man.

As we already read, by taking on a human nature, Jesus raised that nature to a divine dignity. But what exactly does this mean? Well, look at it this way: If God had become an ant, then what would have happened to the dignity of ants? Ants would have been raised to a divine dignity, and in every ant, we would see the face of God. But God didn't become an ant. He became a man. And now we see God in every human face: "Jesus has a unique relationship with every person, which enables us to see in every human face the face of Christ."[267] Indeed, "In every child which is born and in every person who lives or dies we see the image of God's glory. We celebrate this glory in every human being, a sign of the living God, an icon of Jesus Christ."[268] What a beautiful expression! Because of the Incarnation, every human being is a "sign of the living God" and an "icon of Jesus Christ" — now, *that's* divine dignity.

In sum, one of the marvels of the Incarnation is that it makes every human being an even greater wonder than before. So now, we can be amazed at man not only because he is a *person*, not only because he's made in the *image of God*, but also because, by the Incarnation, *human nature itself has been raised to a divine dignity*. And as if this weren't enough, there's yet another reason for our deepest wonder at man: *the Passion of Christ*.

Like the Incarnation, the Passion of Christ also reveals man's true and deepest worth. In particular, it shows how precious we are in the eyes of our Creator, who did not spare his own dearly beloved Son to save us. In *The Gospel of Life*, Pope John Paul II offers a beautiful reflection on how the Passion of Christ (specifically, the shedding of his blood) reveals the wonder of human dignity:

> The blood of Christ, while it reveals the grandeur of the Father's love, *shows how precious man is in God's eyes and how priceless is the value of his life*. The Apostle Peter reminds us of this: "You know that you were ransomed from the futile ways inherited from your fathers, not with perishable things such as silver or gold, but with the precious blood of Christ, like that of a lamb without blemish or spot" (1 Pt 1:18-19). Precisely by contemplating the precious blood of Christ, the sign of his self-giving love (see Jn 13:1), the believer learns to recognize and appreciate the almost divine dignity of every human being and can exclaim with ever renewed and grateful wonder: "How precious must man be in the eyes of the Creator, if he 'gained so great a Redeemer' (*Exsultet* of the Easter Vigil), and if God 'gave his only Son' in order that man 'should not perish but have eternal life!'" (see Jn 3:16).[269]

Yes, indeed, how precious we are! And what great love the Passion of Christ reveals! Do we see it? If not, then how do we come to see it? The Pope answers, "*Precisely by contemplating the precious blood of Christ*." So, for instance, when we ponder in our hearts the blood that flowed down Christ's back after the scourging, that dripped down his face from the crown of thorns, that ran down his arms from the driven nails, and that gushed forth from his pierced side, it's then that we truly learn "to recognize and appreciate the almost divine dignity of every human being." This recognition and appreciation of human dignity in light of the blood of Christ leads us to "exclaim with ever renewed and grateful wonder," "How precious must man be in the eyes of the Creator, since his dearly beloved Son poured out his own blood for us!"

When we contemplate the blood of Christ and come to realize in our hearts the great love that God has for each of us individually, we can't help but love God in return. And when we do turn to God, when we draw close to him and love him, we hear him say, "Now love one another as I have loved you" (see Jn 15:12). Surprisingly, this commandment reveals yet another source of our dignity in Christ, which we'll begin looking at now.

Recall in our section on personalism that one of the ways we come to appreciate the dignity of others is through *empathy*, which, in a sense, is to experience another person within ourselves *as the other person experiences himself*. Also, recall that the basis of empathy is *our own self-experience*. In other words, we saw that we can only show empathy when we ourselves have experienced what the other is experiencing (or, at least, when we've experienced something similar to what the other is experiencing). Well, I believe that loving others with the love of Christ follows a similar dynamic. For how can I love another "as Christ has loved me" unless I myself have experienced the love of Christ?

So, only after we ourselves have experienced God's love for us are we then able to see how much God loves our neighbor. We realize in our hearts, "If God loves me this much, then what great love must he also have for my neighbor — for Christ poured out his blood for him, too." This experience of God's love for us that leads us to see our neighbor's dignity also brings us to respond to our neighbor with the same love that we ourselves have received, "Love one another as I have loved you" (Jn 15:12).

Thus, we're called not only to passively receive the love of Christ but also to become active participants in his love as we love Christ in return and share his love with others. Herein lies another source of our dignity, the one I alluded to earlier. John Paul identifies this source as he continues his reflection on the blood of Christ from the previous citation:

> Furthermore, Christ's blood reveals to man that his greatness, and therefore his vocation, consists in *the sincere gift of self*. Precisely because it is poured out as the gift of life, the blood of Christ is no longer a sign of death, of definitive separation from the brethren, but the instrument of a communion which is richness of life for all. Whoever in the Sacrament of the Eucharist drinks this blood and abides in Jesus (see Jn 6:56) is drawn into the dynamism of this love and gift of life, in order to bring to its fullness the original vocation to love which belongs to everyone (see Gen 1:27; 2:18-24).[270]

So, our greatness and dignity is revealed in our vocation to self-giving love. As the Pope puts it, "Christ's blood reveals to man that his greatness ... consists in the sincere gift of self." Put another way, we are "great" because we're called to participate in the very love of Christ. What a privilege! We don't just passively receive Christ's love. Rather, we're caught up into it, actively share in it, and are called to communicate it to others. Perhaps nothing expresses this amazing reality better than what John Paul brings up at the end of this citation, namely, the Eucharist. For the Eucharist, the sacramental blood of Christ, is not only a sign of Christ's self-giving love, it actually *is* this love, becoming real and active within us. As John Paul so beautifully puts it, he who drinks Christ's blood is *"drawn into the dynamism"* of God's own love, which is the very same dynamism of love of the Most Holy Trinity, a dynamism of love that goes out to others, a dynamism of love that is a "vocation to love which belongs to everyone."

And so, the blood of Christ, flowing from the Cross, reveals the greatness of man. Not only does it show man how much he is loved, but it also draws him into that very love, allowing him to share in God's own activity and divine nature. Indeed, it is from the Cross that Jesus teaches us how to act divinely. In other words, he teaches us the Law of the Gift, namely, that man "can fully discover his true self only in a sincere giving of himself." It is from the Cross, John Paul reminds us, that "Jesus proclaims that *life finds its center, its meaning and its fulfillment when it is given up.*"[271] It's Christ's blood flowing from the Cross that "urges us to imitate Christ and follow in his footsteps."[272] For, indeed, "we too are called to give our lives for our brothers and sisters." And this allows us "to realize in the fullness of truth the meaning and destiny of our existence,"[273] which is a destiny of divine love.

Yes, we are called to love. We are made for love. And we are invited to share in the life and love of the God who is a communion of love. Now, remember, love is a response. In the case of love of neighbor, it's a response that begins by recognizing the dignity, worth, value, and preciousness of every human life. In other words, it begins by fostering in ourselves and in others a contemplative outlook.

Everything seems to begin and flow from the contemplative outlook. Without it, we cannot love our neighbor. Without it, we cannot build the culture of life and the civilization of love. Without it, we cannot proclaim the Gospel. For, indeed, this outlook, according to John Paul II, *is* the Gospel; it *is* Christianity, and so it's the way that all the members of the Church can live out their prophetic mission of communion.

We do well to close this section and indeed this whole chapter on our prophetic mission of communion by once again reflecting on John Paul's summary statement on the contemplative outlook that explains how we can make it real in our lives:

Our proclamation [of the Gospel of life] must also become *a genuine celebration of the Gospel of life.* ...

For this to happen, we need first of all to foster, in ourselves and in others, *a contemplative outlook*. Such an outlook arises from faith in the God of life, who has created every individual as a "wonder" (see Ps 139:14). It is the outlook of those who see life in its deeper meaning, who grasp its utter gratuitousness, its beauty and its invitation to freedom and responsibility. It is the outlook of those who do not presume to take possession of reality but instead accept it as a gift, discovering in all things the reflection of the Creator and seeing in every person his living image (see Gen 1:27; Ps 8:5). This outlook does not give in to discouragement when confronted by those who are sick, suffering, outcast or at death's door. Instead, in all these situations it feels challenged to find meaning, and precisely in these circumstances it is open to perceiving in the face of every person a call to encounter, dialogue, and solidarity.

It is time for all of us to adopt this outlook, and with deep religious awe to rediscover the ability to *revere and honor every person*, as Paul VI invited us to do in one of his first Christmas messages. Inspired by this contemplative outlook, the new people of the redeemed cannot but respond with *songs of joy, praise and thanksgiving for the priceless gift of life*, for the mystery of each individual's call to share through Christ in the life of grace and in an existence of unending communion with God our Creator and Father.[274]

CHAPTER THREE

The Priestly Mission of Communion

*T*HE *PRIESTLY CHARACTER OF THE MASS*. By far, the most crucial life lesson during my entire time in the seminary — yes, even more crucial than the "go eat some pasta" lesson — had to do with my coming to realize the *huge* importance of the Mass. Of course, I'd always been taught that the Mass is important. In fact, even before I entered the seminary, I was very familiar with those famous words from Vatican II that describe the Mass as "the source and summit of the Christian life."[275] Moreover, I myself had experienced the power of the Mass in my own life, and I looked forward to attending it daily.

Having said all this, I'm not sure I'd also go so far as to say that the Mass was the *center* of my life. Now, don't get me wrong. I mean, Mass was surely an important part of my life — but could I actually say that everything flowed into it and out of it and that my whole life revolved around it? Did I really look forward to Mass more than I looked forward to summer break or exciting spectacles like the Super Bowl? Can I honestly say that routine never crept in? I must confess: During my first few years in the seminary, Mass was important to me but not necessarily *hugely* important.

Then, something changed. I can't put my finger on exactly when it happened, but something definitely changed. There was a point during my time in the seminary when I suddenly realized that the Mass had become *the center*, that my life really did revolve around it, and that it truly had become my everything. So, what happened? What changed?

Here's what happened: I came to realize *the priestly character of the Mass.* More specifically, I came to realize my own priestly dignity as a baptized Christian. I don't remember exactly what did it, but at one point, some amazing words from Vatican II became deeply real to me: "[I]n the Eucharistic sacrifice, the source and summit of the Christian life, [all the faithful] *offer the divine victim to God and themselves along with it.*"[276] Without realizing exactly when it happened, those words came to express my reality, and I knew deeply in my heart that even as a seminarian, I shared in the priesthood of Christ. Of course, I knew I wasn't yet an ordained priest, who consecrates the bread and wine, and who then offers to God the transformed Body and Blood of Christ at the altar. Obviously, I knew that only the Bishops and ordained priests could do that. Still, I clearly realized that I wasn't out of the loop. I knew that, with the priest at the altar, I truly could "offer the divine victim to God and myself along with it."

The best way I can describe the impact this realization had on me is to compare it with a realization I mentioned earlier. In Part One, I explained that as a kid, I used to think of heaven, the Beatific Vision, as just a spectator sport. I imagined it as all the saints sitting on some massive grandstand, watching God do whatever God does. But I eventually came to realize that it's not that. Heaven isn't a spectator sport. We won't just be watching the game. Rather, we'll be *in on the action*.

And so it is with the Mass. At Mass, we really and truly get in on the action. What action? The same action that God does in heaven. (This is going to take a little recap and some explaining.)

As we learned in Part One, "God himself is an eternal exchange of love, Father, Son, and Holy Spirit." So, for all eternity, (1) the Father pours himself out in a total gift of self-giving love to the Son, and (2) the Son returns that gift with the same self-giving love — and the love between them is the Holy Spirit. As we also learned in Part One, amazingly, God "has destined us to share in that exchange."[277] In Part Two, we learned that the way we participate in that exchange is by becoming one of the persons of the Most Holy Trinity, the Son, in a transforming communion with him as a member of his Body. But the Mass tells us more of the story.

The Mass, in a sense, reenacts salvation history, what I sometimes call "the drama of the bridging of the gap." What gap? The gap between fallen humanity and the love of the Trinity, the gap separating sinful creatures from the loving Creator. And what did God do about this gap? He bridged it. In his unfathomable mercy, he reached out to us with his Trinitarian love, meaning he gave his Son to fallen humanity, "God so loved the world that he gave his only Son ..." (Jn 3:16).

Now, who is the Son? He's everything that the Father is. So, God truly reached out to us with the eternal action of his own Trinitarian love. In the Incarnation of the Word, he gave himself to us in an act of total self-giving love. The good news, then, is that with the Incarnation, the bridging of the gap begins! Self-giving love is extended to sinful, selfish humanity. And not only is it extended, it goes on to show the way of return. For, on the Cross, Jesus poured himself out in a total gift of self-giving love to the Father.

This is very interesting: The full divine action of the Trinity (mutual, self-giving love) becomes manifested to the world in what I've just described. It doesn't remain veiled in the inaccessible light of eternity. Rather, it illumines our darkened world as (1) God the Father gives himself in love to the world by giving his dearly beloved Son, and then (2) the Son gives himself back to the Father on the Cross, completing the two-stage, eternal exchange of love (with the Holy Spirit himself being the Love).

Great. So the eternal action of the Trinity's exchange of love becomes visible in the Incarnation and the Passion. But what does this have to do with us? Well, if we're baptized and attend Mass, then it has *everything* to do with us. For, again, *the Mass contains the whole drama of the bridging of the gap*, and we in the pews (or at the altar) are right there in the midst of the drama! It works like this: The first "arm" of the Trinity's love is extended to us at the moment of consecration, the moment when the ministerial priest takes the bread and says, "This is my Body," and then takes the wine and says, "This is my Blood." At that moment of consecration, God so loves the world that he gives us his only Son. At that moment, God the Father pours himself out in a gift of self-giving love *to us* by giving us his dearly beloved Son.

Okay, so far so good. But where's the return? Where does Jesus complete the action by giving himself back to the Father in a gift of total self-giving love? Jesus does it when the priest at the altar — who acts "*in persona Christi*" or "in the person of Christ" — takes the Body and Blood of Christ into his hands and offers it back to the Father, saying, "Through him, and with him, and in him, O God, almighty Father, in the unity of the Holy Spirit, all glory and honor is yours, forever and ever."

At that glorious moment, as we say, "Amen!," Jesus returns to the Father, completing the Trinitarian action. But there's something different this time, something that was not part of the invisible Trinitarian action: When the Father reaches down to "pick up" and embrace his Son, he notices that his Son is much *heavier* than before. What I mean is that when he receives the gift of self-giving love of his Son, he receives not only Jesus Christ the Head of the Mystical Body but also *all the members of his Body*. In other words, the Father receives the gift of self-giving love of the "full Christ," namely, all of us in Christ who are uniting ourselves with Christ at the moment of his self-offering to the Father at Mass. Truly, then, "in the Eucharistic sacrifice, the source and summit of the Christian life," we not only "offer the divine victim to God," but also, we offer ourselves "along with it." Truly, the Mass is heaven on earth! It is the visible, sacramental enactment of the invisible, eternal exchange of self-giving love of the Father to the Son and the Son to the Father in the Holy Spirit. And we get in on the action! At least, we're supposed to. For the Second Vatican Council calls us to a "fully conscious and active participation" in the Mass,[278] and this offering of the victim (Christ) and offering of ourselves along with him gets to the heart of this active participation.

My intention for the remainder of this chapter is to help us come to a fully conscious and more active participation in the Mass. I obviously can't cover everything here, so I'm going to stay focused on the priestly character of the Mass. I'll do this by looking at four things that we offer: our praise, our sufferings, our worries, and our whole selves with Mary. As we travel this road, we'll see that these four things help us fulfill our priestly mission of communion in perhaps the deepest and most effective way.

*W*E OFFER OUR PRAISE. Throughout this book, we've reflected on the incredible gift of salvation that God has given us in Christ. We've seen that not only does he forgive us our repented sins, but he raises us up to his own divine life. In fact, we've just read about how intimate our sharing in this life really is: We get to participate in the very action of the Trinity! Okay, so what's our response? What's the only adequate response to such a gift? As we learned in Part One, the angels themselves teach us, especially as they cry out, "Glory to God in the Highest!" We also learn from the Book of Revelation that the appropriate response to such a gift is ardent cries of praise and thanksgiving (see Rev 7:9-12). For, indeed, when we truly realize what God has done for us in Christ, how can we respond otherwise?

But are songs of praise and thanksgiving really an *adequate* response? I mean, doesn't it seem that such an infinitely merciful gift deserves an infinitely powerful response? Yet how can we give infinite praise and thanks? Some verses from Psalm 116 ask a similar question and provide the answer:

> How can I repay the Lord
> for his goodness to me?
> The cup of salvation I will raise;
> I will call on the Lord's name.
>
> My vows to the Lord I will fulfill
> before all his people.
> O precious in the eyes of the Lord
> is the death of his faithful.
>
> Your servant, Lord, your servant am I;
> you have loosened my bonds.
> A thanksgiving sacrifice I make;
> I will call on the Lord's name.
>
> My vows to the Lord I will fulfill
> before all his people,
> in the courts of the house of the Lord,
> in your midst, O Jerusalem (vv. 12-19).

Amazingly, the Psalmist points us to the Mass! Of course, he knew nothing about the Mass, because he lived a millennium before the Mass was instituted. Yet the Holy Spirit prophetically speaks to us today through his words, telling us how we can "make a return" for all the good the Lord has done for us. And how do we make such a return? Again, it's the Mass! After all, where else do we "raise the cup of salvation" and "call on the name of the Lord"? Where else do we "fulfill our vows to the Lord" (the vows of our Baptism, which call us to worship) "before all his people"? Where else do we witness the death of the Lord's most precious faithful one and praise the Lord for "loosening our bonds"? Where else can we make a better "thanksgiving sacrifice"? Where else but the church, where the Mass takes place, is the "house of the Lord"? Sure, the Psalm mentions Jerusalem, but the temple there was destroyed in 70 AD, and now, in a sense, the Church is the New Jerusalem.

So, how do we offer the greatest praise, even infinite praise? It's the Mass. It's especially that moment of the Mass when the priest raises the cup of salvation, the Blood of Christ (with the Body of Christ), and offers it to the Father. It's that super-charged moment of praise when the priest says, "Through him, and with him, and in him, O God, almighty Father, in the unity of the Holy Spirit, all glory and honor is yours, forever and ever." It's that moment when our praise is united to the perfect sacrifice of infinite love of Jesus' own self-offering through his Body and his Blood. Of course, this isn't the Mass' only moment of praise and thanksgiving, but it's a key time when, from our hearts, we can join our own personal prayers of praise with the offering of the Church to the Father.

So, are we ready? When we go to Mass, are our hearts filled with praise? Are we ready to offer our praise "through him, and with him, and in him"? If not, why not? If we're not ready, it may be because we haven't reflected enough on the Lord's blessings. No problem. As a preparation for the next Mass, let's reflect on the Lord's blessings now, so our praise and thanks to God can be fully united to and offered with Christ's own infinitely powerful sacrifice of praise to the Father.

Alright, so we've already looked at the biggest blessing: our salvation in Christ. But what else? For what other blessings should we praise God? How about for the gift of life, the gift of our very existence? After all, if we didn't exist, we wouldn't have *any* blessings. So let's reflect on the gift of our lives. Actually, on this point, we've already had a head start. Recall that we ended the last chapter with a prolonged reflection on how we can develop a "contemplative outlook," an outlook that recognizes human dignity and the gift of every human life. This outlook, as we saw, "arises from faith in the God of life, who has created every individual as a 'wonder.'" It's an outlook "of those who see life in its deeper meaning, who grasp its utter gratuitousness." And when we begin to see life in this way, we "cannot but respond with *songs of joy, praise and thanksgiving for the priceless gift of life.*" Perfect. So let's bring that attitude to Mass. At Mass, let's praise God for the gift of our lives, the gift of the lives of our friends and family, and the gift of every human person we meet.

Okay, so we've got a lot to be thankful for: the gift of our lives and the gift of new life in Christ. Anything else? Of course! There's a whole lot more, and once again, we've already had a head start. Recall how in the last chapter, we learned about the attitude of reverence, an attitude that extends beyond a sense of wonder for the gift of each human being to *all being*. It's an attitude that sees the beauty and goodness of all creation. Well, when we live such an attitude, we can't help but be moved to praise the Creator for the many gifts of beauty and goodness that he has spread out over all the earth. We already touched on this point in Part Two where we saw the connection between the beauty of creation and our vocation as "cosmic priests." Now let's look at that connection more closely in light of the Mass.

The whole earth and the creatures of the earth need the power of our praise. In fact, they've been waiting "with eager longing" for us (Rom 8:19). Why? Because we are the only beings in the whole cosmos who can fully bring the material world back to God. As beings made of both spirit and matter, we're the only ones who can "spiritualize" the material world and raise it up to God, who is himself pure spirit. Alright, so we've already covered all this in Part Two. But here's why it's super important for what we're covering right now: The key place where we raise the material world to God is *at the Mass*, especially, at the supercharged moment I've been talking about. The *Catechism* seems to make this point when it says,

> The Eucharist is also the sacrifice of praise by which the Church sings the glory of God in the name of all creation. This sacrifice of praise is possible only through Christ: he unites the faithful to his person, to his praise ... so that the sacrifice of praise to the Father is offered *through* Christ and *with* him, to be accepted *in* him.[279]

So, at Mass, as the Church, we sing the glory of God in the name of all of creation, and this is only possible through Christ. But does this mean that we can only praise God for his creation when we attend Mass? Of course not. We should always be thanking and praising God for the beauty of creation whenever we encounter it. That being said, it's a good practice to unite such praise and thanks to the offering of all the Masses being said throughout the world. Moreover, it's also a good practice to keep praise in our hearts and, later, to offer it to God when we actually do attend Mass.

Now, these two practices of uniting our praise and thanks to the Masses going on at the time and to the Masses we actually attend do not have to be something complicated. In fact, they can easily flow into our lives if only we develop a kind of "liturgical outlook," whereby we live from the Mass, in anticipation of the Mass, and with the Mass. In other words, we should develop a living liturgical spirituality of doing all things through Christ, with Christ, and in Christ to the glory of God the Father and in the unity of the Holy Spirit. We should foster in ourselves a whole attitude of praise and thanksgiving to God, an attitude that's also a constant movement from and to the "source" and "summit" of the Christian life, the Eucharistic sacrifice. By this liturgical outlook and attitude, we fully live the priestly character of the Mass and allow it to become the true center of our lives.

Before closing this section, I want to point out that our sacrifice of praise and thanks can sometimes be a *real* sacrifice, meaning that it may, indeed, cost us in terms of effort and work. After all, it isn't always easy to recognize the blessings of the Lord.[280] And sometimes, it certainly isn't easy to overcome deep-seated attitudes of complaining and a compulsive focus on the negative. Yet, even after we've developed an attitude of gratitude and have become a people of praise, sometimes praise and thanks will be the farthest things from our lips. That's alright. That's life. Nevertheless, despite the difficulty, we should strive to develop an attitude of gratitude and praise, even in the midst of suffering.

Recall that in Part Two, when treating the Eucharist, we learned that Eucharist means "thanksgiving" and that it gets to the very core of Christian life, *especially as a prayer of thanksgiving in the face of suffering*. Pope Benedict XVI referred to this as the "essential thing" and "fundamental element" of the Last Supper, namely, Jesus' attitude of praise and thanks to the Father *beforehand* for delivering him from his Passion and death through the Resurrection. And so, with Christ, we come to the real crown of praise, namely, when we bless God even for our crosses and thank him in advance (in faith and hope) for how the power of his love will bring good out of our crosses, trials, and sufferings.

In the next point, we'll look at how we can offer suffering itself as a sacrifice of love in and through the Mass.

*W*E OFFER OUR SUFFERING. Perhaps the greatest marvel of the Mass is how it re-presents the sacrifice of Calvary, though in an unbloody manner.[281] This means that while Jesus is definitely not sacrificed again at the Mass, his one sacrifice on Calvary is made truly present to us, even though we're living nearly 2,000 years later. Recall how we explored this marvel of the Mass in Part Two, when we reflected on the remarkable passage of the *Catechism* that spoke of Christ's Paschal mystery (his suffering, death, and Resurrection) as a real event that "abides" and "transcends all times while being made present in them all." Also, recall how we learned that we can have a real contact with the timeless power of that event through faith and love. Well, here I'd like to look more closely at a particular aspect of the power of the Cross, namely, *how our contact with Christ on the Cross at Mass can transform our suffering into a perfect sacrifice of love.* I'd like to begin this treatment with a passage from the *Catechism*:

> *The Eucharist is also the sacrifice of the Church.* The Church which is the Body of Christ participates in the offering of her Head. With him, she herself is offered whole and entire. She unites herself to his intercession with the Father for all men. In the Eucharist the sacrifice of Christ becomes also the sacrifice of the members of his Body. The lives of the faithful, their praise, sufferings, prayer, and work, are united with those of Christ and with his total offering, and so acquire a new value.[282]

This passage repeats for us the amazing idea that in the Mass, we're intimately united with Jesus in his perfect self-offering to the Father. But notice two key lines: (1) "In the Eucharist the sacrifice of Christ becomes also the sacrifice of the members of his Body," and, (2) "The lives of the faithful, their praise, sufferings, prayer, and work, are united with those of Christ and with his total offering, and so acquire a new value." This is truly amazing stuff. Think about it: In the Mass, Christ's sacrifice becomes *our sacrifice* (point 1). And when we take this seriously, when we truly offer this sacrifice and ourselves with it, *our lives acquire a new value* (point 2). This latter point is amazing: United to Christ's sacrifice, our praise, sufferings, prayer, and work *acquire a new value*. What new value? Well, in the previous section, we saw that our praise and thanksgiving, when we offer it through, with, and in Christ, becomes praise of infinite power. So, here, we can expect to find that our suffering and our work also take on infinite power. In fact, that's the "new value," namely, an *infinite power.*

Why infinite power? Because the sacrifice of Calvary is a sacrifice of *infinite love,* and that sacrifice, again, is our sacrifice (point 1). Jesus has placed his infinite love into our hands — literally into the hands of the priest at the altar and spiritually into the hands of the lay faithful who unite their own self-offering with the priest. It's a love that can give infinite value to all our actions, especially our sufferings.

What does it mean that our actions and sufferings have "infinite value"? And why does this even matter? I mean, what's the big deal? To help us realize what it means and why it's a *huge* deal, we need to explore the Christian meaning of human suffering.

Why is there evil? Why do we suffer? Here, we come to some of the greatest of the great questions, and definitely the thorniest. In fact, these kinds of questions have produced more atheists than any other. People say, "How can there be a good, all-powerful God who allows the innocent to suffer?" And, "If God is all-powerful, and he loves us, then why does he allow suffering?" If these questions haven't occurred to us, it might be because we haven't yet experienced great suffering. When we do, we can't help but ask the question, "Why?" Moreover, I suspect that many of us, at least at one time of great suffering or another, may even have gotten angry at God. Well, it's not the end of the world. He can take it. He expects it. And after we express to him what's in our hearts, he gently repeats his answer to our question.

God doesn't give one of the many trite and overly simplistic answers to the question of evil and suffering. He doesn't come down from heaven and give us a lecture. His word on the subject is not simply one among many. Rather, it's *the Word.* It's the Word become flesh. It's the Word become naked, beaten, and bloody flesh, a gaping wound, gasping for air, suffocating, thirsting, seemingly abandoned by God, and crying out in agony. It's Christ on the Cross — with all the gore and brutality. It's God in Christ bearing not just some but *all* the suffering of humanity in his own flesh. This "word of the cross," as St. Paul calls it (1 Cor 1:18), is the deepest answer to the problem of evil and to the "why" of suffering.

Alright, but what does this "word of the cross" actually say? Well, it's hard to tell. After all, it's a mystery. But how do we get our minds around a mystery? And what kind of answer is a crucifix? We've all seen them, and yet our questions remain. We still ask "*why*" when we suffer. Moreover, many of us will likely still get mad at God when we suffer greatly. So maybe this answer isn't good enough — or maybe we just need to pay more attention to the word of the Cross.

What is Jesus saying on the Cross? As we learned in Part Two, it's very simple. He's saying, "I love you." He's also telling us, "I did not come to take away suffering but to transform it into love." Or, more precisely, he's saying, "The suffering I came to take away is the *definitive suffering* of eternal death and hell, and I take it away by transforming temporal suffering into love." Well, this still sounds like the language of mystery — and it is, for the question of the meaning of suffering always remains something of a mystery. Let's delve more deeply into it.

Two questions come to mind: (1) "What does it mean that Jesus came to take away 'definitive suffering'?" and (2) "What does it mean that he transforms temporal suffering into love?" The answer to the first question has to do with Jesus' desire to save us from the definitive suffering of being eternally separated from the communion of love of the Trinity. The reality of sin is that its end result is eternal death, eternal separation from God — hell. This is, indeed, what Jesus came to save us from. Remember how he expressed the desire of his heart of hearts on the night he entered into his Passion? He said, "Father, I desire that they also … may be with me where I AM, to behold my glory." He wants us in the communion of love of the Trinity, and so he prays to the Father "that the love with which thou hast loved me may be in them and I in them." Then, he goes into mind-numbing darkness to keep us from the darkness of hell. This is an important point for us to try to realize. Therefore, before we get to the second question, let's look at this point more closely.

Jesus entered into depths of suffering that are incomparably and even infinitely worse than what any other human being has ever had to endure. This is because Jesus is the God-man. As true God, he could suffer an agony unlike any mere mortal. Pope John Paul II explains:

> [*The*] *Son who is consubstantial with the Father suffers as a man*. His suffering has human dimensions; it also has — unique in the history of humanity — a depth and intensity which, while being human, can also be an incomparable depth and intensity in suffering, insofar as the man who suffers is in person the only-begotten Son Himself: "God from God." Therefore, only He — the only-begotten Son — is capable of embracing the measure of evil contained in the sin of man: in every sin and in "total" sin, according to the dimensions of the historical existence of humanity on earth.[283]

Think of it: Because Jesus is God, he is "capable of embracing the measure of evil contained in the sin of man." As true God, he could see all people of all time, and therefore, he could take in the full "historical existence of humanity." And because he is also true man and loved with a divine and human heart, he felt "incomparable depth and intensity in suffering." Indeed, his Heart was such that it experienced suffering pure and unadulterated. He had none of the protective numbness that comes from having a hardened heart. He had no defense mechanisms that would have allowed him to close or narrow his Heart. In fact, his burning love for fallen humanity caused him to hold nothing back, making his Heart a totally open and vulnerable victim of an endless procession of rejection, blasphemy, and abuse issuing from all people of all times. Finally, this same unconditional openness of heart caused his Heart to bleed with the deepest compassion for the suffering of every human being from the beginning of time to the end of the world. This compassion of Christ for every human person who suffers will help us better understand the second question, "*What does it mean that Jesus transforms temporal suffering into love?*" Let's turn our attention to this second question now.

To understand what it means for Jesus to transform temporal suffering into love, we need to go back to an idea we covered in Part Two. Recall that because Jesus is true God, all his actions are "God events," meaning they have a *huge* significance for man. For instance, as we saw earlier, when God took on a human nature, human nature itself was raised to a divine dignity. When the God-man worked in St. Joseph's workshop, human work itself was raised to a divine dignity. So also, when the God-man suffers out of love, suffering becomes a "God-event," and suffering itself is raised to a divine dignity — specifically, the divine dignity of expressing redemptive, life-giving love:

> Human suffering has reached its culmination in the Passion of Christ. And at the same time it has entered into a completely new dimension and a new order: *it has been linked to love.* ... The Cross of Christ has become a source from which flow rivers of living water.[284]

So, through the Cross of Christ, human suffering, which used to be something without sense or meaning, is transformed into love. This is a very big deal. For, in light of the Cross of Christ, suffering now has worth and dignity. Indeed, by his Cross, Jesus has infused suffering with unfathomable meaning and power, the power of love! And by his Cross, Jesus is lovingly present to each one of us in our suffering, inviting us to discover the meaning and power of suffering. The key question is this: *Are we present to him?* As he lovingly gazes on each one of us from the Cross, are we lovingly gazing back at him from our own crosses? Do we respond to his invitation from the Cross to let him turn our own suffering into divine love? This is one of the great decisions of human life: Will I allow Christ's Passion to transform my suffering into love? Will I participate with Christ in the work of redemption? Will I "make up for what is lacking in the suffering of Christ?" (Col 1:24).

"Wait a minute," someone may say, "Aren't we taking things a bit too far here? I mean, Jesus suffered for all and completed the work of redemption in his own Cross. How can we participate in it? Are you saying that his suffering is incomplete? And really, how dare you say there's something lacking in his suffering? Sure, St. Paul is the one who wrote that, but he must have meant something different."

I'm going to let John Paul II answer these objections by combining two marvelous citations from his masterpiece on the Christian meaning of human suffering, *Salvifici Doloris*:

> Every man has *his own share in the Redemption*. Each one is also *called to share in that suffering* through which the Redemption was accomplished. He is called to share in that suffering through which all human suffering has also been redeemed. In bringing about the Redemption through suffering, Christ *has also raised human suffering to the level of the Redemption*. Thus each man, in his suffering, can also become a sharer in the redemptive suffering of Christ.[285] ...
>
> Does this mean that the Redemption achieved by Christ is not complete? No. It only means that the Redemption, accomplished through satisfactory love, *remains always open to all love* expressed in *human suffering*. In this dimension — the dimension of love — the Redemption which has already been completely accomplished is, in a certain sense, constantly being accomplished. Christ achieved the Redemption completely and to the very limits; but at the same time He did not bring it to a close. In this redemptive suffering, through which the Redemption of the world was accomplished, Christ opened Himself from the beginning to every human suffering and constantly does so. Yes, it seems to be part *of the very essence of Christ's redemptive suffering* that this suffering requires to be unceasingly completed.[286]

In other words, yes, Jesus completed the work of redemption on the Cross, but it's an ongoing work through the members of his Body, the Church, *who open themselves to the transforming power of Christ's Cross.* Christ's Cross is the one source of the redemption. It's Christ on the Cross who transforms suffering into love. And as we'll soon see, when we open ourselves to this love in the midst of our own suffering, we begin to participate in his redeeming work. What's "lacking" in the suffering of Christ, then, is the refusal on the part of Christians to respond to Christ's loving invitation to join him in the work of redemption that he himself accomplished on the Cross. What's lacking is the cooperation of Christians who reject the Cross or who drag their own crosses with constant complaining. What's lacking is those who don't accept the gift of salvation that comes through the Cross.

Let me put it this way. Jesus died for all, and his salvation is superabundantly sufficient to save every human being who ever lived. But does every human being accept the gift of salvation? Not necessarily. Each of us is free to reject Christ. So, in every age, the prayer and suffering of the Church, which is Christ's Body, has the power to open hearts to Christ's love. This is the meaning behind the ancient saying, "The blood of the martyrs is the seed of the Church." For, indeed, the sufferings of the martyrs, united to Christ with love, helped open the hearts of others to accept Christ's saving grace. So, also with us. When we accept the Lord's invitation to lovingly unite our sufferings to him, we become "a multiple subject of His supernatural power" and a "special support for the powers of good" against the powers of evil.[287] Truly, the suffering members of the Church are like so many little powerhouses of grace scattered throughout the world and holding up the world. And these powerhouses are needed today more than ever before.

As we learned earlier, in our day, a great battle for souls is raging, a battle between the culture of life and the culture of death. Jesus wants us to fight on his side, and he gives a most powerful weapon to the children of light and life: the power of the Cross, the power of suffering lovingly united to Christ on the Cross. This is a source of amazing strength and power for the Church, and it's the reason Pope John Paul II appealed in the name of the Church to all those who suffer:

> And we ask all *you who suffer* to support us. We ask precisely you who are weak *to become a source of strength* for the Church and humanity. In the terrible battle between the forces of good and evil, revealed to our eyes by our modern world, may your suffering in union with the cross of Christ be victorious![288]

So, in answer to the perennial question, "Why suffering?" Jesus responds with the word of the Cross, a word that we come to understand only gradually as we become sharers in the suffering of Christ and experience its power. John Paul dramatically explains how this answer unfolds in the life and understanding of the believer:

> The answer which comes through this sharing [in Christ's suffering] is in itself *something more than the mere abstract answer* to the question about the meaning of suffering. For it is above all a call. It is a vocation. Christ does not explain in the abstract the reasons for suffering, but before all else He says: "Follow me!" Come! Take part through your suffering in the work of saving the world, a salvation achieved through my suffering! Through my cross! Gradually, *as the individual takes up his cross*, spiritually uniting himself to the Cross of Christ, the salvific meaning of suffering is revealed before him.[289]

So, let's go! Let's heed the invitation of our Savior. Let's not waste any of our suffering. Through our suffering, lovingly united to Christ, let's take our part in the work of saving the world and allow the meaning of suffering to unfold before us.

See what amazing dignity Jesus gives to us? In saving us, he doesn't simply make us passive recipients of his grace. Rather, he gives us the dignity of taking an active part in the mystery of his love and redemption. In fact, it's by taking this active role that we are saved! For suffering is part of the means of our transformation in Christ, and thus it's an essential ingredient of the Christian life, a fact that Jesus does not hide from his disciples, "If any man would come after me, let him deny himself and take up his cross daily and follow me" (Lk 9:23).

Look at it this way: Our goal is to share in the life of self-giving love of the Trinity. Well, we become self-giving lovers especially through suffering. After all, suffering is what self-giving love looks like. Look at the Cross. That's self-giving love. Do you want to see the Trinity? Look at the Cross. For the love of the Trinity is *self-giving* love, and in the visible world, self-giving love is revealed in the suffering of Christ on the Cross. So, our transforming communion with Christ is not only through faith and the Sacraments, as we learned in Part Two, but also through suffering. And suffering becomes most transformative and powerful when it is lovingly and sacramentally united to the Cross at Mass, which brings us back to our main topic and answers a fear that may be rising up in our hearts.

With all this talk of suffering, maybe you're getting a bit anxious. Maybe questions are beginning to well up from a nervous heart, "Is he saying that I have to be a broken, bruised, and bloody mess? Do I have to be pierced with nails, crowned with thorns, and scourged with a whip?" Well, not exactly. Jesus didn't say, "Take up *my* Cross." He said, "Take up *your* cross, and follow me." How do we take up our crosses and follow Jesus? By accepting the crosses that come our way, offering them up at Mass, and following Jesus to the Father, "through him and with him and in him." Do we have to actually be at Mass to do this? No. We can "offer up" our sufferings at any time and unite them with all the Masses being said throughout the world.

So be not afraid! Our crosses are nothing compared to Jesus' sacrifice on the Cross. Our sufferings cannot compare with his — and they don't need to. Jesus doesn't tell us to carry his infinitely heavy Cross but just our own crosses that are just right for us: not too heavy and not too light. It's our job to accept them, unite them with Jesus on the Cross, and offer them to the

Father. When we do, our little crosses take on infinite value. Indeed, it's as if we ourselves had suffered Jesus' unfathomable agony on the Cross with his own perfect love.

What a gift! This is the gift of the Mass. Through the Mass, the Holy Spirit takes our little offerings of suffering and unites them to Jesus' Passion, which gives them infinite value. As John Paul II puts it, "Those who share in the sufferings of Christ preserve in their own sufferings a very special *particle of the infinite treasure* of the world's redemption."[290] So, while our sufferings are just a particle, when they're united to Christ, they become an infinite treasure and, as John Paul goes on to say, we "can share this treasure with others."

Again, this is the amazing gift of the Mass. We come with our little sufferings, unite them to Christ, offer them to the Father, and then they have infinite value, which we can share with others. Think about this for a moment: *infinite value.* We don't need to torture ourselves with suffering to gain "merits" for souls. Jesus puts the infinite worth and superabundant merit of his entire Passion into our hands at Mass, and he lets us, as it were, "link up" our own little sufferings with his, making them infinitely efficacious for souls. So, what's stopping us from being bold in our prayer for others? We have an ocean of merit at our disposal! Therefore, let me end this section by simply saying this: Don't waste your suffering! Lovingly offer it up daily in union with all the Masses being offered throughout the world, and then bring your sufferings and offer them every time you attend Mass. In this way, your sufferings will have infinite power that can help many, many souls accept the salvation won for them in Jesus Christ, our Lord.

WE OFFER OUR WORRIES. I know, I know. Worries are part of suffering, so they actually belong to the previous section. However, there's something about the suffering of worry that deserves our special attention.

Worry can be one of the great sufferings of life. Many of us worry about all kinds of things: our health, our jobs, our friends and family, our country, and a million other things.

Worries and anxieties are endless! Now, of course, while Jesus wants us to be responsible and take our duties seriously, he doesn't want us to give in to useless worry. Thus, he frequently tells us in Scripture, "Be not afraid." And in what's probably his most important discourse, the Sermon on the Mount, he makes this point very clear:

> Therefore I tell you, do not be anxious about your life, what you shall eat or what you shall drink, nor about your body, what you shall put on. Is not life more than food, and the body more than clothing? Look at the birds of the air: they neither sow nor reap nor gather into barns, and yet your heavenly Father feeds them. Are you not of more value than they? And which of you by being anxious can add one cubit to his span of life. And why are you anxious about clothing? Consider the lilies of the field, how they grow; they neither toil nor spin; yet I tell you, even Solomon in all his glory was not arrayed like one of these. But if God so clothes the grass of the field, which today is alive and tomorrow is thrown into the oven, will he not much more clothe you, O men of little faith? Therefore do not be anxious, saying, "What shall we eat?" or "What shall we drink?" or "What shall we wear?" For the Gentiles seek all these things; and your heavenly Father knows that you need them all. But seek first his kingdom and his righteousness, and all these things shall be yours as well.
>
> Therefore do not be anxious about tomorrow, for tomorrow will be anxious for itself. Let the day's own trouble be sufficient for the day (Mt 6:25-34).

Pretty clear, right? Don't worry. Trust in the Lord. He's going to take good care of us. All we need to do is strive for holiness (which involves doing our daily duties well), and we'll have everything we need. Very simple, right? Yet most of us still don't get it. We tend to worry and give in to useless anxiety. Knowing this, the Lord has done something extraordinary. Just last century, he came to remind us to trust in him. As we learned in Part Two, he appeared to St. Faustina Kowalska and urged her to tell the world about how much he desires that we trust in his goodness, his providential care for us, and his merciful love. To highlight this point, as we also learned in Part Two, he asked Faustina to have an image painted with the signature, "Jesus, I trust in you." This short prayer of trust reminds us to turn to Jesus in all our anxieties. He says to us:

> **The graces of My mercy are drawn by means of one vessel only, and that is — trust. The more a soul trusts, the more it will receive. Souls that trust boundlessly are a great comfort to Me, because I pour all the treasures of My graces into them. I rejoice that they ask for much, because it is My desire to give much, very much. On the other hand, I am sad when souls ask for little, when they narrow their hearts.**[291]

I've always been amazed at how Jesus tells St. Faustina (and other mystics) that by our actions, such as trust or lack of trust, we either comfort him or make him sad. Think of it: We can actually comfort Jesus and give him joy when we trust in him! Here's another example from the *Diary of St. Faustina*: **"You will give Me pleasure if you hand over to Me all your troubles and griefs. I shall heap upon you the treasures of My grace."**[292]

Years ago, after reading several passages like this one, I decided to strive to console Jesus by giving him my trust. Therefore, I frequently pray the prayer, "Jesus, I trust in you," whenever worries oppress me. Or sometimes I pray a prayer composed by a priest whom St. Padre Pio called a saint, Fr. Dolindo Ruotolo, who claimed that Jesus himself taught it to him. Here's the prayer: "*O Jesus, I surrender this to you. You take care of it.*"

According to Fr. Dolindo, Jesus promised that he would take special, even miraculous care of any worries, difficulties, or problems surrendered to him with the words of this prayer.

(The idea behind this promise actually goes back to the words from the Sermon on the Mount cited earlier.) Anyway, I've prayed this prayer many times, and it's never failed me. Of course, things haven't always turned out as I've expected, but I've often noticed that Jesus took care of the situations in a much more beautiful way than I could have imagined.

Still, there are times when I repeat the prayer, "Jesus, I trust in you," over and over, or say, "O Jesus, I surrender this to you. You take care of it," and yet the anxiety and worry remain. During such times, I keep making acts of trust. At the same time, I can't wait to get to Mass. For Mass is the ultimate time and place to offer all our worries to God, "through Christ, with Christ, and in Christ." There's where we can always experience peace. Why? Again, because the offering of the Mass has infinite power. How can our heavenly Father resist the prayers made in view of his Son's perfect sacrifice of love?

Still, some may say, "Well, my worries have to do with my children or family members who have lost the faith and whose souls are in danger, so the worry lingers." Yes, certain worries for loved ones can be a heavy and recurrent burden on our hearts. But still, there's no better place to offer those worries than at Mass, especially at the "through him, with him, and in him" moment. And while, for instance, the heart pain of a mother for her fallen-away children can be intense and even constant, there's the comfort of knowing that the power of the Mass brings infinite mercy, a mercy that continually works to bring good into the lives of those who are offered at Mass.

On the other hand, others may say, "Well, I'm so worried because I have such a long list of people to pray for. It never ends! In fact, I'm worried I may forget someone." To people with this problem, I recommend some remarkable words of St. Thérèse of Lisieux, who also dealt with the issue of having many people for whom she felt responsible to pray:

> Since I have two brothers and my little Sisters, the novices, if I wanted to ask for each soul what each one needed and go into detail about it, the days would not

be long enough and I fear I would forget something important. For simple souls there must be no complicated ways; as I am of their number, one morning during my thanksgiving [after Mass], Jesus gave me a simple means of accomplishing my mission.

He made me understand these words of the Canticle of Canticles: "*DRAW ME, WE SHALL RUN after you in the odor of your ointments*" (1:3). O Jesus, it is not even necessary to say: "*When drawing me, draw the souls whom I love!*" This simple statement: "Draw me" suffices; I understand, Lord, that when a soul allows herself to be captivated by the odor of your ointments, she cannot run alone, all the souls whom she loves follow in her train; this is done without constraint, without effort, it is a natural consequence of her attraction for You. Just as a torrent, throwing itself with impetuosity into the ocean, drags after it everything it encounters in its passage, in the same way, O Jesus, the soul who plunges into the shoreless ocean of Your Love, draws with her all the treasures she possesses. Lord, You know it, I have no other treasures than the souls it has pleased You to unite to mine; it is You who entrusted these treasures to me.[293]

What a remarkable prayer! The saint of childlike confidence always seems to find a way to remain at peace, and what she says here is true. When we give ourselves to God, he blesses those whom we love. When we offer ourselves at Mass, "through him, with him, in him," we are like the soul who "plunges into the shoreless ocean of God's love" and who, thereby, "draws with her all the treasures she possesses." Now, does all this mean we stop praying for our loved ones? Not at all. It's just that when we completely offer ourselves to God at Mass, we need not "fear we would forget something important." The answer, therefore, is really to offer ourselves, to give our whole selves to God — for then, he takes care of everything else. As Jesus said to one holy woman, "You worry only about loving me, and I will take care of everything else to the smallest detail."[294] This is the promise from the Sermon on the Mount that if we seek first the kingdom of God, everything else will be given to us. And what else does it mean to seek first the kingdom of God than to give our whole selves to God without reserve?

Mary helps us to do this, especially when we give ourselves to Jesus through her. Let's look more closely at what this means.

WE OFFER OURSELVES WITH MARY. The spiritual practice of giving oneself totally to Jesus through Mary has a long tradition in the Church and goes by several names. It's sometimes called "Marian consecration," "total consecration to Jesus through Mary," or "Marian entrustment." The best summary of it comes from Jesus' own words when he was dying on the Cross:

> When Jesus saw his mother and the disciple whom he loved standing near, he said to his mother, "Woman, behold, your son." Then he said to the disciple, "Behold, your mother." And from that hour the disciple took her to his own home (Jn 19:26-27).

Who is the beloved disciple mentioned here? It's St. John, the author of the Gospel of John. At the same time, according to Pope John Paul II, "the disciple whom Jesus loved" represents each one of us. And so, with Mary standing near, Jesus says to us, "Behold, your mother." How should we respond? Of course, by accepting the gift! We should respond by accepting Jesus' final parting gift to us: his mother as our spiritual mother. And how do we accept it? According to John Paul, like St. John, we should "take Mary to our own homes." In other words, we should take her into our hearts, meaning we should give her all our joys, sorrows, sufferings, and our very selves, so she can bring us to Jesus.

The idea of giving our whole selves to Jesus through Mary is the essence of Marian consecration, a path that Jesus himself followed and that, from the Cross, he invites us to follow as well. So, it's a solid path, a path Jesus himself took, and one that he desires us to take. Moreover, the Church herself encourages us on this path, saying, "Everyone should have a genuine devotion to [Mary] and entrust his life to her motherly care."[295] Finally, many holy sons and daughters of the Church point us to this path. For instance, St. Louis de Montfort went so far as to say that Marian consecration is "the surest, easiest, shortest, and the most perfect means" to holiness.[296] I would add that there's no better "place" to live out this most perfect means to holiness than in the context of the sacrifice of the Mass.

Why the Mass? Well, look at it this way: Jesus gave us the gift of his mother as our mother on Calvary. And what is the Mass but a re-presentation of the sacrifice of Calvary? And what are we invited to do at Mass? As we read earlier, we're invited to *"offer the divine victim to God and ourselves along with it."* Well, nobody united himself to Jesus and offered himself to God more perfectly than Mary did:

> Thus the Blessed Virgin advanced in her pilgrimage of faith, and faithfully persevered in her union with her Son unto the cross. There she stood, in keeping with the divine plan, enduring with her only begotten Son the intensity of his suffering, joining herself with his sacrifice in her mother's heart, and lovingly consenting to the immolation of this victim, born of her ... .[297]

Like Mary, we're all called to stand at the foot of the Cross at Mass, join ourselves with Jesus' sacrifice, and offer ourselves through him, with him, and in him, in the unity of the Holy Spirit, to the glory of God the Father. And Our Blessed Mother helps us to do this, just as she helped St. John and many other saints throughout the ages. Will we let her help us? If we do, then she'll make all our offerings at Mass, all our sacrifices of praise, suffering, worry, and our very selves even more effective for leading everyone and everything to the Most Holy Trinity. So, let's say yes to Jesus through Mary and allow her to be a mother to us now. (For more information on how you can prepare for and formally make the consecration, see the information pages at the back of this book.)

Now, to conclude this section and this chapter, I'd like to mention one last, important point about how Mary helps a special group of people to offer themselves at Mass and fulfill their priestly mission of communion. The group is called "spiritual mothers for priests."

Spiritual Mothers for Priests. Have you ever wondered why Mary, who is the most perfect of all creatures, the most beloved by Jesus, and the most intimately united with him was not chosen to be a priest at the altar? I mean, she's the one who was standing right there at the altar of the Cross! If anything, this tells us that Jesus' choice to reserve the ordained priesthood to men alone is not based on a superiority of men over women. If it were based on superiority, then Mary clearly would have been the first priest. But she was not. Why not? Because Jesus had another gift for her and for many women: the gift of spiritual motherhood, a vocation in the Church that, unfortunately, is not widely known. Yet it's a vocation that's just as important as the ordained priesthood, at least in the sense that it's not only a privileged source of priestly vocations, but it also sustains them and makes them bear fruit. Actually, there's a sense in which the vocation of being a spiritual mother for priests may be even more important than a priestly vocation. I say this because one spiritual mother can "give birth" to and sustain not just one priestly vocation but *many.*

I said that the priesthood, in a sense, comes from spiritual mothers. Why? Well, let's start with Mary. Without her "yes" to God at the Annunciation, we would not have Jesus Christ, our High Priest. So, without her "yes" to motherhood, there would be no priesthood. Similarly, without the yes of so many hidden spiritual mothers for priests, there would be few (if any) priests. Let me explain.

As I write, I'm well aware that any good or fruitfulness of this writing flows in large part from the prayers and sacrifices of my spiritual mothers. I don't just think this. I know it. I myself have clearly experienced the power of their prayers in my own priestly life and throughout my time in the seminary. It's a given. In a sense, I owe everything to their prayers.

So who are these spiritual mothers? They're consecrated women, married women with families of their own, and single women devoted to the Lord. They come from all walks of life, and again, I know it's their prayers that keep me going as a priest. I also know it's the prayers of such spiritual mothers that keep many other priests going and make their ministries fruitful. Finally, I'm sure that Mary, the first and preeminent spiritual mother, helped keep Jesus going in his priestly mission and assisted in making it fruitful. Let's go more deeply into this point.

I have no doubt that while Jesus was pouring himself out in the toil and labor of preaching the kingdom, healing the sick, raising the dead, and casting out demons, Mary was united with him in prayer and sacrifice. Surely, her motherly heart went out to her Son and to all the people his words and actions would reach. Moreover, I'm convinced that it was the power of her prayers that inspired faith in so many of the people that Jesus healed. The grace for this didn't seem to come directly from Jesus, for he himself was astonished at their faith (see Lk 7:9). So, where did the grace of faith in these Jewish and pagan people come from if not from the Spirit-filled prayers of the perfect disciple whose faith is unsurpassed? For instance, where did the blind man, Bartimaeus, get the courage to repeatedly cry out to Jesus, "Son of David, have pity on me" despite rebukes from crowd? (see Mk 10:46-48). Where did the bleeding woman get the faith that made her reach out to touch Jesus' garment? (Mt 9:20-22). Where did the Syrophoenician woman get the boldness to persevere in faith after being rebuked by Jesus himself? (see Mk 7:25-30). I suggest that these graces came from Mary's prayers, which give birth to faith in faithless men and women.

Similarly, we can ask the questions, "From where does the grace come for a young man to renounce marriage and the world and to embrace a life of toil and service as a priest? From where does the grace come that helps him persevere through the testing and training of the seminary?" And once he becomes a priest, "From where does the grace come that gives power to his words, insights to his mind, and warmth to his heart as he serves God's people?" Of course, the question of where specific graces come is a mystery, and we surely know that the grace of ordination gives a priest everything he needs to fulfill his vocation, but how many extraordinary graces come from spiritual mothers? I'm convinced that many such graces come from them and that their prayers often make the difference between mediocrity in the priesthood and saintly priests.

How much the Church today needs spiritual mothers for priests! In a time when so many convents are empty, Jesus calls out to women from all walks of life to be spiritual mothers for priests. He doesn't just rely on religious sisters and nuns. He calls out to any woman who will beg the harvest master to send out laborers into the vineyard. He calls out to those who feel a desire to help his priests be what he calls them to be. He calls out to those who love the Church and know that the priests have a special calling to and responsibility for the mission of communion. For Jesus knows that without the priests, there is no Mass. He knows that without the priests, there is no Sacrament of Penance, Anointing of the Sick, or Confirmation. He knows that the renewal of the Church comes through a renewal of the priesthood. Furthermore, he knows that the renewal of the priesthood comes from generous women who give themselves as spiritual mothers and exercise their common priesthood by offering themselves through Christ, with Christ, and in Christ for those in the ministerial priesthood.

This offering of oneself for priests does not have to be something scary. For, while it's true that there are many "victim souls" among the spiritual mothers of priests (heroic souls who lovingly offer all kinds of agonies such as cancer and other illnesses), there are also many women who live the vocation simply by offering up their little sufferings. But again, this means so much because, remember, even little sufferings lovingly united to the offering of the Mass take on infinite value. In fact, some of the best spiritual mothers, I believe, are those who offer up things that they might never have realized could bring great holiness to priests. For instance, they can offer their broken motherly hearts if they can't conceive a child or if their children leave the Church and go the way of the world. They can offer their broken spousal hearts if they've been abandoned by husbands who couldn't say no to the culture of death. They can offer their lonely hearts if their husbands are aloof or deceased or if they've never been able to marry. Such women, who may be tempted to think of themselves as motherly failures, can find deep meaning in a vocation of offering up their broken hearts for the sanctification of spiritual fathers.

To all those being called to be spiritual mothers for priests, I say this: *We priests need you!* Priests who are lonely, depressed, discouraged, overworked, overwhelmed, tempted, persecuted, tepid, and brokenhearted need to feel the motherly love of your prayers. *The Church needs you!* It needs you to beg the Master of the harvest for holy priests, men who will say no to the culture of death and embrace a life of self-giving service to God's people. *God's people need you!* They need the holy priests that your prayers will inspire. They need to be fed by priests who have the Heart of the Good Shepherd and the fire of his love.

Just as life begins in mothers, so the life of the Church begins in all you spiritual mothers out there. Just as new life remains hidden in the darkness of the womb, so will your service often remain hidden in the darkness of the world. Just as children often forget the goodness of their mothers, so will you rarely be thanked for your sacrifice. But Jesus sees you, and he will bless you, delight in you, and reward you for your loving service of his mission of communion.

[By the way, this ends Part Three. I'm not going to summarize it here, because a summary is coming in the Conclusion.]

Conclusion

What do you think? Did we do it? Did the super-concept of *communio* work? Did this "one thing" bring it all together? Did it make it all simple? Did it provide a key to the Church's wisdom? Not so fast. Don't answer yet. We're not done.

At this point, your head may be spinning. After all, we've just spent nearly 300 pages covering, well, *everything*. And it's okay if you're feeling a bit overwhelmed. But it's really not so overwhelming. The purpose of this conclusion is to show you that. In fact, I want to tell you what we've really been up to.

I didn't say it at the beginning, but by now, you may have noticed that this whole book has actually been more of a retreat than a theology lesson. By this, I mean that the focus has not been so much on giving notional knowledge as *real knowledge*. It's been about the "enrichment of faith." Don't get me wrong, there's been a lot of theology in these pages, but through the style, I've tried to foster an *experience* of the faith. I tried to do this, for example, by using lots of anecdotes, stories, images, concrete concepts, and an emphasis on the personal. These are the kinds of things that help bring the faith from our heads to our hearts, and that's why this book is more like a retreat. It's also why it doesn't need to feel so overwhelming. I mean, you've had the experience of it. It's with you. Now it's just a matter of properly summarizing and organizing it in your mind and heart.

To summarize and organize what we've learned, I want to put everything into the context of the greatest retreat the Church has to offer, the *Spiritual Exercises of St. Ignatius of Loyola*. By doing so, I hope to make everything we've covered even more simple, clear, and memorable. In fact, by the end of this conclusion, my goal is that each of us will have the essence of what we've learned in our minds and hearts in such a way that we can take it with us.

Let's begin by comparing the author of the *Spiritual Exercises*, St. Ignatius of Loyola, to the author of the *Summa Theologiae*, St. Thomas Aquinas. This comparison will reveal a key to *summarizing* what we've learned. Then, as we look more closely at the *Spiritual Exercises*, we'll find another key to *organizing* what we've learned.

*T*WO *MYSTICAL EXPERIENCES.* In Part Two, we learned that during the last year of St. Thomas's life, while he was writing his *Summa*, he had a mystical experience that caused him to say, "All that I have written seems to me like straw compared to what has now been revealed to me." What we *didn't* learn then is that Thomas stopped writing his *Summa* after this experience and never took it up again. In fact, his students had to finish the last sections for him. Why did he stop? I suspect it's because he realized that the *Summa* couldn't adequately express what he himself had mystically experienced. After all, the *Summa* is written in the style of syllogistic reasoning and theological argument, and while this style is undeniably important, it doesn't measure up to the experience of God.[298]

Saint Ignatius of Loyola also had a life-changing mystical experience. Shortly after his conversion from a life of worldly ambition, he travelled to an isolated town of Spain called Manresa, and for eleven months, he lived a life of intense mortification and prayer. One day during this penitential period, Ignatius decided to make a short pilgrimage to a church outside of town. The road leading to the church followed a river called the Cardoner, and that's where it happened. Ignatius himself, writing in the third person, describes the experience:

> As he went along occupied with his devotions, he sat down for a little while with his face toward the river which was running deep. While he was seated there, the eyes of his understanding began to be opened; though he did not see any vision, he understood and knew many things, both spiritual things and matters of faith and of learning, and this was with so great an enlightenment that everything seemed new to him. Though there were many, he cannot set forth the details that he understood then, except that he experienced a great clarity in his understanding. This was such that in the whole course of his life, through sixty-two years, even if he gathered up all the many helps he had had from God and all the many things

he knew and added them together, he does not think they would amount to as much as he had received at that one time.[299]

This "great enlightenment" was really the culmination and climax of a series of mystical experiences that Ignatius had had during the preceding weeks. It brought together, synthesized, and summarized all those other experiences and gave him a superabundance of wisdom. More specifically, it filled his mind with an understanding of the big picture of reality, or what Fr. Clarke called, "the Great Circle of Being." In the words of one expert of Ignatian spirituality, "What Ignatius understood and grasped then, more than saw, was that everything comes forth from God, everything returns to God, everything — all reality — is to be understood only in God."[300] Another expert describes Ignatius's experience in a similar way, "The descent of creatures from God and their necessary re-ascent and reintegration into their ultimate end, God himself, are among the most vivid experiences of the great enlightenment."[301]

I want to highlight here that both these experts of Ignatian spirituality, who base their conclusions on the testimony of St. Ignatius himself and on the statements of his early companions, describe Ignatius's great mystical experience in the language of "coming forth" and "return," of "descent" and "re-ascent." Recall that in Part Two, I used similar language to describe the Great Circle of Being: "All of creation goes forth from God and then returns to God, making one big, circular movement. This circular movement, or Great Circle, [is] the great movement of all of creation from the Trinity and back to the Trinity." Also, realize that the content of Ignatius's mystical experience reflects the whole organizational structure of Thomas's *Summa*, namely, all reality going forth from God, returning to God, and being understood only in God.

Think of this for a moment. There really must be something to this idea of the "Great Circle" if two of the Church's greatest saints and teachers basically describe all of reality as a great circular movement of descent and re-ascent, of going forth and returning, of *exitus* and *reditus*. Indeed, this idea gets to the heart of their two masterpieces, two of the most influential works in the whole history of the Church: the *Summa Theologiae* and the *Spiritual Exercises of St. Ignatius*, which was composed as a result of Ignatius's "great enlightenment."

And here's another illuminating point to consider: After his great mystical experience, St. Ignatius does the opposite of St. Thomas. For, whereas Thomas *stopped* writing after his mystical experience, Ignatius in effect *begins* writing, meaning that he begins composing in earnest his *Spiritual Exercises* retreat with the goal of communicating to others the same life-changing experience of God that he himself had had. Thomas stopped writing presumably because he recognized that his systematic, logical, syllogistic style of writing couldn't adequately communicate his experience of God. Ignatius begins writing because he recognizes that a retreat *can* help communicate such an experience.

*T*WO *MISSING* *THINGS*. I've tried to make this book a kind of mix between St. Thomas's *Summa* and St. Ignatius's *Spiritual Exercises*. In other words, my goal has been to offer both theology and the experience of theology, both notional and real knowledge. But there's one thing missing, one thing that could complete the work, namely, *having our own synthesizing mystical experience that can bring everything together*. I obviously can't provide this for us. After all, this is not one of Ignatius's retreats, and even then, such an experience can only come as a gift from God. Still, I can at least try to express it for us pictorially.

Of course, looking at a picture is not the same as having a mystical experience, but a picture can help communicate the synthesizing nature of such an experience, meaning it can help bring together into one coherent whole everything we've covered. After all, "a picture is worth a thousand words." So, would you like to see the picture? Would you like to see the last 290 pages brought together onto one page? Well, before I show you, I need to tell you about a second thing that's missing. It has to do with the great principle behind St. Ignatius's whole retreat, a principle that's so great, he called it the "First Principle and Foundation."

What is the First Principle and Foundation? It's basically a summary statement of the whole Christian life, a loose expression of the Great Circle of Being. Its five short paragraphs express who we are, where we've come from, and where we should be going. It's also spiritual gasoline. I say this because for early Jesuits such as Sts. Francis Xavier, Peter Canisius, and Blessed Peter Faber, calling to mind the First Principle and Foundation was like pouring gasoline on the flames of love that already burned in their hearts. Yet, when we read it, it probably doesn't have the same effect. Go ahead and give it a read. See if it starts a raging fire in your heart:

> Man is created to praise, reverence, and serve God our Lord, and by this means to save his soul.
>
> The other things on the face of the earth are created to help him in attaining the end for which he is created.
>
> Hence, man is to make use of them in as far as they help him in the attainment of his end, and he must rid himself of them in as far as they prove a hindrance to him.
>
> Therefore, we must make ourselves indifferent to all created things, as far as we are allowed free choice and are not under any prohibition. Consequently, as far as we are concerned, we should not prefer health to sickness, riches to poverty, honor to dishonor, a long life to a short life. The same holds for all other things.
>
> Our one desire and choice should be what is more conducive to the end for which we are created.[302]

Alright, at this point, we probably don't need to call the fire department. You may be somewhat inspired, but it's likely that your heart isn't ablaze. Why not? Probably because you were not deeply formed in Ignatian spirituality and haven't made the full, 30-day *Spiritual Exercises* retreat. If you were formed in the spirituality and did make the retreat, then like those early Jesuits, you just might be burning with zeal. Let's see what's going on here. Let's see what the link is between the 30-day retreat and the First Principle and Foundation.

The full *Spiritual Exercises* retreat begins with a consideration of the First Principle and Foundation, and then the rest of the retreat is basically a series of ordered meditations that unfold it. The meditations build on one another to create one giant movement from the end for which we are created and then back to it. Indeed, it helps one to *experience* the movement of the Great Circle of Being — and what an experience! Properly made, the retreat provides an occasion for experiencing the kind of life-changing "great enlightenment" that St. Ignatius himself had. If a person has this experience, then the First Principle and Foundation suddenly becomes a powerful reminder, summary, and synthesizing expression of the experience. In other words, the First Principle and Foundation *feels differently at the end than at the beginning*. At the beginning of the retreat, it's simply a consideration of the meaning of life. At the end, it overflows with meaning and has the power to set hearts afire.

Okay, so what does this have to do with us? Actually, a lot. Did you notice that we started this book with the seeds of our own First Principle and Foundation for theology? I called it "The Three Points of Communion." At the beginning, however, I didn't summarize these three points. I just named them. Then, for the rest of the book, I've been unpacking their meaning. The whole book has simply been one long three-point meditation!

Well, now we've come to the time when we can look back on this nearly 300 page meditation and begin to see the Three Points of Communion with new eyes. We can see them as suddenly packed with meaning. Problem is, it may seem that they're too packed with meaning, too overwhelming. This is because we haven't yet provided *a summary statement* of these Three Points. We haven't yet made them into a "First Principle and Foundation." That's what we're going to do here. And when we do, the Three Points of Communion will provide us with a brief, easy-to-carry, and power-packed Principle and Foundation that summarizes *everything*. Alright, but before I give this summary, we'll first look at the grand summary picture (and my explanation of it).

So, the remainder of this conclusion will simply provide two missing things: first, the summarizing picture of the big picture and then, the *organizing* three-point summary. Put differently, we're going to try to have a synthesizing experience that can bring together everything we've learned (the picture) and then end with a First Principle and Foundation (the summary paragraphs of the Three Points).

1. Picture of the Big Picture

First, we'll look at the "picture of the big picture" and then my explanation of it. Here's the picture:

Now, I'd like to explain this picture, commenting on its different parts. (See the inside back cover for a larger, full-color version of this image.)

(a) The Trinity

Those three interlocking rings at the top of the image are meant to represent the Trinity, the source from which all creation goes forth and to which it returns (lines to the left and right, respectively). The other lines that radiate from the three rings in different directions, like the rays of the sun, represent the radiance of Trinitarian glory. Saint Ignatius seemed to envision something like this in one of his mystical experiences, which he described (in the third person) as follows:

> One time the manner in which God had created the world was revealed to his understanding with great spiritual joy. He seemed to see something white, from which some rays were coming.[303]

(b) Creation

In his *Spiritual Exercises* retreat, at the end of the very last meditation, it seems that St. Ignatius wants those who make his retreat to experience something similar to what he himself experienced in his vision of creation. For he instructs the retreatant to meditate as follows:

> [C]onsider all blessings and gifts as descending from above. Thus, my limited power comes from the supreme and infinite power above,

and so, too, justice, goodness, mercy, etc., descend from above as the rays of light descend from the sun, and as the waters flow from their fountains, etc.[304]

In the picture, the lines that go out from the left of the three rings represent many streams of life gushing forth from the Trinity at the moment of creation, like waters flowing from a great fountain and descending from above. Notice that there are many lines (streams) that go out from the Trinity. These represent the multitude of creatures that God creates. (Recall that, as we learned in Part Two, God creates such a multitude because a superabundance of creatures better reflects the divine glory.)

Now, notice the arm, hand, and finger that extend out from the left side of the Trinity. That arm is meant to represent the special creative action of God in making "the only creature on earth ... willed for its own sake,"[305] the only creature made in the very image of God, which is man. Man is represented as the finger that is being touched (created) by the arm of God. (Think of Michelangelo's fresco in the Sistine Chapel, "The Creation of Adam.")

Finally, recall that in his role as "cosmic priest," man was supposed to bring all of creation back to God with his praise and thanks. However, instead of choosing to obey God, offer creation and himself, and return back to God, man chose to be selfish. We see that happening in the next part of the picture.

(c) The Fall

Notice how the figure representing man is shaped not like a full circle but a semi-circle. This reveals that while the curve back to God is beginning (from the pointing finger around to the other hand), the hand on the right, instead of completing the circle by opening up to praise and adoration of God, curls back on itself in a selfish gesture.

Thus, tragically, man doesn't complete the circle. And in his sinful turning back on himself, he descends into a dark spiral of sin and death. That black "X" at the bottom of the spiral represents man's seemingly hopeless situation after the fall — yet it's not actually hopeless. For God himself comes to save us. (See "Redemption" and "Glorification" below.)

(d) Redemption

The figure at the foot of the Cross represents fallen humanity. (He has literally fallen to the bottom, just about as far from communion with the Trinity as possible.) The hand covering the face is meant to depict man's sorrow, shame, and spiritual blindness after the fall. (The covered face is significant, because the human face most clearly represents the image of God in man, which, here, has become obscured by sin.) Also, this figure of fallen man is not looking up at the Creator but downward, toward the stream of creatures. (All sin involves turning one's back on God and turning toward creatures.) The hole in the figure's back with the hand reaching out represents the restlessness of man's heart, which still reaches out to God, the Trinity, despite man's sinful turning toward creatures. For, man is made in God's image and cannot find satisfaction except in God.

Thus, fallen man is really a kind of split personality. One part of him turns away from God toward creatures. Another part, his heart, is always reaching out toward God, because "You made us for yourself, O God, and our hearts are restless until they rest in you."

Of course, the figure on the Cross represents Christ, the Incarnate Son, who has descended from the glory of God above down into the darkness of fallen humanity. Why does he come? Because he's on a mission to bring us (and the rest of creation) back into communion with the Trinity.[306] The stream flowing from Christ's side represents all the graces and mercies won for us by his suffering, death, and Resurrection. For instance, it's the Sacraments that forgive us and heals us. It's also the grace that meets our restless hearts and moves us to faith.

(e) Glorification

The stream of sacramental grace flowing from Christ's pierced side not only heals and forgives us, but it transforms us and gathers us into the communion of Christ's own Body, the Church, which is represented by the large figure on the right that bears Christ's wounds in the wrists. By God's grace, we thus become a glorious new  creation. Moreover, through our ongoing transformation in Christ, which includes living a mission of communion, we ascend through Christ, with Christ, and in Christ, in the unity of the Holy Spirit, back into communion with the Trinity, our final end. The open hands of the figure suggest an attitude of praise, and the three streams that go up from the hands suggest that this praise is threefold, namely, to the Father; through, with, and in Son; and by the power of the Holy Spirit.

(f) The Trinity, Again

Heaven is the Trinity: Father, Son, and Holy Spirit. So where are we? As we learned in Part Two, we share in the life of the Trinity through our transforming communion with the Son by the power of the Holy Spirit. We are sons and daughters of God in the Son! And for all eternity, we will receive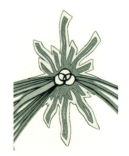

everything that we are from the Father and return his gift with our praise and thanks through Christ, with Christ, and in Christ, by the power of the Holy Spirit. As members of Christ's Body, we will be in eternal communion with the Trinity, taking part in its very action of love, provided that we believe in and follow Christ.

2. The Three Points of Communion Summary

Okay, now that we've reflected on the meaning of the picture of the big picture, I hope it has helped bring things together into a more coherent whole. All that we need now is our summary statement of everything we've covered, and then we'll be all set. Ready? Alright, but before we begin, just know that I'm keeping the statements short, so they can stay with us, and so we can easily review them. (Don't let their shortness fool you: Because of everything we've covered, each sentence is now packed with meaning.) Also, I'm keeping the statements in the voice of the first person, so they'll be more personal and real and, thus, better enrich our faith.

Point One
COMMUNION WITH THE TRINITY

I am created in the image of God, the Most Holy Trinity: Father, Son, and Holy Spirit. Therefore, my heart is restless until I enjoy eternal communion with God, which is my final end. Because I am a sinner, I try (and fail) to satisfy my restless heart with creatures rather than the Creator. All the while, God calls me to be totally for him and to return to communion with him. Yet, without his merciful help, I can do nothing and would remain forever separated from him, which is hell.

POINT TWO
TRANSFORMING COMMUNION WITH CHRIST

The Second Person of the Trinity, the eternal Son, became man, lived in the world, suffered, died, resurrected, and ascended into heaven to bring me back to communion with God. Through faith and the Sacraments, I receive the saving power of his Paschal mystery. Specifically, Jesus Christ redeems me by forgiving me of my sins and giving me the grace to avoid sin. He "glorifies" me by transforming me into his very Body, the Church. This transformation in Christ, begun in my Baptism and nourished by the Eucharist, is an ongoing process. It aims to make me fully "through Christ, with Christ, and in Christ," in the unity of the Holy Spirit, to the glory of God the Father.

POINT THREE
MISSION OF COMMUNION

Filled with gratitude for the gift of salvation and as a member of Christ's Body, I should desire with Christ, the Head of the Body, "that all may be one" in the communion of love of the Most Holy Trinity. This desire should spur me on to action, to a mission of communion, a mission of bringing others and all of creation back to God through, with, and in Jesus Christ, by the power of the Holy Spirit. I fulfill this mission as a priest, prophet, and king according to my state of life and personal vocation in Christ.

THE END? Alright, so what do you think? Did we do it? Are we all set? Are our minds and hearts filled with the Church's wisdom? Now that we've covered the two "missing things" (the Picture of the Big Picture and the Three Points of Communion Summary), I hope we can all answer, "Yes!"

But we're still not done. I mean, we now have these two great tools, but will we use them?

First, we've got a picture worth 100 thousand words, a picture that summarizes everything we've covered, but will we look at it again and again? Will we bring it into our everyday lives? Will we ponder it while making dinner or sitting on the subway? Through our times of prayer and meditation, will we impress it on our minds and hearts, so it can be something we always have with us?

Second, we've got our Three Points Summary, which is basically a modern-day First Principle and Foundation. Since we've read this whole book, the Three Points are now packed with meaning. But will we frequently refer to them, just like the Jesuit saints frequently called to mind their First Principle and Foundation? Will we let our Three Points Summary truly influence how we live and work? Will we keep the Three Points of Communion prayercard[307] where we can see it and ponder it often? If we keep the Three Points of Communion in mind, then they can keep us rooted and remind us of who we are, where we've come from, and where we're going. If we keep them in our hearts, then they can influence how we approach just about everything.

Before closing, I want to emphasize that while we now have what we need to bring together all that we've learned, we can always go deeper. After all, just as our transformation in Christ is a lifelong process so also is growing in wisdom. In fact, the two go together, because, as we learned earlier, the more we make the faith our own, the more it becomes real and part of us, which makes us more fully transformed in Christ. Also, the more we know God, the more we can love him, for knowledge and love go together.

So, keep learning about the faith. Keep enriching your faith. And keep up the good work! The effort you've made to read this book has given you a whole skeletal structure of theology. Well, now I invite you to go deeper. Appendix One, "The Great Oyster," will help you do just that, so I encourage you to read it. Also, keep an eye out for a forthcoming group-study program that will help deepen your understanding of this book while building communion with others. In the meantime, may the Lord bless you and give you a superabundance of his wisdom. I ask this in the name of the Father, and of the Son, and of the Holy Spirit. Amen.

APPENDIX ONE

The Great Oyster

Pearl divers brim with joy when, on opening an oyster, they find a little white prize. Their joy doubles when, on very rare occasions, one oyster yields two pearls. Now, imagine if there were an oyster that contained *hundreds* of pearls. That'd be a truly great oyster.

Throughout this book, we've been doing two things. First, we've been following a golden thread of the Church's wisdom, the super-concept of *communio*. Second, we've been reading pearls of wisdom from wise theologians whose quotes are scattered throughout. Put these things together, and we've got a beautiful treasure: dozens of pearls of wisdom hanging on the golden thread of *communio*. If we look more closely, though, we'll see that this golden thread is a very long one, meaning there's room for a lot more pearls. So, where can we find more pearls to add to it? Showing us where we can find them is what this appendix is all about. Let's see how it works.

*H*OW THIS APPENDIX WORKS. In this appendix, I'd like to recommend the book or books for each section of *The 'One Thing' Is Three* that contain many pearls of wisdom. Occasionally, I'll point out a book that deserves the honorary title, "The Great Oyster," meaning it overflows with a superabundance of pearls of wisdom on a given topic. Actually, I may recommend more than just books. Sometimes a CD, film, or a piece of art may be "The Great Oyster" for a given section. After all, art has a way of wordlessly conveying wisdom, and lots of it. So, even an artistic work can win the title, "The Great Oyster."

Before we begin, I want to say something about my recommendations. Each one will be ranked according to two rating systems. The first one is what I call the "Pearl-of-Wisdom (POW) Scale," which measures how many pearls of wisdom a given book has. This rating system runs on a scale of 1 to 5 pearls. So, for example, if I give a book one pearl (⬤◯◯◯◯), then, in my opinion, it has only one or a few great pearls of wisdom. If I give a book five pearls (⬤⬤⬤⬤⬤), then, in my opinion, the book is filled to the brim with wisdom. Every now and then, I'll point out "The Great Oyster" for a given category, meaning that this particular book totally overflows with pearls of wisdom.

The second rating system is what I call the "Level-of-Difficulty (LOD) Scale," which measures how difficult a given book is. This rating system runs on a scale of 1 to 10. So, for example, if I give a book a "1," then even little kids can understand it. On the other hand, if I give a book a "10," then it's the kind of book that only the Pasta Priest can understand, and I've included it only because I had help grasping its meaning.

*T*HE TOP THREE "*GREAT OYSTERS.*" Now, before we begin, I should mention that, of course, the *Greatest* Oyster is the Bible, which is the inspired Word of God, and it should be our daily companion. I recommend the Catholic edition of the Revised Standard Version (RSV) translation, which is one of the most faithful to the original languages. The *Second Greatest* Oyster is the *Catechism of the Catholic Church*, which contains the official teaching of the Church on just about everything. Because of this, under the different categories of this appendix, my first recommendation will always be the relevant sections of the *Catechism*.[308] The *Third Greatest* Oyster is, arguably, the *Summa Theologiae of St. Thomas Aquinas.* So, under the different categories, I will frequently recommend the relevant sections of the *Summa*. Because I'll be including such recommendations, I should say a bit more on this point.

The *Summa Theologiae* can be a daunting and difficult work. It's daunting because of its sheer size: four massive volumes. It's difficult because of its technical, syllogistic language, which takes some getting used to. Moreover, the way it's divided can seem confusing at first, but it doesn't take long to figure out. The whole work is divided into three parts — though, practically speaking, it's really four parts, because the Second Part is divided into two. So it's like this: I, I-II, II-II, and III. Each Part is divided into Treatises on specific theological topics such as "The One God," "The Creation," "On Man," and their related subtopics. Finally, the Treatises are made up of different Questions, which are further divided into Articles. So, one typically sees references to the *Summa* cited as follows: Part, Question, Article (for example, I-II, q. 1, a. 2).

As I mentioned in Part Two, the key to appreciating the *Summa* is its overall organizational structure, which is the Great Circle of Being, the great exit and return of all creatures going forth from God and returning to God. I found a diagram and chart that are particularly helpful for navigating the *Summa*, which is more of a reference book than something you'll want to read all the way through. I'm going to provide these two tools below: (a) the exit-return diagram of the Summa, and (b) the chart that shows the organization of all the treatises and the numeration of the questions for all three parts. Finally, to help you better appreciate the *Summa*, I'm gong to begin my book recommendations with a section called "*Summa* Summaries." This section will highlight the best books on the *Summa* that helped me to eventually dive in and come up with lots of pearls. Anyway, to begin, here's the diagram and chart followed by the "*Summa* Summaries."

(a) The exit-return diagram of the *Summa*[309]

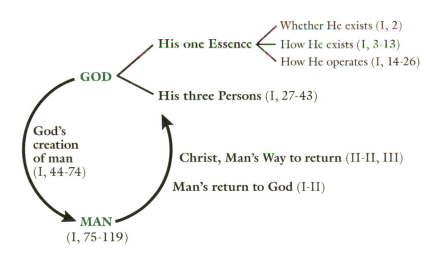

(b) Organizational chart of the Summa[310]

QUESTION

Sacred Doctrine. What it is and to what it extends.
All things are treated in it under the idea of God, either because they are God Himself or because they have some relation to God.......... 1. Sacred doctrine.......... 1

PART 1

1. GOD (Threefold consideration)

1st Concerning things that pertain to the divine essence..........
- 2. The one God.......... 2-26

2nd Concerning things that pertain to the distinction of Persons..........
- 3. The Most Holy Trinity.......... 27-43

3rd Concerning those things that pertain to the PRODUCTION of CREATURES by GOD

  1st The PRODUCTION of CREATURES..........
- 4. The creation.......... 44-46

  2nd The DISTINCTION of CREATURES

    1st The distinction of things *in general*..........
- 5. The distinction of things in general.......... 47

      (a) The distinction of *good and evil*..........
- 6. The distinction of good and evil.......... 48-49

    2nd The distinction of things *in particular*

      (b) The distinction of *corporeal and spiritual creatures*
- 1st The *creature* purely *spiritual.* — 7. The angels.......... 50-64
- 2nd The *creature* purely *corporeal.* — 8. The creature purely corporeal 65-74
- 3rd The *creature composed of body and spirit,* i.e., *man.* — 9. On man.......... 75-102

  3rd The PRESERVATION and GOVERNMENT of CREATURES.......... 10. The conservation and government of creatures...... 103-119

PART 2

Ia 2ae

2. The ADVANCE of the RATIONAL CREATURE to GOD. (Twofold consideration) Those things should be considered by means of which man attains to or deviates from his end, i.e., HUMAN ACTS.

THE END OF MAN.......... 11. The end of man and beatitude 1-5

1st The ACTS THEMSELVES.

Some acts are peculiar to man; some are common to man and other living creatures; and since beatitude is the peculiar good of man inasmuch as he is rational, the acts that are peculiar to him have a more intimate connection with that good than those that are common to man and living creatures.

  (a) Acts that are PECULIAR to MAN.......... 12. Human acts.......... 6-21
  (b) Acts that are COMMON to MAN and other ANIMALS.......... 13. The passions.......... 22-48

2nd The PRINCIPLES of ACTS.

  (a) INTRINSIC PRINCIPLES

The intrinsic principles are POWERS of the soul and HABITS; but powers have already been treated in the 1st part. Therefore, now the consideration of HABITS:

    1st HABITS in GENERAL.......... 14. Habits in general.......... 49-54

    2nd HABITS in PARTICULAR
- *Good* habits, i.e., virtues — 15. The virtues.......... 55-70
- *Evil* habits, i.e., vices. — 16. On vices and sins.......... 71-89

  (b) EXTRINSIC PRINCIPLES

The extrinsic principle of GOOD is GOD, who instructs man by His *law* and helps and moves man by *grace.* The external principle of EVIL is the DEVIL. But he was treated in the 1st part; therefore it remains to treat of:
- 1st LAWS.......... 17. On laws.......... 90-108
- 2nd GRACE.......... 18. On grace.......... 109-114

Summa Summaries

~ The Great Oyster ~

Title: *Thomas Aquinas: Spiritual Master (Vol. 2)*

Author: Fr. Jean-Pierre Torrell, OP

Rating: POW = ●●●●●
              LOD = 8

Description: Best summary tour of the *Summa* I've ever read.
              While it's not for beginners, it's full of wisdom.
              Treats the *Summa* as a spirituality. (422 pages.)

Title: *Tour of the Summa*

Author: Msgr. Paul Glenn

Rating: POW = ●●●●●
              LOD = 7.5

Description: Offers a complete, chapter-by-chapter restate-
              ment of the entire *Summa* that's brief enough
              to fit into one volume. (466 pages.)
                     For a more advanced tour of the *Summa*, see
              Walter Farrell, OP's *Companion to the Summa*.
                     Available Online ...
              Glenn:
              www.catholictheology.info/summa-theologica/index.php
              Farrell:
              www.catholicprimer.org/farrell/compfram.htm

Title: *Knowing the Love of Christ:*
              An Introduction to the Theology of
              St. Thomas Aquinas

Author: Michael Dauphinais and Matthew Levering

Rating: POW = ●●●○○
              LOD = 5.5

Description: This is the best short introduction to the *Summa*
              and St. Thomas's theology I've read. (146 pages.)

INTRODUCTION

Going Deeper with Scripture

Catechism: "Sacred Scripture," nn. 100-133.

～ The Great Oyster ～

Title: *The Gospel According to John* (CD)

Author: Leonardo Defilippis

Rating: POW = ●●●●●
                LOD = 4-10

Description: This audio CD contains the entire Gospel of John
                in a dramatic presentation that's accompanied by
                what, in my opinion, is one of the most beautiful
                pieces of music ever composed, Rachmaninov's
                Vespers. I've happily listened to this CD more than
                70 times, especially the Farewell Discourse.

                I also recommend the excellent *Truth and
                Life Dramatized Audio Bible* available as a CD set
                or an iTunes download.

Title: *The Ignatius Catholic Study Bible: New Testament*

Author: Scott Hahn and Curtis Mitch

Rating: POW = ●●●●●
                LOD = 4-10

Description: In my opinion, this is the best Catholic study Bible
                and the best translation — the Revised Standard
                Version (RSV), Catholic edition. (Presently, only
                the New Testament is available.)

Title: *Jesus of Nazareth* Trilogy

Author: Pope Benedict XVI

Rating: POW = ●●●●●
                LOD = 8

Description: Pope Benedict's reflections on the mysteries of the
                 life of Christ in three volumes. Not always easy
                 reading, but it's filled with the highest wisdom.
                 For an easier to understand version of Christ's
                 life, I highly recommend Fulton Sheen's *Life of
                 Christ* and Mel Gibson's film *The Passion of the
                 Christ*. Romano Guardini's *The Lord* is also good,
                 but it's not as easy to understand as Sheen's book.

Title: *A Father Who Keeps His Promises:*
                 God's Covenant Love in Scripture

Author: Scott Hahn

Rating: POW = ●●●●○
                 LOD = 5

Description: This 293-page summary of all of salvation history
                 is the best "big picture" approach to Sacred Scrip-
                 ture I've ever read. *The Great Adventure* Catholic
                 Bible study by Jeff Cavins is also excellent.

Title: *The Consuming Fire:*
                 A Christian Introduction to the Old Testament

Author: Michael Duggan

Rating: POW = ●●●●○
                 LOD = 7

Description: This goes more deeply into the Old Testament
                 than does *A Father Who Keeps His Promises*. It
                 summarizes the different books of the Old Testa-
                 ment and is geared toward Theology students.

Companions to the *Catechism*

Title: *Living the Catechism of the Catholic Church*

Author: Cardinal Christoph Schönborn

Rating: POW = ●●●●○
                 LOD = 5.5

Description: From the editor of the *Catechism* come these four
              short volumes of brief yet profound reflections on
              the four parts of the *Catechism*. For those who
              want to go deeper with the *Catechism*, these
              volumes are particularly insightful companions.

Title: *Catholicism* (10-part DVD series)

Author: Fr. Robert Barron

Rating: POW = ●●●○○
              LOD = 2-3

Description: A stunning video tour of our Catholic faith by a
              wise and articulate priest. If I were giving Great
              Oysters for beauty, this would get it.

Title: *Catholic Christianity:*
              A Complete Catechism of Catholic Beliefs
              Based on the Catechism of the Catholic Church

Author: Peter Kreeft

Rating: POW = ●●●●○
              LOD = 4-5

Description: Peter Kreeft makes the faith easy to understand
              without sacrificing profundity. This is his com-
              mentary on the *Catechism*. (426 pages.)

Title: *YOUCAT*

Author: Cardinal Christoph Schönborn (editor)

Rating: POW = ●●●●○
              LOD = 4

Description: Written for adolescents and young adults, this
              book is a contemporary expression of the Catholic
              faith that's keyed to the *Catechism of the Catholic
              Church* for easy cross-referencing. Filled with vivid
              photos, question-and-answers, and quotes from
              saints and others in the margins. (300 pages.)

POINT ONE
COMMUNION WITH THE TRINITY

On the Trinity

Catechism: nn. 232-267.

Summa: Part I, Questions 27-43.

∾ The Great Oyster ∾

Title: "Holy Trinity" (Icon)

Artist: Andrei Rublev

Rating: POW = ⬤⬤⬤⬤⬤
             LOD = 1-10

Description: All the experts agree that this is the greatest icon
             in the world in terms of its beauty, symbolic
             richness, and power for theological synthesis. For
             a profound and detailed explanation, see Gabriel
             Bunge's book, *The Rublev Trinity: The Icon of the
             Trinity by the Monk-painter Andrei Rublev.* (120
             pages.) For a brief explanation, visit:
             www.wellsprings.org.uk/rublevs_icon/rublev.htm

Title: *The Trinity:
             An Introduction to Catholic Doctrine on
             the Trinity*

Author: Fr. Gilles Emery, OP

Rating: POW = ⬤⬤⬤◯◯
             LOD = 7.5

Description: This is the best scholarly introduction to the Trinity
             I've ever read. It's not an easy read, but it's not an
             easy subject. Having said this, the author writes
             clearly and presents the topic in a digestible format.
             Written from a Thomistic perspective. (203 pages.)

Title: *Contemplating the Trinity:*
                The Path to the Abundant Christian Life

Author: Fr. Raniero Cantalamessa, OFM Cap.

Rating: POW = ●●○○○
                LOD = 5

Description: A brief, readable, and rich reflection on the Most
                Holy Trinity by a prominent preacher. (124 pages.)

On Sin

Catechism: "The Fall," nn. 385-421.
                "Sin," nn. 1846-1876.

Summa: Part I-II, Questions 71-89.

Title: *The Concept of Sin*

Author: Josef Pieper

Rating: POW = ●●●○○
                LOD = 7.5

Description: A thorough treatment of the concept of sin by one
                of Pope Benedict XVI's favorite philosopher-
                theologians. Not an easy read for non-theologians,
                but the writing style and translation by Fr. Edward
                T. Oakes, SJ, is very clear. (116 pages.)

Title: *The Screwtape Letters*

Author: C.S. Lewis

Rating: POW = ●●○○○
                LOD = 4-5

Description: This spiritual classic is written as an exchange of
                letters between two demons and provides amaz-
                ingly perceptive insights into temptation, sin, and
                the strategy of the enemy of our salvation. (209
                pages.) I also recommend Lewis's book *The Great
                Divorce*, which covers similar themes.

On the Angels

Catechism: "The Angels,"   nn. 328-336.

Summa: Part I, Questions 50-64.

Title: *The Angels and Their Mission*
Author: Cardinal Jean Daniélou
Rating: POW = ●●○○○
                LOD = 6.5

Description: A Biblical treatment of the role of the angels in man's salvation that also draws heavily from the teachings of the Fathers of the Church. Written by a key theologian of 20th century Catholic theology, this book is widely regarded as one of the best books on angelology. (144 pages.)

Title: *Angels and Demons:*
                What Do We Really Know About Them?
Author: Peter Kreeft
Rating: POW = ●●○○○
                LOD = 4-5

Description: Written in Kreeft's popular style, this book answers 100 questions about the angels, for example: What do angels do all day? How do angels communicate with each other? How do they move? Why do people often arrange angels into nine levels or "choirs"? How many angels are there? How do angels affect our minds? What difference do guardian angels make? What can demons do? How did angels fall and become demons? Can demons possess cats? What about computers? (157 pages.)

POINT TWO

TRANSFORMING COMMUNION
WITH CHRIST

On Creation ("The Journey Out")

Catechism:	nn. 279-384.

Summa:	Part I, Questions 44-46.

Title:	"The Creation of Adam" (Sistine Chapel, Vatican)
Artist:	Michelangelo
Rating:	POW = ●●●●○ LOD = 1-8
Description:	The most famous artistic depiction of creation.

On Faith

⌇ The Great Oyster ⌇

Catechism:	"'I Believe'—'We Believe,'" nn. 26-184.
Description:	This masterful opening to the *Catechism* not only explains what faith is but provides the context of faith. The progression of the three chapters is brilliant: (1) Man's Capacity for God; (2) God Comes to Meet Man; (3) Man's Response to God. Faith itself only appears in chapter three, but the previous chapters help us fully appreciate what it means that faith is "man's response to God." (See also nn. 1814-1816.)

Summa:	Part II-II, Questions 1-16.

∾ The Great Oyster ∾

Title: *Parochial and Plain Sermons*

Author: Cardinal John Henry Newman

Rating: POW = 🟢🟢🟢🟢🟢
               LOD = 7

Description: As I say in the text, Newman's sermons are "so many power-packed presentations communicating *real* knowledge. In each sermon, he covers one thing, one familiar topic, one single, theological point. And what wonders he works with a single point! Being one of the best prose writers in the English language, he unpacks his topic using all his marvelous powers of persuasion, rhetoric, and communication. When you read Newman's sermons, you actually experience the faith." (All the sermon texts are available online from www.thenewmanreader.org.)

On the Sacraments

Catechism: Part Two:
                The Celebration of the Christian Mystery

Summa: Part III, Questions 60-68.

Title: *Living the Sacraments: Grace into Action*

Author: Bert Ghezzi

Rating: POW = 🟢🟢🟡🟡🟡
                LOD = 4-5

Description: Written in an accessible and personal style, this book covers all seven Sacraments. The author draws upon his own experience, Sacred Scripture, the writings of the saints, and the *Catechism* to give a fresh look at the meaning of the Sacraments and how to live them. (176 pages.)

On the Eucharist

Catechism:	nn. 1322-1419.

Summa:	Part III, Questions 73-83.

Title:	Encyclical Letter, *Ecclesia de Eucharistia*
Author:	Pope John Paul II
Rating:	POW = ●●●○○
	LOD = 6-7
Description:	Pope John Paul II's encyclical letter on the Eucharist and its relationship to the Church.

Title:	*The Lamb's Supper: The Mass as Heaven on Earth*
Author:	Scott Hahn
Rating:	POW = ●●●○○
	LOD = 5-6
Description:	A profound and easy-to-read commentary on the Book of Revelation and the Mass. (174 pages.)

Title:	*Jesus and the Jewish Roots of the Eucharist*
Author:	Brant Pitre
Rating:	POW = ●●●○○
	LOD = 7
Description:	An excellent and inspiring description of the Old Testament roots of our belief in the Eucharist. (240 pages.)

Title:	*7 Secrets of the Eucharist*
Author:	Vinny Flynn
Rating:	POW = ●●●○○
	LOD = 5
Description:	An easy-to-read book built on seven pearls of wisdom regarding the Eucharistic mystery. (130 pages.)

Divine Mercy

～ The Great Oyster ～

Title: *Diary of St. Maria Faustina Kowalska:*
                Divine Mercy in My Soul

Author: St. Faustina Kowalska

Rating: POW = ●●●●●
                LOD = 4-5

Description: The testimony of one of the most important saints
                and mystics of modern times to the power and
                greatness of God's mercy. I often hear people say
                about this book, "After Sacred Scripture, nothing
                has nourished my soul more." (700 pages.)

                Read *Consoling the Heart of Jesus* if you want
                a distillation of the spirituality of St. Faustina (and
                St. Thérèse). It includes an appendix of important
                quotes from the *Diary*. Also, see "Appendix Two:
                Divine Mercy 101," found in this book.

Title: *Story of A Soul:*
                The Autobiography of St. Thérèse of Lisieux

Author: St. Thérèse of Lisieux

Rating: POW = ●●●●●
                LOD = 4-5

Description: The testimony of a Doctor of the Church and
                one of the most important saints of modern
                times to the power and greatness of God's
                mercy. I recommend the translation by John
                Clarke, OCD. (306 pages.) Read *I Believe in*
                Love by Jean C.J. d'Elbée for a marvelous distil-
                lation of Thérèse's teaching.

Title: Encyclical Letter, *Dives in Misericordia*
                    (*Rich in Mercy*)

Author: Pope John Paul II

Rating: POW = ●●●●◐
               LOD = 6-7

Description: A masterful teaching on God's mercy revealed in
               Sacred Scripture. (Available online.)

POINT THREE

MISSION OF COMMUNION

On the Church

Catechism: Part One, Article 9:
               "I Believe in the Holy Catholic Church"

Title: *The Splendor of the Church*

Author: Henri de Lubac

Rating: POW = ●●●●◐
               LOD = 7

Description: One of the great works on the Church by a pre-
               eminent theologian of the 20th century. Written as
               a personal testimony of love for the Church, its
               insights contributed to the Vatican II's Dogmatic
               Constitution on the Church, *Lumen Gentium*,
               which I also recommend. (384 pages.) *The Spirit
               of Catholicism* by Karl Adam is another classic work
               on the Church that's worth reading. (260 pages.)

Title: *Loving the Church*
Author: Cardinal Christoph Schönborn

Rating: POW = ●●●◐◐
               LOD = 5.5

Description: A Lenten retreat preached to Pope John Paul II
               by the editor of the *Catechism*. Draws from
               Scripture, the *Catechism*, and the lives of the
               Saints to bring the reader to a deeper love for the
               Church. Accessible and enjoyable. (218 pages.)

On the Three States of Life

Catechism: Christ's Faithful:
              Hierarchy, Laity, Consecrated Life, nn. 871-945.

Title: Post-Synodal Apostolic Exhortations:
              • *Pastores Dabo Vobis* (*I Will Give You Shepherds*)
              • *Vita Consecrata* (*Consecrated Life*)
              • *Christifideles Laici* (*The Lay Christian Faithful*)

Author: Pope John Paul II

Rating: POW = ●●●●○
              LOD = 6.5

Description: The most authoritative documents on the priest-
              hood, consecrated life, and laity after the Second
              Vatican Council. (Available online.)

On Defending the Faith (Apologetics)

∿ The Great Oyster ∿

Title: *The Handbook of Christian Apologetics:*
              Reasoned Answers to Questions of Faith

Author: Peter Kreeft and Fr. Ronald Tacelli, SJ

Rating: POW = ●●●●●
              LOD = 5-6

Description: From the introduction: "Outlines and summarizes
              all the major arguments for all the major Christian
              teachings that are challenged by unbelievers today
              — such as the existence of God, the immortality of
              the soul, the trustworthiness of Scripture, the
              divinity and Resurrection of Christ — and answers
              the strongest and commonest objections against
              these doctrines." (494 pages.)

Title: *Mere Christianity*

Author: C.S. Lewis

Rating: POW = ●●●●◐
                  LOD = 6

Description: This modern classic is one of the best expressions
                  of the central beliefs of Christians. Not only has it
                  helped convert many atheists and agnostics to
                  Christianity, but it has also strengthened the faith
                  of countless believers. (352 pages.)

Title: *Christianity for Modern Pagans:*
                  Pascal's Pensées, Edited, Outlined, and Explained

Author: Peter Kreeft

Rating: POW = ●●●●◐
                  LOD = 5-6

Description: A commentary by one of the best modern
                  apologists on the great work of the first modern
                  apologist. I read Pascal's *Pensées* in high school,
                  and it changed my life. This book beautifully
                  presents and highlights Pascal's life-changing
                  wisdom. (341 pages.)

Title: *Rome Sweet Home: Our Journey to Catholicism*

Author: Scott and Kimberly Hahn

Rating: POW = ●●●◐◐
                  LOD = 4-5

Description: This huge bestseller has lead to the conversion of
                  many Protestants to Catholicism and has enkindled
                  greater zeal for the faith in innumerable Catholics.
                  I recommend it as an introduction to Catholic
                  Apologetics. (210 pages.)
                       For a detailed list of apologetics topics and
                  resources, see Hahn's website:
                  www.scotthahn.com/apologetics-topics.html

On Other Religions

Title:	*The World's Religions*
Author:	Huston Smith
Rating:	POW = ●●●○○
	LOD = 6
Description:	Widely regarded as the best book on comparative religions, it gives a fair and accurate account of all the major religions of the world. (399 pages.)

On the Culture War

Title:	Encyclical Letter, *Evangelium Vitae* (*The Gospel of Life*)
Author:	Pope John Paul II
Rating:	POW = ●●●●○
	LOD = 6
Description:	John Paul's masterpiece on building the culture of life in the midst of a culture of death. (Available online.)

Title:	*How to Win the Culture War: A Christian Battle Plan for a Society in Crisis*
Author:	Peter Kreeft
Rating:	POW = ●●○○○
	LOD = 4
Description:	A brief, popular treatment of the culture wars. (120 pages.)

Title:	*Man and Woman He Created Them: A Theology of the Body*
Author:	Pope John Paul II (translated by Michael Waldstein)
Rating:	POW = ●●●●●
	LOD = 8-9

Description: The Theology of the Body is perhaps Pope John Paul II's most important teaching. It's his answer to the "sexual revolution" and explains man's destiny and meaning. While it's incredibly rich, it's also very difficult. You might want to begin reading one of the many popularizations of the Theology of the Body. (768 pages.)

On Baptizing the Imagination

Title: *Letter to Artists*

Author: Pope John Paul II

Rating: POW = ●●○○○
              LOD = 5

Description: A relatively brief letter by Pope John Paul II "to all who are dedicated to the search for new 'epiphanies' of beauty so that through their creative work as artists they may offer these as gifts to the world." (Available online.)

Title: *The Chronicles of Narnia*

Author: C.S. Lewis

Rating: POW = ●●○○○
              LOD = 2-3

Description: Lewis's seven-volume children's classic that wraps the truth in a fictional story. (Good for adults, too.)

Title: *The Lord of the Rings*

Author: J.R.R. Tolkien

Rating: POW = ●●●○○
              LOD = 5

Description: Tolkien's three-volume masterpiece that expresses the truth in a fictional story. See also the epic *Lord of the Rings* film series directed by Peter Jackson.

Title:	*Babette's Feast* (film)
Author:	Gabriel Axel (screenplay, director)
Rating:	POW = ⬤⬤◯◯◯
	LOD = 4-5
Description:	Perhaps the best film on the power of Catholic Culture. The POW rating is low, because it's not exactly packed with truths. Nevertheless, the truths it does convey are masterfully expressed. (Subtitled.)

Personalism

∽ The Great Oyster ∽

Title:	*The Selfhood of the Human Person*
Author:	John F. Crosby
Rating:	POW = ⬤⬤⬤⬤⬤
	LOD = 8-9
Description:	This book explores the mystery of the human person in his uniqueness and dignity. Crosby writes with a clear and understandable style, but if you're not a student of philosophy, it's a difficult read. (313 pages.) See also Crosby's *Personalist Papers* in which he continues the project he begins in *Selfhood*.

Title:	*Person and Being*
Author:	Fr. W. Norris Clarke, SJ
Rating:	POW = ⬤⬤⬤⬤◯
	LOD = 8-9
Description:	This marvelous little book explores the mystery of the human person within St. Thomas's metaphysics. Fr. Clarke writes with a clear and understandable style, but if you're not a student of philosophy, it's a difficult read. (121 pages.)

I also recommend his textbook on metaphysics, *The One and The Many: A Contemporary Thomistic Metaphysics*, which is clearly written but not so easy for those who are unfamiliar with philosophy. (324 pages.)

Title: *The Art of Living*

Author: Dietrich and Alice von Hildebrand

Rating: POW = ⬤⬤⬤◯◯
LOD = 7

Description: While not being a book on "personalism" *per se*, this is a good introduction to the thought of a great personalist philosopher. (139 pages.) I also recommend his book *The Heart: An Analysis of Human and Divine Affectivity.* (160 pages.)

Title: *The Weight of Glory*

Author: C.S. Lewis

Rating   POW = ⬤◯◯◯◯
LOD = 5

Description: This little essay receives only one pearl, because it's so short and only covers one main point. That point is the dignity of the human person in light of our divine calling, and it's memorably expressed by one of Christianity's greatest apologists. (Available online.)

On the Meaning of Suffering

∾ The Great Oyster ∾

Title: Apostolic Exhortation, *Salvifici Doloris*
(*On the Christian Meaning of Human Suffering*)

Author: Pope John Paul II

Rating: POW = ⬤⬤⬤⬤⬤
LOD = 6.5

Description: John Paul's masterpiece on the Christian meaning of human suffering. This is the shortest work to win the title, "The Great Oyster," which means it's fully packed with wisdom on a difficult subject. (Available online.)

Title: *Arise from Darkness:*
              When Life Doesn't Make Sense

Author: Fr. Benedict Groeschel, CFR

Rating: POW = ●●●○○
              LOD = 5

Description: Drawing on years of experience as a priest and psychologist, Fr. Groeschel offers help and guidance for those troubled or weighed down by life and those struggling with "fear, anxiety, grief, loss of loved ones, hurt, anger or anything that makes life difficult and dark." Full of practical suggestions on how to keep going and growing through such times, with God's help. (184 pages.)

              Also, see Father's book *The Tears of God: Persevering in the Face of Great Sorrow or Catastrophe*, which is geared for those going through extraordinary suffering. (107 pages.)

Title: *Making Sense Out of Suffering*

Author: Peter Kreeft

Rating: POW = ●●●●○
              LOD = 5.5

Description: A more philosophical and popular approach to the question of the meaning of suffering that includes the Christian answer. (184 pages.)

CONCLUSION

On Ignatian Spirituality

∾ The Great Oyster ∾

Title: *The Spiritual Exercises of St. Ignatius of Loyola*

Author: St. Ignatius of Loyola

Rating: POW = ●●●●●●
              LOD = 1-10

Description: This book is not supposed to be read, except by
              the director of an Ignatian retreat. It's supposed
              to be experienced. Therefore, this recommenda-
              tion is to make an Ignatian retreat. It's not always
              easy (or affordable) to make the full retreat of 30
              days or a directed retreat in one's daily life (3-6
              months), so I also recommend the "do-it-your-
              self" version that follows.

Title: *Retreat with the Lord:*
              A Popular Guide to the Spiritual Exercises of
              Ignatius of Loyola

Author: Fr. John A. Hardon, SJ

Rating: POW = ●●○○○○
              LOD = 6

Description: This book will help you make the *Spiritual
              Exercises* in your daily life or at a retreat house.
              It's not as powerful as a directed retreat, but it
              gives one a taste of Ignatius's famous retreat
              from a popular Jesuit retreat master. (225 pages.)
              Another popular version is called *A Do-It-at-
              Home-Retreat: The Spiritual Exercises of St. Ignatius
              of Loyola* by André Ravier, SJ. (235 pages.)

Title: *All My Liberty: Theology of the Spiritual Exercises*

Author: Fr. John A. Hardon, SJ

Rating: POW = ●●●○○
                 LOD = 6

Description: This book provides a theological assessment and
                 explanation of the *Spiritual Exercises*. (201 pages.)
                 For a more advanced theology of Ignatian Spir-
                 ituality, see the work by Fr. Joseph de Guibert, SJ,
                 The Jesuits: Their Spiritual Doctrine and Practice.
                 (692 pages.) For clear, easy-to-understand, and
                 faithful treatments of specific aspects of Ignatian
                 Spirituality, see the many excellent books by Fr.
                 Timothy Gallagher, OMV. Finally, for an amazing
                 story of a modern day Jesuit, read *He Leadeth Me*
                 by Fr. Walter Ciszek, SJ. (202 pages.)

Be a Pearl Diver

There are many more great Catholic books, filled with pearls of
wisdom, sitting on the shelves of Catholic bookstores, waiting
for you to discover them. Check your local listings, and visit the
one that's closest to you. Not only will you be supporting a
Catholic apostolate for the new evangelization, but you'll also
be able to browse and discover unfamiliar books in a way that's
impossible to do on the Internet. There's nothing like walking
among the book displays, having a cover catch your eye, picking
up the book, flipping through its pages, and randomly diving in
here and there in search of hidden pearls.

Appendix Two

Divine Mercy 101

JESUS I TRUST IN YOU

Just as *The 'One Thing' Is Three* is a crash course in theology, so this appendix is a crash course in Divine Mercy. Think of it as "Divine Mercy 101." And while this crash course certainly can't tell us everything there is to know about the Divine Mercy message and devotion, it does give a substantial summary of the essentials. Before we get to "the message and devotion" part, let's start with Divine Mercy in general.

*D*IVINE MERCY IN GENERAL. Divine Mercy gets to the heart of Sacred Scripture. In fact, as the *Catechism of the Catholic Church* teaches, "The Gospel is the revelation in Jesus Christ of God's mercy to sinners."[311] Right there: That summarizes it. Divine Mercy is the Gospel. It's the good news. And so, it gets to the very center of our faith. Moreover, in the words of Pope Benedict XVI, "Divine Mercy is not a secondary devotion, but an integral dimension of Christian faith and prayer."[312] Benedict even goes so far as to say, "[M]ercy is the central nucleus of the Gospel message."[313]

Okay, so what is Divine Mercy? What is this thing that gets to the heart of Sacred Scripture and to the very center of our faith? To begin, mercy is "love's second name."[314] It's a particular kind of love, a particular mode of love when it encounters suffering, poverty, brokenness, and sin. *Divine* Mercy is when God's love meets us and helps us in the midst of our suffering and sin. In fact, because this side of eternity we're all sinners and because suffering is our lot in life, God's love for us here always takes the form of mercy. It's always the Lord stepping out in compassion to help us poor, weak, and broken sinners. From our perspective, then, *every good we receive* is an expression of Divine Mercy. (See the following endnote for some of Pope John Paul II's statements on the meaning of Divine Mercy.)[315]

*T*HE MESSAGE OF DIVINE MERCY. The *message* of Divine Mercy is something that's most associated with a Polish nun who died in 1938, about a year before the start of World War II. She's known today as St. Maria Faustina Kowalska. Now, St. Faustina was a mystic. In other words, she received extraordinary experiences of the Lord Jesus in prayer. In fact, Jesus appeared to her and even spoke with her.

Of course, Jesus didn't reveal some new Gospel when he appeared to St. Faustina. I mean, he already revealed everything he needed to say 2,000 years ago to the Apostles and through Sacred Scripture. So, why did he do it? Why did he appear to Faustina? Actually, why does he appear to *any* mystic for that matter?

God sometimes appears to mystics because he has a prophetic message for a particular time in history, and he uses particular men and women to share his message. Sometimes it's to remind us of something that's been forgotten. At other times, it's a warning or a call to conversion. Still other times, it's simply a message of comfort and consolation. Whatever it is, it doesn't change the Bible. Rather, it brings us back to it at a certain period of history.

Okay, so what's the particular and important message that God wants to give to us in our modern time through St. Faustina? Simple. He wants to remind us of the heart of Sacred Scripture, namely, *his mercy for us sinners.* In fact, he's saying to us sinners, "Now is the time of mercy. Now is a time of *extraordinary* mercy! Now is a time when I want give especially great graces to the human race. I want to pour out my mercy in a big way."

Why would God say this? Why would he want to give such great graces in our time? I think St. John Paul II explained it best. First, he pointed out something we all know: namely, that there are all kinds of blessings in our contemporary society. For instance, modern technology has done so much to make life easier for us. Just think of e-mail, cell phones, smartphones, and air-conditioning. All these things are blessings. Yet, in the midst of these blessings and in some ways, because of the very same advances in technology that brought them, John Paul would say that *evil has a reach and power in our day like never before.* Indeed, our time, sadly, is marked by unprecedented evil. Despite this, John Paul would also say, "Be not afraid." Why should we not be afraid? Because of what St. Paul writes in Romans, "Where sin increased, grace abounded all the more" (5:20). In other words, God is not outdone by evil. So, in a time of great evil, God wants to give even greater graces, and in our time, the graces are *huge*, precisely because there's so much sin.

Basically, then, what I want to share in the remainder of this crash course on Divine Mercy, this Divine Mercy 101, is how we can tap into the extraordinary graces of our time. Which makes sense, right? I mean, if there are tons of graces available to us, why not gather them in?

*T*APPING INTO THE GRACES. Alright, so how do we do it? How do we get the great graces of Divine Mercy in our time? One important way to get them is to live out a devotion to Divine Mercy, and learning how to live it out is easy. All you need to know is one little word — actually, it's a little bird: finch. F-I-N-C-H. Finch. If you remember this word, you've got it. But now I've got to explain it. Okay, so let's get started with **F-I-N-C-H**,[316] beginning with "**F**."

F = Feast. What feast? The Feast of Divine Mercy, also known as Divine Mercy Sunday. Divine Mercy Sunday falls on the Second Sunday of Easter, which is my favorite day of the year. I hope that by the time I finish explaining it, it will be your favorite day also.

What's so great about Divine Mercy Sunday? Well, look at it this way: What's the most important feast day of the year? Easter, right? And how many days is Easter? We celebrate it for eight full days, which is why we call it the *Octave* of Easter. But the last day is the greatest of all. The eighth day. It's the climax of the whole feast. Well, Divine Mercy Sunday is the eighth day of Easter, the climax of the entire Easter celebration. In a sense, it's the most important day of the most important feast![317]

Now, Divine Mercy Sunday existed *way* before St. Faustina. In fact, it has its roots in the Easter celebrations of the early Church.[318] Well, when Jesus told Faustina that he wanted the feast celebrated, she asked some priests and theologians about it, and they told her, "There already is such a feast." So, Faustina went back to Jesus and told him, "They tell me that there already is such a feast, and so why should I talk about it?" Jesus responded, **"And who knows anything about this feast? No one!"**[319] In other words, the great feast of mercy had been forgotten and was almost completely unknown.

So, I imagine Jesus saying to Faustina, "Look, I want people to know and celebrate this feast. And to sweeten the deal, I promise to give great graces on Divine Mercy Sunday." Specifically, he told her:

On that day [Divine Mercy Sunday], **the very depths of My tender mercy are opened. I pour out a whole ocean of graces upon those souls who approach the fount of My mercy. ... On that day, all the divine floodgates through which graces flow are opened.**[320]

When I first read about these promises of grace attached to celebrating Divine Mercy Sunday, I decided to test it out. So, when the day arrived, I prayed all day long for my dad who was in need of conversion. Well, his conversion happened that very day! And 15 years later, it has still stuck. Now, of course, it doesn't always work like that, but thousands upon thousands of people attest to the super-power of prayer offered on Divine Mercy Sunday. ... But I still haven't gotten to my favorite part of Divine Mercy Sunday, what I call "the clean slate grace."

Regarding Divine Mercy Sunday, Jesus told St. Faustina, **"The soul that will go to Confession and receive Holy Communion shall obtain complete forgiveness of sins and punishment."**[321] Now, that's a big deal. It means that if we were to die right after receiving this grace, then we wouldn't have to go to purgatory! In other words, our slate is wiped clean. In fact, the theologian who was assigned by the future Pope John Paul II to investigate the question "What is the grace of Mercy Sunday?" likened the grace to *a second baptism*.[322] Of course, it's not the same as Baptism, but it is an extraordinary grace of being cleansed of sin and the punishment due to sin.

Unfortunately, a lot of people confuse the great grace of Divine Mercy Sunday with a plenary indulgence. It's not the same thing. To get a plenary indulgence, you need to do the indulgenced act, pray for the intentions of the Holy Father, go to confession (within 20 days), receive Holy Communion, and be detached from all sin.

That last one is the kicker. Are we detached from all sin? I don't know. But I once read a story that St. Philip Neri was speaking to a large crowd of people who had gathered for some Church event to receive a plenary indulgence, and the Holy Spirit told St. Philip that only two people in the whole crowd were going to receive the plenary indulgence: Philip himself and a seven-year-old boy — presumably because everyone else was attached to sin.

Now, the good news about the grace of Divine Mercy Sunday is that to receive it, you simply need to go to confession before or on the feast — the experts say that sometime during Lent suffices — be in the state of grace (no mortal sin), and receive Holy Communion with the intention of obtaining the promised grace. Of course, we should also do acts of mercy such as forgiving people, praying for others, and having the intention to be more merciful to our neighbor.

Okay, so that explains the feast. Now, let's look at the next letter, "I," as in F-I …

I = Image. What image? The Image of Divine Mercy. Jesus told St. Faustina to have an image painted just as he looked when he appeared to her. She obeyed and had it painted by a Polish artist, Eugene Kazimirowski. It took him more than 12 tries before Faustina accepted it as satisfactory.[323]

As you can see, Jesus' right hand is raised in blessing. Also, he's taking a step toward us, and two rays of light issue from his Heart: a red ray and a pale ray, representing the blood and water that gushed forth from his pierced side on the Cross. At

Jesus, I Trust in You

the bottom of the image, Jesus wanted a prayer to be written, "Jesus, I trust in you." He also promised to give great graces through it. For instance, one time, he said:

I am offering people a vessel with which they are to keep coming for graces ... that vessel is this image with the signature, Jesus, I trust in You." By means of this image, I shall be granting many graces to souls.[324]

I've met tons of people who have experienced special graces through the Divine Mercy image. One grace that comes through the image is this: It heals the way people often mistakenly view God. Here's what I mean. People too often have a false image of God. They're afraid of him and see him as some mean ogre just out to ruin their fun. Well, the Image of Divine Mercy helps to change that. In it, we discover our Merciful Savior who surely calls us to conversion but who also blesses us, loves us, and is deserving of all of our trust.

Next, we come to the letter "N," as in F-I-**N** ...

N = Novena. What novena? The Novena to Divine Mercy. A novena is basically nine days of prayer in a row. Jesus taught St. Faustina a novena that he wanted her to pray and that we can all pray. Each day, he asked that a different group of people be entrusted to him (for example, "all sinners" on day one and "all priests and religious" on day two). The words of the novena are beautiful, but we don't have time to go through them here. At the end of this crash course, I'll share with you information about where you can learn more.[325]

For now, I'd just like to answer a question that people often ask about the novena: "When should I begin?" Well, it can be prayed at any time, but a special time to pray it is in preparation for Divine Mercy Sunday. The starting date for the novena, combined with praying the Chaplet of Divine Mercy, is Good Friday, and it ends on the Saturday after Easter Sunday, the day before Divine Mercy Sunday. (Novenas typically end the day before the feast.) While you don't have to pray this novena to obtain the grace of Divine Mercy Sunday, it is a good way to prepare, and Jesus promised, **"By this novena, I will grant every possible grace to souls."**[326]

Now, we come to letter "C" as in F-I-N-**C** ...

C = Chaplet. What chaplet? The Chaplet of Divine Mercy. This is a prayer that's prayed on ordinary rosary beads, and it's pretty popular today — perhaps because it can be prayed in a short amount of time (about seven minutes).

I think another reason why the chaplet is so popular is because it's such an incredibly powerful prayer. Why is it so powerful? Because it draws its strength from the holiest and mightiest prayer there is: the Mass. In other words, the Chaplet of Divine Mercy is a kind of extension of the prayer of the Mass. In fact, it's an extension of what I call the "supercharged moment of the Mass." Here's what I mean: It's an extension of that moment when the priest at the altar takes the Body and Blood of Christ into his hands and offers it up to the Father with these words:

> Through him, and with him, and in him, O God, almighty Father, in the unity of the Holy Spirit, all glory and honor is yours forever and ever. Amen.

That's supercharged because, at the Mass, Jesus is giving himself Body, Blood, Soul, and Divinity into our hands: literally, in the hands of the priest and spiritually, in the hands of all the lay faithful who are uniting their own sacrifices to the offering of the priest at the altar. Together, each in his own way, we offer Jesus' infinite sacrifice of love to the Father. That's the power of the Mass. It's Jesus' own sacrifice of love in our hands, held up to the Father, and the Father can't resist such a perfect sacrifice of love. It really is the perfect prayer.

Now, the chaplet is an extension of that moment of the Mass, because on the "Our Father" beads of the rosary, we pray, "Eternal Father, I offer You the Body and Blood, Soul and Divinity of Your dearly beloved Son, our Lord Jesus Christ in atonement for our sins and those of the whole world." Also, notice that it's a bold prayer. We're not simply praying for our families or our comunities but "*for the whole world*"! And it can be so bold, because it relies on infinite merits: Christ's infinite sacrifice of love on the Cross. Alright, so this explains the "Our Father" beads.

On each "Hail Mary" bead, we pray, "For the sake of His sorrowful Passion, have mercy on us and on the whole world." In other words, as we're holding up to the Father his Son's infinite sacrifice of love, we keep repeating: "Mercy, mercy, mercy." More specifically, we keep praying, "Have mercy on us and on the whole world." And this is powerful. Believe me. I've seen it's power. I've heard the testimonies. And you know who it's most powerful for? The dying. Our Heavenly Father said to St. Faustina,

> **When this chaplet is said by the bedside of a dying person ... unfathomable mercy envelops the soul, and the very depths of My tender mercy are moved for the sake of the sorrowful Passion of My Son.**[327]

Also, Jesus made several comforting promises to those who pray the chaplet:

> **Say unceasingly the chaplet that I have taught you. Whoever will recite it will receive great mercy at the hour of death. ... Even if there were a sinner most hardened, if he were to recite this chaplet only once, he would receive grace from My infinite mercy.**[328]

> **The souls that say this chaplet will be embraced by My mercy during their lifetime and especially at the hour of their death.**[329]

> **Oh, what great graces I will grant to souls who say this chaplet; the very depths of My tender mercy are stirred for the sake of those who say the chaplet.**[330]

> **My daughter, encourage souls to say the chaplet which I have given to you. It pleases Me to grant everything they ask of Me by saying the chaplet. When hardened sinners say it, I will fill their souls with peace, and the hour of their death will be a happy one.**[331]

Okay, that was C for the Chaplet of Divine Mercy. To learn how to pray it, see this endnote.[332] Now, on to the last letter: "H," as in F-I-N-C-**H** ...

H = Hour. What hour? The Hour of Great Mercy. Because Jesus died on the Cross for us at 3 p.m., every day between 3-4 in the afternoon is known as the Hour of Great Mercy. During this hour, Jesus asked St. Faustina to pray the Stations of the Cross, provided her duties permitted it.[333] But he went on to say:

> **If you are not able to make the Stations of the Cross, then at least step into the chapel for a moment and adore, in the Blessed Sacrament, My Heart, which is full of mercy; and should you be unable to step into the chapel, immerse yourself in prayer there where you happen to be ... and if only for a brief moment, immerse yourself in My Passion, particularly in My abandonment at the moment of agony.**[334]

I love that. What Jesus wants above all through this devotion is that we have mercy on him![335] In other words, he wants us to recall his sacrifice of love. He wants us to think about what he did for us on the Cross. He simply wants our love. So, let's get "the three o'clock habit" and remember Jesus' sacrifice of love for us, even if only for a moment.

Oh, and one other thing about the Three O'clock Hour: Jesus promised that it's a huge time of grace: **"This is the hour of great mercy for the whole world. ... I will refuse nothing to the soul that makes a request of Me in virtue of My Passion."**[336] Thus, I look at this hour as a kind of mini-Mercy Sunday that we have *every day*. So, it's also a great time to pray for our loved ones, especially for the conversion of unrepentant sinners, and to recite the Chaplet of Divine Mercy. For a summary of the ways we can observe the Hour of Great Mercy, see this endnote.[337]

*C*ONCLUSION. Okay, so there we go: Divine Mercy 101. Now you have everything you need to know about the Divine Mercy *devotion* and how to tap into the great graces God offers us through it. Just remember FINCH, F-I-N-C-H, where F = Feast of Divine Mercy; I = Image of Divine Mercy; N = Novena of Divine Mercy; C = Chaplet of Divine Mercy; and H = Hour of Great Mercy.

During this crash course, you've also learned some of the basics of the Divine Mercy *message*. But there's a bit more I'd like to explain about how to live it. Fr. George Kosicki's teaching tool, the "A-B-C's of Mercy," will help us.

By the way, before we begin, I should mention that living the Divine Mercy message and devotion to the full presupposes that one actively participates in the Sacraments. For the Sacraments are the true sources and fountains of God's mercy.

A = Ask for mercy. In Sacred Scripture, Jesus tells us, "Ask and it will be given to you ... for everyone who asks receives" (Mt 7:7, 8). In the *Diary of St. Faustina*, Jesus reminds us of this idea:

> **Souls that make an appeal to My mercy delight Me. To such souls I grant even more graces than they ask. I cannot punish even the greatest sinner if he makes an appeal to My compassion.**[338] **[B]eg for mercy for the whole world.**[339] **No soul that has called upon My mercy has been disappointed.**[340]

B = Be merciful in deed, word, and prayer. As we learned earlier, mercy is love's second name. It's a particular kind of love, a particular mode of love when it encounters suffering, poverty, brokenness, and sin. But it's not just a movement of the heart. It's not just feeling compassion for someone. To be true, mercy must also be put into action. So, mercy is really two movements: heart and arms. The "heart" part is the movement of compassion — it's something we feel. The "arms" part is the movement to alleviate the suffering of another — it's something we do. And what should we do? Jesus tells us in the *Diary*:

I am giving you three ways of exercising mercy toward your neighbor: the first — by deed, the second — by word, the third — by prayer. In these three degrees is contained the fullness of mercy, and it is an unquestionable proof of love for Me. By this means a soul glorifies Me and pays reverence to My mercy.[341]

So, mercy in action is mercy in deed, word, and prayer. And whenever our hearts are moved to compassion, wherever we are, we can always put this compassion into action either by some deed that helps alleviate another person's suffering, by some word that comforts or assists them, or by prayer. As St. Faustina wrote: "If I cannot show mercy by deeds or words, I can always do so by prayer. My prayer reaches out even there where I cannot reach out physically."[342] Of course, one of the great prayers of mercy, as we learned earlier, is the Chaplet of Divine Mercy.

C = Completely Trust. Trust in the mercy of God gets to the heart of the message of Divine Mercy, which is why the Image of Divine Mercy has the prayer at the bottom, "Jesus, I trust in you." Now, trust does not mean that we have license to go about sinning as we please. Rather, it implies that we repent of our sins. Anyway, here are some beautiful quotes from the *Diary* that have to do with trust:

Encourage the souls with whom you come in contact to trust in My infinite mercy. Oh, how I love those souls who have complete confidence in Me — I will do everything for them.[343]

Why are you fearful and why do you tremble when you are united to Me? I am displeased when a soul yields to vain terror. Who will dare to touch you when you are with Me? Most dear to Me is the soul that strongly believes in My goodness and has

complete trust in Me. I heap My confidence upon it and give it all it asks.[344]

I desire that the whole world know My infinite mercy. I desire to grant unimaginable graces to those souls who trust in My mercy.[345]

I am Love and Mercy itself. When a soul approaches Me with trust, I fill it with such an abundance of graces that it cannot contain them within itself, but radiates them to other souls.[346]

Sooner would heaven and earth turn into nothingness than would My mercy not embrace a trusting soul.[347]

Alright, now that we know our ABC's of mercy and FINCH, we're all set to live the Divine Mercy message and devotion to the full. For more information on Divine Mercy, I invite you to visit TheDivineMercy.org. Also, if you have a smartphone, you can download the Marian's fully-loaded and free "Divine Mercy" app for Apple and Android mobile devices. For information about getting the *Diary of St. Faustina Kowalska* or other Divine Mercy resources, see the information pages at the back of this book. If you're interested in purchasing high quality, affordable canvas Divine Mercy images and prints, visit DivineMercyArt.com. Finally, to learn how you can solemnly celebrate Divine Mercy Sunday at your parish, visit CelebrateMercySunday.org. May God bless you with his mercy!

Endnotes

INTRODUCTION

[1] To St. Faustina, Jesus sometimes spoke of our modern era as a "time of mercy" (*Diary of St. Maria Faustina Kowalska: Divine Mercy in My Soul.* [Stockbridge, MA: Marian Press, 1987.], nn. 1160; 1261). As if to emphasize this point, he said to her:

> **In the Old Covenant I sent prophets wielding thunderbolts to My people. Today I am sending you with My mercy to the people of the whole world. I do not want to punish aching mankind, but I desire to heal it, pressing it to My Merciful Heart. ... Before the Day of Justice I am sending the Day of Mercy** (Ibid., 1588).

Pope John Paul II echoed this idea that ours is a time of mercy during a homily he gave in his native Poland (Błonie, Kraków) on August 18, 2002, for the occasion of the beatification of four of his countrymen. He said:

> From the beginning of her existence the Church, pointing to the mystery of the Cross and the Resurrection, has preached the mercy of God, a pledge of hope and a source of salvation for man. Nonetheless, it would appear that we today have been particularly called to proclaim this message before the world. We cannot neglect this mission, if God himself has called us to it through the testimony of Saint Faustina.
>
> God has chosen our own times for this purpose. Perhaps because the twentieth century, despite indisputable achievements in many areas, was marked in a particular way by the "mystery of iniquity." With this heritage both of good and of evil, we have entered the new millennium. New prospects of development are opening up before mankind, together with hitherto unheard of dangers. Frequently man lives as if God did not exist, and even puts himself in God's place. He claims for himself the Creator's right to interfere in the mystery of human life. He wishes to determine human life through genetic manipulation and to establish the limit of death. Rejecting divine law and moral principles, he openly attacks the family. In a variety of ways he attempts to silence the voice of God in human hearts; he wishes to make God the "great absence" in the culture and the conscience of peoples. The "mystery of iniquity" continues to mark the reality of the world.
>
> In experiencing this mystery, man lives in fear of the future, of emptiness, of suffering, of annihilation. Perhaps for this very reason, it is as if Christ, using the testimony of a lowly Sister, entered our time in order to indicate clearly the source of relief and hope found in the eternal mercy of God.
>
> The message of merciful love needs to resound forcefully anew. The world needs this love. The hour has come to bring

Christ's message to everyone: to rulers and the oppressed, to those whose humanity and dignity seem lost in the mysterium iniquitatis. The hour has come when the message of Divine Mercy is able to fill hearts with hope and to become the spark of a new civilization: the civilization of love (n. 3).

[2] See Final Report of the Extraordinary Assembly of the Synod of Bishops, II, C.1: *L'Osservatore Romano*, December 10, 1985, 7, cited in the encyclical letter of John Paul II, *Ecclesia de Eucharistia*, n. 34.

[3] Unless otherwise indicated, all Bible translations are from the Revised Standard Version (RSV), Catholic Edition.

[4] *Confessions*, Book X:27.

[5] English translation of the *Catechism of the Catholic Church: Modifications from the Editio Typica* (Washington, D.C./Vatican: United States Catholic Conference, Inc./Libreria Editrice Vaticana, 1997), n. 125.

[6] Ant. 1, Morning Prayer, Feast of St. John, Apostle and Evangelist, December 27.

[7] For instance, in the prologue to his *Commentary on the Gospel of John*, St. Thomas Aquinas writes: "Because secrets are revealed to friends ... Jesus confided his secrets in a special way to that disciple who was specially loved. ... [I]t is John who sees the light of the Incarnate Word more excellently and expresses it to us" (trans. James A. Weisheipl, OP [Albany: Magi Books, Inc., 1998]).

[8] *The Diary of St. Maria Faustina Kowalska: Divine Mercy in My Soul* (Stockbridge: Marian Press, 1987), n. 684.

[9] Benedict XVI, *Jesus of Nazareth: From the Baptism in the Jordan to the Transfiguration*, trans. Adrian J. Walker (New York: Doubleday, 2007), p. xiv.

[10] If you're wondering, "Where's the Holy Spirit in all this?" He's right there at the center of the "greatest passage." For he is the Love that proceeds from the Father and the Son, "I made known to them thy name, and I will make it known, that the *love* with which thou hast *loved* me may be in them, and I in them" (Jn 17:26). Emphasis added.

POINT ONE

COMMUNION WITH THE TRINITY

[11] *Catechism*, n. 234.

[12] Ibid., n. 221.

[13] G.K. Chesterton, *The Everlasting Man* (San Francisco: Ignatius Press, 1993), p. 17.

[14] Ibid.

[15] Plato, *The Republic and Other Works*, trans. Benjamin Jowett (New York: Doubleday, 1960), p. 208.

[16] *Catechism*, n. 261.

[17] In comparing the fruitful communion of love in the Holy Trinity to the fruitful communion of love in the human nuclear family (as does Blessed

Pope John Paul II), I want to make clear that the latter is a created analogy of and participation in the former. I emphasize this point, because what will naturally arise in the minds of some readers is this question: "If the human family is meant to mirror the divine, Trinitarian communion, then why isn't the divine triad properly understood as Father-Mother-Child rather than Father-Son-Holy Spirit?" I want to remind such readers that analogies are not the same as direct correspondence. Analogy is based on there being some likeness between two things, but it does not mean or imply that the two things are equivalent. The relationship between the Father, Son, and Holy Spirit involves begetting and love proceeding, which bears some resemblance to what goes on in marriage and family, but God's Word and the Christian Tradition do not use the language of Father, Mother, and Child to describe God in himself. So, again, we're dealing here with an analogy and not direct correspondence.

[18] *Catechism*, n. 1994.

[19] Ibid., nn. 397-398.

[20] Ibid., n. 399.

[21] Ibid., n. 400.

[22] Ibid.

[23] C.S. Lewis, *Perelandra* (London: HarperCollins, 2005), pp. 271-279.

[24] C.S. Lewis, *The Weight of Glory and Other Addresses* (New York: Macmillan Publishing, 1949), pp. 16-17.

[25] *Catechism*, n. 221.

[26] Ibid., n. 398.

[27] The divinization theme of the early Fathers of the Church is repeated in the Liturgy in many ways, for instance, on the final day of the Octave of Christmas, the Solemnity of the Mother of God, the psalms of evening prayer begin with the following antiphon: "O marvelous exchange! Man's Creator has become man, born of a virgin. We have been made sharers in the divinity of Christ who humbled himself to share in our humanity." Also, at every Mass, when the priest or deacon pours a droplet of water into the chalice containing the wine, he prays, "By the mystery of this water and wine may we come to share in the divinity of Christ who humbled himself to share in our humanity."

[28] St. Athanasius, *De Incarnatione Verbi Dei*, n. 54:3. Of course, man becomes "god" not by nature but by sheer grace. This nuance will become clearer in the next chapter.

[29] Cited in John Paul II, encyclical letter, *Evangelium Vitae*, March 25, 1995, n. 80. Also, the *Catechism* has many passages that speak to the theme of divinization. I'm grateful to Vinny Flynn for compiling this list of them for me:

> The Father's power 'raised up' Christ his Son and by doing so perfectly introduced his Son's humanity, including his body, into the Trinity (n. 648).
>
> The ultimate end of the whole divine economy is the entry of God's creatures into the perfect unity of the

Blessed Trinity. But even now we are called to be a dwelling for the Most Holy Trinity: "If a man loves me," says the Lord, "he will keep my word, and my Father will love him, and we will come to him and make our home with him" [Jn 14:23] (n. 260).

By the grace of Baptism "in the name of the Father and of the Son and of the Holy Spirit," we are called to share in the life of the Blessed Trinity (n. 265).

The Word became flesh to make us "partakers of the divine nature" [2 Pet 1:4]: "For this is why the Word became man, and the Son of God became the Son of man: so that man, by entering into communion with the Word and thus receiving divine sonship, might become a son of God" [St. Irenaeus]. "For the Son of God became man so that we might become God" [St. Athanasius]. "The only-begotten Son of God, wanting to make us sharers in his divinity, assumed our nature, so that he, made man, might make men gods" [St. Thomas Aquinas] (n. 460).

We are brethren [of Christ] not by nature, but by the gift of grace, because that adoptive filiation gains us a real share in the life of the only Son (n. 654).

"The eternal Father ... chose to raise up men to share in his own divine life," to which he calls all men in his Son (n. 759).

Those who die in God's grace and friendship and are perfectly purified life forever with Christ. They are like God forever, for they "see him as he is," face to face [1 Jn 3:2] (n. 1023).

Now that you share in God's own nature, do not return to your former base condition by sinning [St. Leo the Great] (n. 1691).

Christians participate in the life of the Risen Lord (n. 1694).

[E]ach of us is called to enter into the divine beatitude (n. 1877).

Grace is a participation in the life of God. It introduces us into the intimacy of Trinitarian life (n. 1997).

The grace of Christ is the gratuitous gift that God makes to us of his own life, infused by the Holy Spirit into our soul to heal it of sin and to sanctify it (n. 1999).

[30] *The Weight of Glory*, p. 3.
[31] Ibid., pp. 3-4.
[32] According to St. Thomas Aquinas, humans are by nature lower than the angels but higher by grace. See *Summa Theologiae*, I, q. 108, a. 8; q. 117, a. 2, 3; *Scriptum super libros sententiarum*, II, dist. ix, q. 1, a. 8.
[33] Translation from the Douay-Rheims Catholic Bible.

POINT TWO

TRANSFORMING COMMUNION WITH CHRIST

[34] See diagram on page 307, which closely resembles the one that was on my computer screen.

[35] St. Thomas Aquinas, *The Book of the Sentences*, I, dist. 14, q. 2, a. 2.

[36] W. Norris Clarke, S.J., *The One and the Many: A Contemporary Thomistic Metaphysics* (South Bend, Ind.: University of Notre Dame Press, 2001), p. 305.

[37] *Catechism*, n. 293.

[38] Ibid., n. 258.

[39] Ibid. Emphasis added.

[40] See the *Catechism*, n. 260: "The ultimate end of the whole divine economy is the *entry* of God's creatures into the perfect unity of the Blessed Trinity."

[41] *Summa Theologiae* I, q. 47, a. 2. (Unless otherwise indicated, all citations from the *Summa* are from the translation by the Fathers of the English Dominican Province.)

[42] Peter J. Kreeft, *Catholic Christianity* (San Francisco: Ignatius Press, 2001), p. 51.

[43] This citation is from the Grail Translation of the Psalms and Canticles (1963).

[44] Cited in the article by Kallistos Ware, "The Unity of the Human Person According to the Greek Fathers" in A. Peacocke, *Persons and Personality* (New York: Blackwell, 1987), p. 204.

[45] *Summa Theologiae*, III, q. 62, a. 6, trans. by Abbot Anscar Vonier in *A Key to the Doctrine of the Eucharist* (Bethesda, Md.: Zaccheus Press, 1925), p. 28.

[46] Ibid., III, q. 46, a. 2.

[47] Ibid., a. 3.

[48] Ibid. Also, St. Thomas says, "From the beginning of his conception, Christ merited our eternal salvation; but on our side there were some obstacles, whereby we were hindered from securing the effect of his preceding merits: consequently, in order to remove such hindrances, it was necessary for Christ to suffer" (*Summa* III, q. 48, a. 1, ad. 2).

[49] Roch Kereszty, O. Cist., *Jesus Christ: Fundamentals of Christology* (New York: Alba House, 1991), pp. 289-290.

[50] Romanus Cessario, OP, *The Godly Image: Christ and Salvation in Catholic Thought from Anselm to Aquinas* (Petersham, Mass.: St. Bede's Publications, 1990), p. 165.

[51] *Catechism*, n. 1085. Emphasis added.

[52] "About the Production," The Passion of the Christ, n.d., tinyurl.com/PassionMovie (accessed January 5, 2012).

[53] Ibid.

[54] See John Paul II, apostolic letter, *Rosarium Virginis Mariae*, October 18, 2002, n. 15.

[55] *Catechism*, n. 478.

[56] *A Key to the Doctrine of the Eucharist*, p. 3.

[57] Blaise Pascal, *Pensées*, trans. A. J. Krailsheimer (London: Penguin Classics, 1966), n. 277.

[58] *A Key to the Doctrine of the Eucharist*, p. 5.

[59] Ibid.

[60] *Summa Theologiae*, III, q. 62, a. 6, emphasis added. See also *De Veritate* q. 27, a. 4, which speaks to the concrete manner in which everything that the Savior did and suffered in the flesh reaches us "spiritually through faith and bodily through the sacraments, for Christ's humanity is simultaneously spirit and body in order that we might be able to receive into ourselves [we who are spirit and body] the effect of the sanctification that comes to us through Christ" (cited in Jean-Pierre Torrell, *Saint Thomas Aquinas: Spiritual Master*, trans. Robert Royal [Catholic University of America Press, 1996], p. 139).

[61] *Catechism*, n. 1131.

[62] Ibid., n. 1127. Emphasis added.

[63] Colman E. O'Neill, OP, *Meeting Christ in the Sacraments*, ed. Romanus Cessario, OP (New York: Alba House, 1991), p. 66.

[64] Ibid., pp. 55-56.

[65] Ibid., p. 58.

[66] John Paul II, encyclical letter, *Ecclesia de Eucharistia*, April 17, 2003, n. 5.

[67] A number of recent surveys indicate that as many as 70 percent of Catholics do not believe in Jesus' Real Presence in the Eucharist.

[68] *A Key to the Doctrine of the Eucharist*, pp. 27-29.

[69] *Summa Theologiae*, III, q. 62, a. 5, trans. by Abbot Vonier, *A Key to the Doctrine of the Eucharist*, p. 29.

[70] Ibid., q. 69, a. 2, trans. by Abbot Vonier, *A Key to the Doctrine of the Eucharist*, p. 34.

[71] Ibid.

[72] *A Key to the Doctrine of the Eucharist*, p. 34.

[73] Liturgy of the Hours, Office of Readings, Thursday within the Octave of Easter.

[74] Pope Benedict XVI, post-synodal apostolic exhortation, *Sacramentum Caritatis*, February 22, 2007, n. 11.

[75] On the Eucharist as a re-presentation of the sacrifice of Calvary, we read: "The Eucharist is indelibly marked by the event of the Lord's passion and death, of which it is not only a reminder but the sacramental re-presentation. It is the sacrifice of the Cross perpetuated down the ages" (John Paul II, *Ecclesia de Eucharistia*, n. 11). And, "[O]ur Savior instituted the Eucharistic sacrifice of His Body and Blood. He did this in order to perpetuate the sacrifice of the Cross throughout the centuries until He should come again" (Second Vatican Council, Constitution on the Sacred Liturgy, December 4, 1963, *Sacrosanctum Concilium*, n. 47).

[76] Joseph Cardinal Ratzinger, *On the Way to Jesus Christ* (San Francisco: Ignatius Press, 2005), p. 126.

[77] Ibid.

[78] Benedict XVI, *Jesus of Nazareth: Holy Week: From the Entrance into Jerusalem to the Resurrection*, trans. Vatican Secretariat of State (San Francisco: Ignatius Press, 2011), p. 140.

[79] *On the Way to Jesus Christ*, p. 110.

[80] *Jesus of Nazareth: Holy Week*, p. 141. In referring to the prayer of praise and thanksgiving of the Eucharistic Liturgy as its "fundamental element," Pope Benedict XVI is actually citing the words of the great liturgical scholar, Joseph Andreas Jungmann, SJ.

[81] Benedict XVI, encyclical letter, *Deus Caritas Est*, December 25, 2005, n. 13.

[82] *On the Way to Jesus Christ*, pp. 115-116.

[83] Ibid., pp. 117-118.

[84] *Catechism*, n. 255.

[85] The *Catechism*'s treatment of mortal sin falls under the heading, "The Gravity of Sin: Mortal and Venial Sin," and can be found in numbers 1854-1864. Here's an excerpt from the first two paragraphs of those numbers:

> Sins are rightly evaluated according to their gravity. The distinction between mortal and venial sin, already evident in Scripture, became part of the tradition of the Church. It is corroborated by human experience.
>
> *Mortal sin* destroys charity in the heart of man by a grave violation of God's law; it turns man away from God, who is his ultimate end and his beatitude, by preferring an inferior good to him. ... Venial sin allows charity to subsist, even though it offends and wounds it (nn. 1854-1855).

The *Catechism* goes on to speak about the three conditions for committing a mortal sin:

> For a *sin* to be *mortal*, three conditions must together be met: "Mortal sin is sin whose object is grave matter and which is also committed with full knowledge and deliberate consent" (n. 1857).

The first condition, grave matter, is specified by the Ten Commandments. I recommend reading the *Catechism's* treatment of the Ten Commandments (nn. 2052-2557) to get a clear idea of what specific sins are meant as "grave." (Reading this treatment is also a great way to form one's conscience.) Regarding the second and third conditions, full knowledge and deliberate consent, we read the following:

> Mortal sin requires *full knowledge* and *complete consent*. It presupposes knowledge of the sinful character of the act, of its opposition to God's law. It also implies a consent sufficiently deliberate to be personal choice. Feigned ignorance and hardness of heart do not diminish, but rather increase, the voluntary character of sin.

Unintentional ignorance can diminish or even remove the imputability of a grave offense. But no one is deemed to be ignorant of the principles of the moral law, which are written in the conscience of every man. The promptings of feelings and passions can also diminish the voluntary and free character of the offense, as can external pressures or pathological disorders (nn. 1859-1860).

The *Catechism* provides a more concrete explanation of how the "voluntary and free character of the offense" may be diminished when it treats the sin of masturbation, that is, "the deliberate stimulation of the genital organs in order to derive sexual pleasure." Masturbatory acts, it says, are "intrinsically and gravely disordered" (n. 2352). Having said this, the *Catechism* then goes on to teach the following:

> To form an equitable judgment about the subjects' moral responsibility and to guide pastoral action, one must take into account the affective immaturity, force of acquired habit, conditions of anxiety, or other psychological or social factors that can lessen, if not even reduce to a minimum, moral culpability.

[86] The following passages on the Sacrament of Confession come from the *Diary of St. Faustina*. The words in boldface are from the Lord. The words in regular type are from St. Faustina:

> The confessor will sometimes say something he had never intended to say, without even realizing it himself. Oh, let the soul believe that such words are the words of the Lord Himself! Though indeed we ought to believe that every word spoken in the confessional is God's, what I have referred to is something that comes directly from God. And the soul perceives that the priest is not master of himself, that he is saying things that he would rather not say. That is how God rewards faith (n. 132).
> **Pray for souls that they be not afraid to approach the tribunal of My mercy** [i.e., the Sacrament of Confession] (n. 975).
> **Write, speak of My mercy. Tell souls where they are to look for solace; that is, in the Tribunal of Mercy** [i.e., the Sacrament of Confession]. **There the greatest miracles take place [and] are incessantly repeated. To avail oneself of this miracle, it is not necessary to go on a great pilgrimage or to carry out some external ceremony; it suffices to come with faith to the feet of My representative and to reveal to him one's misery, and the miracle of Divine Mercy will be fully demonstrated. Were a soul like a decaying corpse so that from a human standpoint there would be no [hope of] restoration and**

everything would already be lost, it is not so with God. The miracle of Divine Mercy restores that soul in full (n. 1448).

Daughter, when you go to confession, to this fountain of My mercy, the Blood and Water which came forth from My Heart always flows down upon your soul and ennobles it. Every time you go to confession, immerse yourself entirely in My mercy, with great trust, so that I may pour the bounty of My grace upon your soul. When you approach the confessional, know this, that I Myself am waiting there for you. I am only hidden by the priest, but I myself act in your soul. Here the misery of the soul meets the God of mercy. Tell souls that from this fount of mercy souls draw graces solely with the vessel of trust. If their trust is great, there is no limit to My generosity (n. 1602).

My daughter, just as you prepare in My presence, so also you make your confession before Me. The person of the priest is, for Me, only a screen. Never analyze what sort of a priest it is that I am making use of; open your soul in confession as you would to Me, and I will fill it with My light (n. 1725).

Finally, I recommend reflecting on the moment when Jesus gave us the Sacrament of Confession, which is found in the Gospel of John (20:19-23). This beautiful scene is depicted in the Image of Divine Mercy:

On the evening of that day, the first day of the week, the doors being shut where the disciples were, for fear of the Jews, Jesus came and stood among them and said to them, "Peace be with you." When he had said this, he showed them his hands and his side. Then the disciples were glad when they saw the Lord. Jesus said to them again, "Peace be with you. As the Father has sent me, even so I send you." And when he had said this, he breathed on them, and said to them, "Receive the Holy Spirit. If you forgive the sins of any, they are forgiven; if you retain the sins of any, they are retained.

[87] Second Vatican Council, Pastoral Constitution on the Church in the Modern World, *Gaudium et Spes*, December 7, 1965, n. 43.
[88] Karol Wojtyła, *Sources of Renewal*, (New York: Harper & Row, 1980) p. 16.
[89] Ibid., p. 17
[90] Ibid., p. 18.
[91] Ibid., pp. 420-421.
[92] Ibid., p. 18.
[93] Ibid., p. 18.
[94] Ibid., p. 18.

[95] John F. Crosby, *The Personalist Papers*, (Washington, D.C.: The Catholic University of America Press, 2004), p. 231.

[96] Cited by Ian Kerr in *John Henry Newman: A Biography*, (Oxford: Oxford University Press, 1988), p. 619.

[97] John Henry Newman, *Grammar of Assent* (New York: Doubleday, 1958), p. 29

[98] Cited in *John Henry Newman*, p. 113.

[99] Cited in Ibid., p. 114.

[100] Cited in Ibid., p. 92.

[101] Cited in Ibid., p. 113.

[102] Cited in Ibid., p. 509.

[103] Cited in Ibid., pp. 320, 324.

[104] *Grammar of Assent*, p. 29.

[105] Here are some examples of how Newman brings out the real from the notional:

(1) Regarding the notional idea that God has a plan for each human person,

> God has created me to do Him some definite service. He has committed some work to me which He has not committed to another. I have my mission. I may never know it in this life, but I shall be told it in the next. I am a link in a chain, a bond of connection between persons. He has not created me for naught. I shall do good; I shall do His work. I shall be an angel of peace, a preacher of truth in my own place, while not intending it if I do but keep His commandments. Therefore, I will trust Him, whatever I am, I can never be thrown away. If I am in sickness, my sickness may serve Him, in perplexity, my perplexity may serve Him. If I am in sorrow, my sorrow may serve Him. He does nothing in vain. He knows what He is about. He may take away my friends. He may throw me among strangers. He may make me feel desolate, make my spirits sink, hide my future from me. Still, He knows what He is about. (Source: Newman Reader, "Meditations on Christian Doctrine," March 6, 1848, tinyurl.com/NewmanMeditation (accessed October 1, 2012.)

(2) Regarding the notional idea that each Christian is to witness to Christ,

> Dear Jesus, help us to spread your fragrance everywhere we go. Flood our souls with your spirit and life. Penetrate and possess our whole being, so utterly, that our lives may only be a radiance of yours. Shine through us, and be so in us, that every soul we come in contact with may feel your presence in our soul. Let them look up and see no longer us, but only Jesus! Stay with us, and then we shall begin to shine as you

shine; so to shine as to be a light to others; the light, O Jesus, will be all from you, none of it will be ours; it will be you shining on others through us. Let us thus praise you in the way you love best by shining on those around us. Let us preach you without preaching, not by words but by our example, by the catching force, the sympathetic influence of what we do, the evident fullness of the love our hearts bear to you. Amen. (Cited in *Works of Love are Works of Peace: Mother Teresa of Calcutta and the Missionaries of Charity* [San Francisco: Ignatius Press, 1996], pp. 202-203.)

(3) Regarding the notional idea that martyrdom bears fruit,

Can we religiously suppose that the blood of our martyrs, three centuries ago and since, shall never receive its recompense? Those priests, secular and regular, did they suffer for no end? or rather, for an end which is not yet accomplished? The long imprisonment, the fetid dungeon, the weary suspense, the tyrannous trial, the barbarous sentence, the savage execution, the rack, the gibbet, the knife, the cauldron, the numberless tortures of those holy victims, O my God, are they to have no reward? Are Thy martyrs to cry from under Thine altar for their loving vengeance on this guilty people, and to cry in vain? Shall they lose life, and not gain a better life for the children of those who persecuted them? Is this Thy way, O my God, righteous and true? Is it according to Thy promise, O King of saints, if I may dare talk to Thee of justice? Did not Thou Thyself pray for Thine enemies upon the cross, and convert them? Did not Thy first Martyr win Thy great Apostle, then a persecutor, by his loving prayer? And in that day of trial and desolation for England, when hearts were pierced through and through with Mary's woe, at the crucifixion of Thy body mystical, was not every tear that flowed, and every drop of blood that was shed, the seeds of a future harvest, when they who sowed in sorrow were to reap in joy? (Sermon: "The Second Spring," delivered 13 July 1852, from *Sermons Preached on Various Occasions*, 1857, in *A Newman Treasury*, ed. Charles Frederick Harrold [London: Longmans Green and Co., 1943], p. 220).

[106] *Grammar of Assent*, p. 86.

[107] *Personalist Papers*, p. 231.

[108] *John Henry Newman*, p. 211. Newman seems to be using hyperbole in this quote. I don't think he really believed that deductive reason has "no power of persuasion" at all. In the context of his thought as a whole, I think what he meant was that it has no power of forming deep commitment in the human soul all by itself: It needs all the other factors he mentioned as well (the influence of the heart and mind) to end in true personal commitment.

[109] Mother Teresa's letter to the Missionaries of Charity family, 25th March 1993 © 2011 Missionaries of Charity Sisters, c/o Mother Teresa Center.

[110] *Sermon Notes of John Henry Cardinal Newman*, 1849-1878, ed. Fathers of the Birmingham Oratory, (London: Longman's, Green, and Co., 1913), p. 119.

[111] *John Henry Newman: A Biography*, p. 692.

[112] Ibid., p. 621.

[113] John Paul II, *Regina Caeli* Address, April 10, 1994.

[114] John Paul II, Address to the Sisters of Our Lady of Mercy at the Shrine of the Divine Mercy in Kraków-Lagiewniki, Poland on June 7, 1997.

[115] Here's the fuller citation: "The message of Divine Mercy has always been near and dear to me. [I took it] with me to the See of Peter and ... in a sense [it] forms the image of this Pontificate. ... I pray unceasingly that God will have "mercy on us and on the whole world" (Ibid.)

[116] Here's the fuller citation: "Right from the beginning of my ministry in St. Peter's See in Rome, I considered this message [of Divine Mercy] my special task. Providence has assigned it to me in the present situation of man, the Church and the world. It could be said that precisely this situation assigned that message to me as my task before God" (John Paul II, Public Address at the Shrine of Merciful Love in Collevalenza, Italy, November 22, 1981).

[117] Benedict XVI, *Regina Caeli* Address for Divine Mercy Sunday, April 23, 2006.

[118] John Paul II's preeminent biographer, George Weigel, in his book *The End and the Beginning: Pope John Paul II — The Victory of Freedom, the Last Years, the Legacy* (New York: Doubleday, 2010), suggests that John Paul's emphasis on the Divine Mercy devotion is just what the Church has needed in our time:

> That the Divine mercy devotion outlined by Saint Faustyna Kowalska became, during the pontificate of John Paul II, a means for the recovery of devotional life in Catholic parishes throughout the world suggested that John Paul II's pastoral intuitions about the imperative of the Church's preaching God's mercy at the turn into a new millennium were squarely on target (p. 438).

[119] *Diary*, n. 1732. (Note: All citations that include Jesus' words from the *Diary of St. Faustina* will appear in bold-face print to conform with the practice of all Marian Press publications of the *Diary*.)

[120] On this topic, the following note, adapted from my book, *Consoling the Heart of Jesus*, may be helpful ...

Jesus is alive and speaks to us today. Of course, he — and also the Holy Spirit — speaks to us whenever we hear or read his Word, that is, Sacred Scripture. Yet he can also speak to us in many other ways such as through people, events, and through the peace and joy he puts in our hearts. Some of the people through whom God speaks to us are the prophets. Of course, we've all heard of prophets in the Old Testament, people such as Jeremiah, Isaiah, and Ezekiel. However, we may be surprised to learn that there have been prophets throughout the Church's history, even up to our own day. (The surprise often comes despite the fact that St. Paul writes in his letters about the charism of prophecy in the life of the Church: See Eph 2:20; 4:11-12; 1 Cor 14:1-5, 22-25, 29-32.) In fact, even though they aren't frequently thought of as prophets, well-known saints such as Francis of Assisi, Ignatius of Loyola, Thérèse of Liseiux, Faustina Kowalska, and Mother Teresa of Kolkata truly had prophetic missions. In other words, they (and many other saintly people) had powerful experiences of God that they were then called to share at a given time for the strengthening of other people's faith, hope, and love. Sometimes their experiences of God came through extraordinary mystical experiences, such as in the case of St. Faustina. At other times, their experiences came through the silent, hidden action of the Holy Spirit, such as in the case of St. Thérèse. Whatever the nature of his experience of God, if a prophet is authentic — of which only the Church has the authority to make a final, definitive determination — then his experience becomes a gift for the people of his time.

By the way, St. Faustina's testimony is a powerful prophetic witness for our day. Pope John Paul II makes this point in the following excerpt from his homily on the occasion of the dedication of the Shrine of Divine Mercy in Krakow–Łagiewniki on August 17, 2002:

> Today, therefore, in this Shine, I wish *solemnly to entrust the world to Divine Mercy.* I do so with the burning desire that the message of God's merciful love, proclaimed here through Saint Faustina, *may be made known to all the peoples of the earth* and fill their hearts with hope. May this message radiate from this place to our beloved homeland and throughout the world. May the binding promise of the Lord Jesus be fulfilled: from here there must go forth "the spark which will prepare the world for his final coming" (cf. *Diary,* 1732). This spark needs to be lighted by the grace of God. This fire of mercy needs to be passed on to the world. *In the mercy of God the world will find peace and mankind will find happiness!* (n. 5).

Having said that the charism of prophecy has been alive and active in the life of the Church through the ages, I'd now like to make an important point: The words of post–Biblical prophets do not carry the same weight as Divine Revelation, which is communicated to us through Sacred Scripture and Sacred Tradition. Thus, we should always consider the words of prophetic saints in light of Divine Revelation and keep in mind that their words do not contain the same fullness of authority as, for instance, the words of Jesus in the Gospels or the teachings of the Magisterium of the Church. Still, the Church may decide that the prophetic testimony of a saint (or group of saints) contributes to and comprises a part of Sacred Tradition (for instance, when a saint is made a Doctor of the Church). The testimony of such a saint would then have greater weight. On this topic, it may be helpful to meditate on words from the Dogmatic Constitution on Divine Revelation, *Dei Verbum* (n. 8) as it teaches about the role of believers in the development of Sacred Tradition:

> This Tradition which comes from the apostles develops in the Church with the help of the Holy Spirit. For there is a growth in the understanding of the realities and the words which have been handed down. *This happens through the contemplation and study made by believers, who treasure these things in their hearts* (cf. Lk 2:19, 51), *through a penetrating understanding of the realities which they experience,* and through the preaching of those who have received through Episcopal succession the sure gift of truth. For as the centuries succeed one another, the Church constantly moves forward toward the fullness of divine truth until the words of God reach their complete fulfillment in her (emphasis added).

For an excellent and thorough study of prophecy and its role in the life of the Church, see Niels Christian Hvidt's *Christian Prophecy: The Post Biblical Tradition,* foreword by Joseph Cardinal Ratzinger (Oxford/New York: Oxford University Press, 2007).

[121] John Paul II, Homily at the Dedication of the Shrine of Divine Mercy in Krakow-Lagiewniki, Poland, August 17, 2002. Emphasis added.

[122] Here's the full citation: "The Servant of God Pope John Paul II ... wanted the Sunday after Easter to be dedicated in a special way to divine mercy, and providence disposed that he should die precisely on the vigil of that day in the arms of divine mercy" (Benedict XVI, *Regina Caeli* Address for Divine Mercy Sunday, April 23, 2006).

[123] *Regina Caeli* Address for Divine Mercy Sunday, prepared by Pope John Paul II but delivered as the Homily for the Mass for the repose of his soul on April 3, 2005.

[124] Peter Seewald, *Light of the World: The Pope, the Church and the Signs of the Times* (San Francisco: Ignatius Press, 2010), pp. 180-181.

[125] Kereszty, *Jesus Christ,* p. 359.

[126] This idea of the Lord's coming as including our going to him does not contradict the Church's traditional faith that Christ will, in fact, return to earth (see *Catechism* n. 677). Somehow it can be true that the Lord's "coming down" from heaven includes our being "taken up" to heaven. In view of this "somehow," we can ponder the following reflection by Pope Benedict on the Liturgy of the Eucharist:

> Every Mass is ... an act of going out to meet the One who is coming. In this way, his coming is also anticipated, as it were; we go out to meet him—and he comes, anticipatively, already now. I like to compare this with the account of the wedding at Cana. The first thing the Lord says to Mary there is "My hour

has not yet come." But then, in spite of that, he gives the new wine, as it were, anticipating his hour, which is yet to come. This eschatological realism becomes present in the Eucharist: we go out to meet him—as the One who comes—and he comes already now in anticipation of this hour, which one day will arrive once and for all. If we understand this as we should, we will go out to meet the Lord who has already been coming all along, we will enter into his coming—and so will allow ourselves to be fitted into a greater reality, beyond the everyday (*Light of the World*, p. 180).

POINT THREE
MISSION OF COMMUNION

[127] John Paul II, encyclical letter, *Redemptoris Missio*, December 7, 1990, n. 23.

[128] Here are other Johannine references for Jesus as the one "sent by the Father": 1:33; 4:34; 5:23, 37; 5:30, 36; 6:38, 39, 44, 47; 7:16, 18, 28, 33; 8:16, 18, 29; 9:4; 10:36; 12:44, 45, 49; 13:20; 14:24; 15:21; 16:5; 17: 18, 21, 25.

[129] On the relationship between the Church and the kingdom of God, Pope Benedict XVI (as Joseph Ratzinger) writes, "The kingdom of God has begun in the Church of Christ in this world, and the Church is the only and the authentic instrument of God's kingdom in this world. The Church, however, is not identical with this kingdom, which is greater than this world in space and time." [*Dogmatic Theology: The Church: The Universal Sacrament of Salvation*, trans. Michael Waldstein (Washington, D.C.: Catholic University of America Press, 1993), p. 476.] In the same book, on pages 475-476, Benedict summarizes the kingdom as follows:

> In contemporary theological language the phrase "kingdom of God" expresses all that can be known of God, his being and his knowledge, his will and activity; of the goal, end, and means of his actions; of his power, which is his self-abandoning love. The world's creation, conservation, and government, the redemption of the fallen world in the history of salvation through Jesus Christ, the incarnate Son of God, the fulfillment and sanctification of the world in the Church through the Holy Spirit, who is sent by the Father and the Son, and the final fulfillment of all creation at the end of time through and in and with God — all these elements are summarized in the phrase "kingdom of God."

The Pope then goes on to explain that the importance of the Church with regard to the kingdom of God "is most simply and clearly expressed in the Vatican II description of the Church as the universal sacrament of salvation in this world," an idea that will be explained further on in the text.

[130] John Paul II, post-synodal apostolic exhortation, *Christifideles Laici*,

December 30, 1988, n. 64.

[131] *Catechism*, n. 1567.

[132] Ibid., n. 1554.

[133] Ibid., n. 897.

[134] For a description of each one of these forms, see *Catechism*, nn. 920-930.

[135] *Catechism*, n. 882.

[136] Paul VI, apostolic exhortation, *Evangelii Nuntiandi*, December 8, 1975, n. 65.

[137] *Catechism*, n. 882.

[138] Second Vatican Council, Dogmatic Constitution on the Church, *Lumen Gentium*, November 21, 1964, n. 36.

[139] *Catechism*, n. 2447.

[140] *Redemptoris Missio*, n. 62.

[141] *Evangelii Nuntiandi*, n. 14.

[142] Ibid., n. 15. Emphasis added.

[143] Ibid., n. 53.

[144] Ibid., n. 57.

[145] Ibid.

[146] Ibid.

[147] *Redemptoris Missio*, n. 34.

[148] Ibid., n. 33.

[149] Second Vatican Council, Decree on the Missionary Activity of the Church, *Ad Gentes*, December 7, 1965, nn. 11, 15.

[150] Second Vatican Council, Declaration on the Relation of the Church to Non-Christian Religions, *Nostra Aetate*, October, 28, 1965, n. 2.

[151] *Gaudium et Spes*, nn. 10, 15, 22.

[152] *Redemptoris Missio*, n. 55.

[153] *Evangelii Nuntiandi*, n. 53. Also, see *Lumen Gentium*, n. 16, which speaks of the difficulties non-Christians face who have not heard the Gospel.

[154] *Mere Christianity*, pp. 55-56.

[155] *Redemptoris Missio*, n. 86.

[156] St. Francis Xavier, SJ, "Letter from Cochin to Members of the Society in Rome" (January 15, 1544) in *Monumenta Historica Societatis Iesu* 67 (1944), pp. 166-167.

[157] *Redemptoris Missio*, n. 33.

[158] Ibid.

[159] *Evangelii Nuntiandi*, n. 46.

[160] See the following documents from the Second Vatican Council: Declaration on Religious Liberty, *Dignitatis Humanae*, n. 14; Decree on the Church's Missionary Activity, *Ad Gentes*, n. 35; Dogmatic Constitution on the Church, *Lumen Gentium*, n. 17.

[161] John Paul II, Post-Synodal Apostolic Exhortation on the Formation of Priests, *Pastores Dabo Vobis*, March 25, 1992, n. 38.

[162] See *Ad Gentes*, n. 38.

[163] *Catechism*, n. 891. The bishops, acting as a body with the Pope, also have the grace of being free from error in their teaching. (Take, for example, the case of an ecumenical council.)

[164] *Lumen Gentium*, n. 25.

[165] Ibid.

[166] To minister to the large number of Protestant clergy and laity who are seeking to reunite with the Catholic Church today, there is, for example, The Coming Home Network International, "a fellowship of clergy and lay converts to the Catholic Church and those who are on the journey home." Visit www.chnetwork.org for more information.

[167] *Lumen Gentium*, n. 14.

[168] *Redemptoris Missio*, n. 90.

[169] Cited by John Paul II in *Christifideles Laici*, n. 9.

[170] Second Vatican Council, Decree on the Apostolate of Lay People, *Apostolicam Actuositatem*, November 18, 1965, n. 33.

[171] *Christifideles Laici*, n. 3.

[172] *Evangelii Nuntiandi*, n. 70.

[173] *Gaudium et Spes*, n. 21.

[174] John Paul II, message to participants in the seventh international meeting of the "Catholic Fraternity of Covenant Communities and Fellowships," Nov. 9, 1996, n. 4.

[175] *Christifideles Laici*, n. 18.

[176] *Lumen Gentium*, n. 1.

[177] *Christifideles Laici*, n. 29.

[178] Lutheran World Federation and the Catholic Church, *Joint Declaration on the Doctrine of Justification*, 1999.

[179] See the *Catechism*, "The Gospel is the revelation in Jesus Christ of God's mercy to sinners" (n. 1846).

[180] John Paul II, post-synodal apostolic exhortation on the consecrated life, *Vita Consecrata*, March 25, 1996, n. 33.

[181] Ibid., n. 109.

[182] Ibid., n. 20.

[183] Congregation for Institutes of Consecrated Life and Societies of Apostolic Life, *Fraternal Life in Community*, 1994, n. 12.

[184] *Vita Consecrata*, n. 46.

[185] Ibid., n. 41.

[186] Ibid., n. 51.

[187] Ibid., n. 46.

[188] *Evangelium Vitae*, n. 5.

[189] Ibid., n. 11.

[190] Ibid., n. 12.

[191] Ibid., n. 95.

[192] Ibid., nn. 12, 17.

[193] Ibid., n. 18.

[194] Ibid., n. 28.

[195] Ibid.

[196] Ibid., n. 91.

[197] Karol Cardinal Wojtyła, "Notable & Quotable," in *The Wall Street Journal* (Nov. 9, 1978).

[198] John Paul II, homily at the Mass for the 8th World Youth Day in Cherry

Creek State Park of Denver, Colo., August 15, 1993, n. 6.

[199] John Paul II, Address to UNESCO, June 2, 1980, n. 11.

[200] Ibid., n. 12.

[201] For more on the natural law, see the *Catechism*, nn. 1950-1986.

[202] Pragmatism is a system of moral philosophy that evaluates the moral goodness or badness of an action based on the possibility of practical success and not on objective truth. Social Darwinism is the theory that the social order can be defined by the laws of evolution, the most important of which is natural selection. Atheistic humanism is a philosophical worldview that exalts humanity, effectively replacing God with man.

[203] See endnote n. 17.

[204] *Gaudium et Spes*, n. 22.

[205] John Paul II, encyclical letter, *Redemptoris Hominis*, March 4, 1979, nn. 8-9.

[206] Ibid., n. 10.

[207] *Evangelium Vitae*, n. 25.

[208] *Redemptoris Hominis*, n. 10.

[209] Ibid., n. 14.

[210] Ibid., n. 12.

[211] Karol Wojtyła, *Love and Responsibility*, (San Francisco: Ignatius Press, 1993), p. 199.

[212] *Evangelium Vitae*, n. 83.

[213] See Dietrich von Hildebrand, *The Heart: An Analysis of Human and Divine Affectivity*, especially Part I, ch. 8.

[214] George Weigel, *Witness to Hope: The Biography of Pope John Paul II* (New York: HarperCollins, 1999), p. 102.

[215] "J.R.R. Tolkien: Lord of the Imagination," *Catholic Education Resource Center*, n.d., accessed August 5, 2012, tinyurl.com/TolkienFaith.

[216] Ibid.

[217] Mars Hill Review, "A Baptism of Imagination: A Conversation with Peter Kreeft," *Catholic Education Resource Center*, 1996, accessed August 5, 2012, tinyurl.com/KreeftWriters.

[218] See the Second Vatican Council, Declaration on the Relation of the Church to Non-Christian Religions, *Nostrae Aetate*, October 26, 1965, n. 2, which reads:

> Likewise, other religions found everywhere try to counter the restlessness of the human heart, each in its own manner, by proposing "ways," comprising teachings, rules of life, and sacred rites. The Catholic Church rejects nothing that is true and holy in these religions. She regards with sincere reverence those ways of conduct and of life, those precepts and teachings which, though differing in many aspects from the ones she holds and sets forth, nonetheless often reflect a ray of that Truth which enlightens all men.

[219] Buttiglione, *Karol Wojtyła: The Thought of the Man Who Became Pope John Paul II* (Grand Rapids: Eerdmans Publishing Company, 1997), p. 194.

[220] Ibid., p. 191.

[221] John Paul II, *Rise, Let Us Be On Our Way* (New York: Warner Books, 2004), p. 67. For instances of the Greek word, "*plēthos*" ("multitude" in English), see Mk 3:7; Lk 6:17; Acts 2:6, 14:1, and elsewhere.

[222] *Catechism*, n. 478.

[223] John Henry Newman, "The Individuality of the Soul," *Parochial and Plain Sermons* (London: Rivingtons, 1869), IV, 81-83, cited in John F. Crosby, *Selfhood of the Human Person*, (Washington, D.C.: Catholic University of America Press, 1996), pp. 51-52.

[224] Ibid., p. 51.

[225] Ibid., p. 52.

[226] Ibid.

[227] John Paul II, apostolic letter, *Novo Millennio Ineunte*, 2000, n. 8. Translation of the Latin prayer: "I will sing of the mercies of the Lord forever."

[228] *Rise, Let Us Be On Our Way*, p. 65.

[229] John F. Crosby, *Personalist Papers* (Washington, D.C.: The Catholic University of America Press, 2004), p. ix.

[230] *Gaudium et Spes*, n. 24.

[231] *Love and Responsibility*, p. 41.

[232] Ibid., p. 42.

[233] John Paul II, trans. Michael Waldenstein, *Man and Woman He Created Them: A Theology of the Body* (Boston: Pauline Books and Media), n. 5:5-6.

[234] W. Norris Clarke, SJ, *Person and Being* (Marquette: Marquette University Press, 1993), p. 44.

[235] See Fr. Clarke's more technical explanation in *Person and Being*:

> This identity or coincidence of knower and known in the one act when we say "I" is one of the evidences brought forward by St. Thomas, together with many later thinkers, for asserting that the inner principle of such action must be a spiritual soul. For one essential note of material being is dispersal over extended space, which does not allow any part of a material being to coincide or be identical with any other part, or with any part of itself. To coincide fully with oneself, so that both the subject and the object of the same act are identical, as in the act of self-awareness, reveals that the subject of such an activity must transcend the self-dispersal, or "spread-outness," of the material mode of being as such, pointing to a more intense and concentrated level of self-presence that we call "spiritual being" (pp. 44-45).

[236] Ibid., p. 55.

[237] Ibid., p. 51.

[238] John F. Crosby, "Worthy of Respect: The Personalist Norm," *Lay Witness Magazine* (March 2000), pp. 54-55.

[239] *Person and Being*, pp. 46-47.

[240] Ibid., p. 47.

[241] Ibid.

[242] *Confessions*, Book I:1.

[243] Dietrich and Alice von Hildebrand, *The Art of Living* (Chicago: Franciscan Herald Press, 1965), p. 4.

[244] Dietrich von Hildebrand, *The Nature of Love* (South Bend, Ind.: St. Augustine's Press, 2009), p. 16n.

[245] *The Art of Living*, p. 5.

[246] Ibid.

[247] Ibid., p. 4.

[248] Ibid., p.5

[249] Ibid., pp. 5-6.

[250] Ibid., p. 6.

[251] *Rise, Let Us Be On Our Way*, p. 95.

[252] *The Art of Living*, p. 6.

[253] Ibid., p. 7.

[254] Ibid.

[255] Ibid.

[256] See Blaise Pascal, *Pensées*, trans. A. J. Krailsheimer (London: Penguin Classics, 1966), n. 200, which reads:

> Man is only a reed, the weakest in nature, but he is a thinking reed. There is no need for the whole universe to take up arms to crush him: a vapor, a drop of water is enough to kill him. But even if the universe were to crush him, man would still be nobler than his slayer, because he knows that he is dying and the advantage the universe has over him. The universe knows none of this.

[257] *Personalist Papers*, p. 21.

[258] I say this side of eternity, because in heaven, according to John Paul II, we as the one Body of Christ *will* be able to experience the subjectivity of each other in a "perfect intersubjectivity of all" — a stunning thought (*Theology of the Body*, n. 68:4).

[259] See *Love and Responsibility*, p. 126.

[260] *Gaudium et Spes*, n. 24.

[261] *Theology of the Body*, n. 19:4.

[262] By "enjoyed to the full," John Paul II would especially mean, enjoyed in harmony, which can be a challenge for the man especially because of his "shorter curve of arousal" compared to the "more gradual curve of arousal" of the woman. As Cardinal Karol Wojtyła, he makes this point in his book *Love and Responsibility*:

> [I]t is necessary to insist that intercourse must not serve merely as a means of allowing sexual excitement to reach its climax in one of the partners, i.e. the man alone, but that climax must be reached in harmony, not at the expense of one partner, but with both partners fully involved. ... [L]ove demands that the

reactions of the other person, the sexual partner be fully taken into account.

... There exists a rhythm dictated by nature itself which both spouses must discover so that climax may be reached both by the man and by the woman, and as far as possible occur in both simultaneously.

... [T]here is a need for harmonization, which is impossible without good will, especially on the part of the man, who must carefully observe the reactions of the woman. If a woman does not obtain natural gratification from the sexual act there is a danger that her experience of it will be qualitatively inferior, will not involve her fully as a person. This sort of experience makes nervous reactions only too likely, and may for instance cause secondary sexual frigidity. Frigidity is sometimes the result of an inhibition on the part of the woman herself, or of a lack of involvement which may even at times be her own fault. But it is usually the result of the egoism of the man, who failing to recognize the subjective desires of the woman in intercourse, and the objective laws of the sexual process taking place in her, seeks merely his own satisfaction, sometimes quite brutally.

In the woman this can produce an aversion to intercourse, and a disgust with sex which is just as difficult or even more difficult to control than the sexual urge. It can also cause neuroses and sometimes organic disorders ... . Psychologically, such a situation causes not just indifference but outright hostility. A woman finds it very difficult to forgive a man if she derives no satisfaction from intercourse. It becomes difficult for her to endure this, and as the years go her resentment may grow out of all proportion to its cause. This may lead to the collapse of the marriage. ... [T]he woman's frigidity and indifference is often the fault of the man, when he seeks his own satisfaction while leaving the woman unsatisfied, something which masculine pride should in any case forbid (pp. 272-274).

[263] According to a German study published online as "Human Reproduction Today" on February 21, 2007, the sympto-thermal method of natural family planning is as effective for preventing pregnancy as the contraceptive pill.

[264] John and Barbara Willke, in their book, *Why Can't We Love Them Both?*, describe the abortifacient nature of the contraceptive pill, which causes "micro-abortion":

An abortifacient is a drug or device which causes an abortion within the first one or two weeks of a human's life. An abortifacient acts after human life has begun and produces a micro-abortion. There are over 30 "contraceptive" pills on the market, each differing a little from the others. They "prevent" pregnancy through three separate functions. 1) They thicken the mucous plug at the cervix. If this is the primary effect, then it truly is contraceptive because it prevents sperm from entering. 2) They prevent release of the ovum. If this is the primary effect, then the function is "temporary" sterilization. 3) They render the lining of the womb hostile to the implantation of the tiny new human at one week of life. These are micro-abortions caused by an abortifacient. The earlier high-estrogen pills largely prevented ovulation. The newer low-estrogen pills allow "break-through" ovulation in up to 20% or more of the months used. Such a released ovum is fertilized 10% or more of the time. Most of these tiny new lives which result, do not survive. The reason is that at one week of life this tiny new boy or girl cannot implant in the womb lining and dies. [tinyurl.com/abortifacient (accessed on September 29, 2012)].

[265] In light of this paragraph, read Romans 1:18-32, which clearly reflects our present situation, living in the culture of death.

[266] *Gaudium et Spes*, n. 22. Emphasis added.

[267] *Evangelium Vitae*, n. 81.

[268] Ibid., n. 84.

[269] Ibid., n. 25.

[270] Ibid.

[271] Ibid., n. 51.

[272] Ibid.

[273] Ibid.

[274] Ibid., n. 83.

[275] *Lumen Gentium*, n. 11.

[276] Ibid. Emphasis added.

[277] *Catechism*, n. 221.

[278] Paul VI, Constitution on the Sacred Liturgy, *Sacrosanctum Concilium*, December 4, 1963, n. 14.

[279] *Catechism*, n. 1361.

[280] As an aid to recognizing the blessings of each day, I recommend making a daily examination of conscience. The examination of conscience (also called "examen") should be made sometime toward the end of the day. Most people make it shortly before going to bed. It's basically a mental review of the previous 16 hours or so of consciousness — thus, some people prefer to call the examination of conscience an examination of *consciousness.*

To make the examen, first, we should put ourselves in the presence of God. In other words, we should begin with the attitude that the examen is a time of prayer, not just a mental exercise. Devoutly making the Sign of the Cross may be enough to do this.

Next, we just have to remember one word: baker, B-A-K-E-R, baker. Actually, we also have to remember what each letter of this word stands for. Let's start with "B."

B stands for "blessings." According to St. Ignatius, this is the most important of the five points. Here we simply review our day, survey the many blessings God has given us throughout it, and then praise and thank him for these blessings. For instance, maybe we had a great conversation with someone at lunch. During the examen, we might want to reflect on that gift and praise and thank God for it. Of course, we don't have to go through every single blessing of the day. That would take way too much time. The key is to let one's heart roam about and settle on the particular peaks of joy and blessing of the day, what Ignatius calls "consolation." One more thing: We shouldn't forget to thank God for the crosses of the day, which are also blessings.

If we get into the habit of praising and thanking God like this every day during our examen, then we'll begin to better recognize the blessings of our day as they happen, and thus, we'll develop a continual attitude of gratitude. In other words, our praise and thanks won't begin to flow simply when we make our examen — it'll flow all day long. Furthermore, as God sees our efforts to recognize and thank him for his many gifts, he'll send us more and more. But be careful, for if we keep it up, we might end up like St. Ignatius.

Because he was so faithful to the examen, St. Ignatius developed an attitude of gratitude to a remarkably high degree. He became so sensitive to the countless blessings God constantly poured out on him that he was always on the verge of tears. Mind you, Ignatius was a former soldier and had a will of iron. He was no wimp. Nevertheless, he was always on the brink of being overwhelmed by the immense love that he recognized God was always showering down upon him. It got so "bad" that when he was in public, he would sometimes have to distract himself from seeing the blessings to prevent his torrents of tears from flowing. But don't worry. We're still far behind Ignatius, as the next two points may remind us.

A stands for "Ask." Although we already placed ourselves in the presence of God when we began the examen, here we need to ask for a special grace from the Holy Spirit, the grace to recognize our sins. Without the help of the Holy Spirit, we'll remain blind to our sinfulness. Thus, when we get to this second point, we need to ask the Holy Spirit to help us recognize our sinfulness, which brings us to the next point.

K stands for "Kill." Why "kill"? Because it was our sins that killed and crucified Jesus. During this third point, we look at our sinfulness (weaknesses and attachments, too). So, again, we gaze across the conscious hours of our day. This time, however, we look not for peaks but valleys, what Ignatius calls "desolation." In other words, we pay attention to those times during our day when our hearts dropped. Why might they have dropped? Maybe because of someone else's sin. Maybe someone said something unkind to us. Fine. Did we forgive them? If so, good. If not, well, the examen is a good time to deal with it.

Now, let's keep looking. Here's another time our hearts dropped. It was this afternoon at work, standing by the water cooler. Hmmm. Why did our hearts drop then? Ah, yes (thanks, Holy Spirit), that's when we stuck

Bob with a verbal barb. Let's see, anything else? Yes, there's another heart dropper: We didn't accept the traffic jam on our way home as a small sharing in the Cross. We should have been more peaceful about it and offered it up as a prayer for others.

Okay, so after remembering all those heart-dropping moments, we may feel pretty down. In the past, such feelings might have made us want to run away from Jesus. But now it's different, right? Now we know that when the weight of our sinfulness drags us down, that's the best time to go to Jesus, sinfulness and all — which brings us to the next point.

E stands for "embrace." This is to allow Jesus to embrace us, sinners that we are, with the rays of his merciful love. While praying over this point, it may be helpful to think of the Image of Divine Mercy. I like to imagine the rays of this image embracing me with forgiveness. I also like to remember Jesus' words that it rests his Heart to forgive and that when I go to him with my sinfulness, I give him the joy of being my Savior. I believe that at this point of the examen, we greatly console Jesus when we simply let him embrace us with his merciful love — and of course, we, too, are consoled. I recommend spending some time lingering on this point (in the embrace) before moving on to the next.

R stands for "Resolution." During this last point of the examen, we take what we've learned from the previous points and look ahead to the next day, ready to make resolutions. For instance, having recognized during "K" that we stuck Bob with a verbal barb at the office today, we might resolve that tomorrow morning we'll make it up to him by going to his cubicle, slapping him on the back, and congratulating him on how his football team did earlier this evening. Also, having remembered that we were impatient during the traffic jam today, we can resolve to bite our tongues if the sea of brake lights appears again tomorrow. Finally, because during "B" we realized that God was speaking to us during our lunchtime conversation with Sally, giving light on a certain problem, we can resolve to act on that light by looking up the online article she recommended. (I think we get the idea.)

[281] *Catechism*, nn. 1365-1366.

[282] Ibid., n. 1368.

[283] John Paul II, apostolic letter, *Salvifici Doloris*, February 11, 1984, n. 17.

[284] Ibid., n. 18.

[285] Ibid., n. 19.

[286] Ibid., n. 24.

[287] Ibid., n. 27.

[288] Ibid., n. 31.

[289] Ibid., n. 26.

[290] Ibid., n. 27.

[291] *Diary*, n. 1578.

[292] Ibid., n. 1485.

[293] John Clarke, OCD, *Story of a Soul* (Washington, D.C.: ICS Publications, 1996), p. 254.

[294] "You, worry only about loving me ..." The original words are in Italian,

"Tu pensa solo ad amarmi, lo penserò a tutto il resto, fino ai minimi particolari." They can be found in the book by Fr. Lorenzo Sales, II *Cuore di Gesù al Mundo* (Vatican City: Liberia Editrice Vaticana, 1999), p. 172. Jesus said something similar to St. Margaret Mary, "Take care of my interests and I shall take care of yours" (cited by Jean C.J. d'Elbée in *I Believe in Love: A Personal Retreat Based on the Teaching of St. Thérèse of Lisieux*, trans. Marilyn Teichert and Madeleine Stebbins (Manchester, N.H.: Sophia Institute Press, 2001), p. 103).

[295] Second Vatican Council, Decree on the Apostolate of Lay People, *Apostolicam Actuositatem*, November 18, 1965, n. 4.

[296] *True Devotion to Mary*, trans. Frederick W. Faber (Rockford, Ill.: TAN Books, 1985), n. 55. See also nn. 152-168.

[297] *Lumen Gentium*, n. 58.

CONCLUSION

[298] Having said that the *Summa* does not measure up to Aquinas's own experience of God, I should point out that Fr. Jean-Pierre Torrell, OP, in his book *St. Thomas Aquinas: Spiritual Master* (Washington, D.C.: Catholic University of America Press, 2003), argues that the *Summa* does communicate a profound spirituality. See chapter one, "Theology and Spirituality."

[299] *The Autobiography of St. Ignatius of Loyola*, trans. Joseph F. O'Callaghan (New York: Fordham University Press, 2005), pp. 39-40.

[300] Herbert Alphonso, SJ, "The Jesuit/Ignatian Charism: A Personal Synthesis and Tribute to Fr. P. Arrupe," *Review of Ignatian Spirituality*, v. 116, p. 51.

[301] Pedro Leturia, SJ, "Génesis de los Ejercicios … y su influjo en la fundación de la Compañía de Jesús," *Archivum historicum Societatis Iesu* 10 (1941): 32 as cited and translated by Pedro Arrupe, SJ, in his essay, "The Trinitarian Inspiration of the Ignatian Charism" in *Studies in the Spirituality of the Jesuits*, 33/3 (May 2001), p. 9.

[302] *The Spiritual Exercises of St. Ignatius of Loyola*, trans. Louis J. Puhl, SJ (Chicago: Loyola Press, 1951), n. 23.

[303] *The Autobiography of St. Ignatius of Loyola*, p. 38.

[304] *The Spiritual Exercises*, n. 237.

[305] *Gaudium et Spes*, n. 24.

[306] Describing Christ's mission of salvation, the *Catechism* states: "The whole history of salvation is identical with the history of the way and the means by which the one true God, Father, Son, and Holy Spirit, reveals himself to men 'and reconciles and unites with himself those who turn away from sin'" (n. 234). And, "The ultimate end of the whole divine economy is the entry of God's creatures into the perfect unity of the Blessed Trinity" (n. 260).

[307] This prayercard often comes with this book. In some instances, it may not. To order more, see information pages at the end.

[308] When I give the numbers from the *Catechism* in this appendix, they will

not always include all the *Catechism* numbers that apply to a given topic. This is because the *Catechism* has an excellent cross-reference system that readers who want to go even deeper can easily use. They'll simply need to look up the cross-reference numbers printed in the margins by the *Catechism* numbers I give.

[309] The concept for this diagram comes from Peter Kreeft. The original appears in his book *Summa of the Summa* (San Francisco: Ignatius Press, 1990), p. 15. Reproduced with permission.

[310] Organizational chart of the *Summa* from the *New Catholic Encyclopedia*. Vol. 14 (Washington, DC: The Catholic University of America Press, 1967), p. 112.

[311] *Catechism*, n. 1849.

[312] Benedict XVI, *Regina Caeli* Address, Divine Mercy Sunday, April 23, 2006.

[313] Ibid., Divine Mercy Sunday, March 30, 2008.

[314] *Dives in Misericordia*, n. 7.

[315] Definitions of mercy from John Paul II's encyclical letter, *Dives in Misericorida*:

1. It restores to value.

> [M]ercy is manifested in its true and proper aspect when it restores to value, promotes and draws good from all the forms of evil existing in the world and in man. Understood in this way, mercy constitutes the fundamental content of the messianic message of Christ and the constitutive power of His mission. His disciples and followers understood and practiced mercy in the same way. Mercy never ceased to reveal itself, in their hearts and in their actions, as an especially creative proof of the love which does not allow itself to be "conquered by evil," but overcomes "evil with good" (cf. Rom 12:21). The genuine face of mercy has to be ever revealed anew. In spite of many prejudices, mercy seems particularly necessary for our times (n. 6).
>
> ... merciful love which, by its essence, is a creative love (n. 14).

2. It's a particular mode of love when it meets suffering.

> The truth, revealed in Christ, about God the "Father of mercies," (2 Cor 1:3) enables us to "see" Him as particularly close to man especially when man is suffering, when he is under threat at the very heart of his existence and dignity (n. 2).
>
> This love makes itself particularly noticed in contact with suffering, injustice and poverty — in contact with the whole historical "human condition," which in various ways manifests man's limitation and frailty, both physical and moral. It is precisely the mode and sphere in which love manifests itself

that in biblical language is called "mercy."

… [Christ is the] incarnation of the love that is manifested with particular force with regard to the suffering, the unfortunate, and sinners, [which] makes present and thus more fully reveals the Father, who is God "rich in mercy" (n. 3).

In the preaching of the prophets, mercy signifies a special power of love, which prevails over the sin and infidelity of the chosen people (n. 4).

In the eschatological fulfillment mercy will be revealed as love, while in the temporal phase, in human history, which is at the same time the history of sin and death, love must be revealed above all as mercy and must also be actualized as mercy (n. 8).

For mercy is an indispensable dimension of love; it is as it were love's second name and, at the same time, the specific manner in which love is revealed and effected vis-a-vis the reality of the evil that is in the world, affecting and besieging man, insinuating itself even into his heart and capable of causing him to perish in Gehenna" (Mt 10:28) (n. 7).

3. Mercy is Hesed and Rahamim.

In describing mercy, the books of the Old Testament use two expressions in particular, each having a different semantic nuance. First there is the term *hesed*, which indicates a profound attitude of "goodness." When this is established between two individuals, they do not just wish each other well; they are also faithful to each other by virtue of an interior commitment, and therefore also by virtue of a faithfulness to themselves. Since *hesed* also means "grace" or "love," this occurs precisely on the basis of this fidelity. The fact that the commitment in question has not only a moral character but almost a juridical one makes no difference. When in the Old Testament the word *hesed* is used of the Lord, this always occurs in connection with the covenant that God established with Israel. This covenant was, on God's part, a gift and a grace for Israel. Nevertheless, since, in harmony with the covenant entered into, God had made a commitment to respect it, *hesed* also acquired in a certain sense a legal content. The juridical commitment on God's part ceased to oblige whenever Israel broke the covenant and did not respect its conditions. But precisely at this point, *hesed*, in ceasing to be a juridical obligation, revealed its deeper aspect: it showed itself as what it was at the beginning, that is, as love that gives, love more powerful than betrayal, grace stronger than sin.

This fidelity vis-a-vis the unfaithful "daughter of my people"(cf. Lam. 4:3, 6) is, in brief, on God's part, fidelity to Himself. This becomes obvious in the frequent recurrence together of the two terms *hesed we'e met* (= grace and fidelity), which could be considered a case of hendiadys (cf. e.g. Ex. 34:6; 2 Sm. 2:6; 15:20; Ps. 25[24]:10; 40[39]:11-12; 85[84]:11; 138[137]:2; Mi. 7:20). "It is not for your sake, O house of Israel, that I am about to act, but for the sake of my holy name" (Ez. 36:22). Therefore Israel, although burdened with guilt for having broken the covenant, cannot lay claim to God's *hesed* on the basis of (legal) justice; yet it can and must go on hoping and trusting to obtain it, since the God of the covenant is really "responsible for his love." The fruits of this love are forgiveness and restoration to grace, the reestablishment of the interior covenant.

The second word which in the terminology of the Old Testament serves to define mercy is *rahamim*. This has a different nuance from that of *hesed*. While *hesed* highlights the marks of fidelity to self and of "responsibility for one's own love" (which are in a certain sense masculine characteristics), *rahamim*, in its very root, denotes the love of a mother (*rehem* = mother's womb). From the deep and original bond — indeed the unity — that links a mother to her child there springs a particular relationship to the child, a particular love. Of this love one can say that it is completely gratuitous, not merited, and that in this aspect it constitutes an interior necessity: an exigency of the heart. It is, as it were, a "feminine" variation of the masculine fidelity to self expressed by *hesed*. Against this psychological background, *rahamim* generates a whole range of feelings, including goodness and tenderness, patience and understanding, that is, readiness to forgive.

The Old Testament attributes to the Lord precisely these characteristics when it uses the term *rahamim* in speaking of Him. We read in Isaiah: "Can a woman forget her suckling child, that she should have no compassion on the son of her womb? Even these may forget, yet I will not forget you" (Is. 49:15). This love, faithful and invincible thanks to the mysterious power of motherhood, is expressed in the Old Testament texts in various ways: as salvation from dangers, especially from enemies; also as forgiveness of sins — of individuals and also of the whole of Israel; and finally in readiness to fulfill the (eschatological) promise and hope, in spite of human infidelity, as we read in Hosea: "I will heal their faithlessness, I will love them freely" (Hos. 14:5) (endnote n. 52).

[316] I'm grateful to Fr. Dan Cambra, MIC, for sharing this acronym with me.
[317] See next note.
[318] Divine Mercy Sunday has its roots in the Octave Day of Easter, which was celebrated in the early Church. The great theologian Gregory of Nazianzen even taught a rather bold concept that the Easter Octave Day is

the "New Sunday." He distinguished the Pasch or Easter from its octave, affirming "that Sunday [meaning Easter Day] was the day of salvation, but this Sunday [meaning the Octave of Easter] is the birthday of salvation." This early Church theologian considered the Octave Day of Easter to be "more sublime" and "more wonderful" without in any way depreciating Easter Sunday itself.

It's no wonder, then, that St. Augustine in his sermons calls the whole Octave of Easter "days of mercy and pardon" and the Octave Day itself "the compendium of the days of mercy." In his *Summa Theologiae*, St. Thomas Aquinas echoes the early Fathers when he describes the Octave Day as the goal and the second perfection of Easter. For a penetrating analysis of this topic, see "A Contribution to the Discussion on the Feast of The Divine Mercy" by Fr. Seraphim Michalenko, MIC, in *Divine Mercy: The Heart of the Gospel* (Stockbridge: Marian Press, 1999), p. 117-133.

[319] *Diary*, n. 341.

[320] Ibid., n. 699.

[321] Ibid., n. 699.

[322] See the judgment of the theologian censor on the writings attributed to the Servant of God, Faustina Kowalska in *Sacra Congregatio Pro Causis Sanctorum P.n. 1123 Cracovien. Beatificationis et canonizationis servae dei Faustinae Kowalska Instituti Sororum B.M.V.A. Misericordia (1905-1938)*, pp. 429-430.

[323] That original image now hangs in the Holy Spirit Church in Vilnius, Lithuania. An interesting fact about this particular image is that if you superimpose it over the Shroud of Turin, it makes nearly a perfect match!

[324] *Diary*, nn. 327, 742.

[325] The text of the Novena to Divine Mercy can be found in the *Diary of St. Faustina*, nn. 1209-1229.

[326] Ibid., n. 796.

[327] Ibid., n. 811.

[328] Ibid., n. 687.

[329] Ibid., n. 754.

[330] Ibid., n. 848.

[331] Ibid., n. 1541.

[332] How to pray the Chaplet of Divine Mercy:

1. Make the Sign of the Cross
In the name of the Father, and of the Son, and of the Holy Spirit. Amen.

2. Optional Opening Prayers
You expired, Jesus, but the source of life gushed forth for souls, and the ocean of mercy opened up for the whole world. O Fount of Life, unfathomable Divine Mercy, envelop the whole world and empty Yourself out upon us. O Blood and Water, which gushed forth from the Heart of Jesus as a fountain of Mercy for us, I trust in You.

3. Our Father
Our Father, who art in heaven, hallowed be thy name; thy kingdom come;

thy will be done on earth as it is in heaven. Give us this day our daily bread; and forgive us our trespasses, as we forgive those who trespass against us; and lead us not into temptation, but deliver us from evil. Amen.

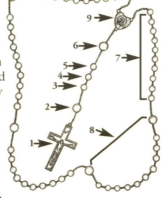

4. Hail Mary
Hail Mary, full of grace; the Lord is with thee; blessed art thou among women, and blessed is the fruit of thy womb, Jesus. Holy Mary, Mother of God, pray for us sinners, now and at the hour of our death. Amen.

5. The Apostle's Creed
I believe in God, the Father almighty, Creator of heaven and earth, and in Jesus Christ, his only Son, our Lord, who was conceived by the Holy Spirit, born of the Virgin Mary, suffered under Pontius Pilate, was crucified, died and was buried; he descended into hell; on the third day he rose again from the dead; he ascended into heaven, and is seated at the right hand of God the Father almighty; from there he will come to judge the living and the dead. I believe in the Holy Spirit, the holy catholic Church, the communion of saints, the forgiveness of sins, the resurrection of the body, and life everlasting. Amen.

6. The Eternal Father
Eternal Father, I offer You the Body and Blood, Soul and Divinity of Your Dearly Beloved Son, Our Lord, Jesus Christ, in atonement for our sins and those of the whole world.

7. On the Ten Small Beads of Each Decade
For the sake of His sorrowful Passion, have mercy on us and on the whole world.

8. Repeat for the remaining four decades
Say the "Eternal Father" (6) on the "Our Father" bead and then 10 "For the sake of His sorrowful Passion" (7) on the following "Hail Mary" beads.

9. Conclude with Holy God (Repeat three times)
Holy God, Holy Mighty One, Holy Immortal One, have mercy on us and on the whole world.

10. Optional Closing Prayer
Eternal God, in whom mercy is endless and the treasury of compassion — inexhaustible, look kindly upon us and increase Your mercy in us, that in difficult moments we might not despair nor become despondent, but with great confidence submit ourselves to Your holy will, which is Love and Mercy itself. Amen.

[333] *Diary*, n. 1572.

[334] Ibid., nn., 1572, 1320.

[335] Can we really have mercy on Jesus? In a remarkable passage from *Dives in Misericordia*, Pope John Paul II teaches that we not only can but should:

> The events of Good Friday and, even before that, in prayer in Gethsemane, introduce a fundamental change into the whole course of the revelation of love and mercy in the messianic mission of Christ. The one who "went about doing good and healing" and "curing every sickness and disease" now Himself seems to merit the greatest mercy and to *appeal for mercy*, when He is arrested, abused, condemned, scourged, crowned with thorns, when He is nailed to the cross and dies amidst agonizing torments. It is then that He particularly deserves mercy from the people to whom He has done good, and He does not receive it ...
>
> [T]he cross will remain the point of reference for other words too of the Revelation of John: "Behold, I stand at the door and knock; if anyone hears my voice and opens the door, I will come in and eat with him and he with me." In a special way, God also reveals His mercy when He invites man to have "mercy" on His only Son, the crucified one.
>
> ... Christ, precisely as the crucified one, is the Word that does not pass away, and He is the one who stands at the door and knocks at the heart of every man, without restricting his freedom, but instead seeking to draw from this very freedom love, which is not only an act of solidarity with the suffering Son of man, but also a kind of "mercy" shown by each one of us to the Son of the eternal Father. In the whole of this messianic program of Christ, in the whole revelation of mercy through the cross, could man's dignity be more highly respected and ennobled, for, in obtaining mercy, He is in a sense the one who at the same time "shows mercy"? (nn. 7-8).

[336] *Diary*, n. 1320.

[337] Three Ways to Keep the Three O'clock Hour:
(Based on *Diary*, nn. 1320, 1570)

> 1. We can *immerse ourselves in the Lord's Passion, especially in his abandonment on the Cross.* We can do this briefly (even "for an instant") or for a longer period of time. For example, we can simply look at a crucifix, think of Jesus in his Passion, or pray the Three O'clock Prayer:
>
> > You expired, Jesus, but the source of life gushed forth for souls, and the ocean of mercy opened up for the whole world. O Fount of Life, unfathomable Divine Mercy, envelop the whole world and empty Yourself out upon us. ... O

Blood and Water, which gushed forth from the
Heart of Jesus as a fount of mercy for us, I trust
in You.

If we have more time, we can pray the sorrowful mysteries of the Rosary or make the Stations of the Cross.

2. We can *present our petitions to the Father by virtue of his Son's
Passion.* Our petitions should be made with bold confidence
because of the indescribable power of Jesus' Passion and the
great promises attached to the Hour of Great Mercy. I recommend presenting one's petitions in the context of praying the
Divine Mercy Chaplet. (Don't forget to pray for unrepentant
sinners and the dying, especially for unrepentant sinners who
are dying.)

3. The three o'clock hour is a great time to *visit Jesus, truly
present in the Blessed Sacrament.*

[338] Ibid., n. 1146.
[339] Ibid., n. 570.
[340] Ibid., n. 1541.
[341] Ibid., n. 742.
[342] Ibid., n. 163.
[343] Ibid., n. 294.
[344] Ibid., n. 453.
[345] Ibid., n. 687.
[346] Ibid., n. 1074.
[347] Ibid., n. 1777.

Index

Y

MARIAN PRESS
STOCKBRIDGE, MA

All proceeds go to support the good works of the Marians of the Immaculate Conception

Your Trustworthy Resource for Publications on Divine Mercy and Mary

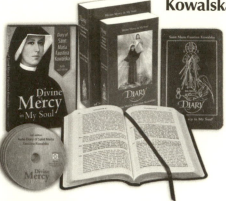

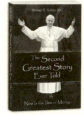

MORE FROM FR. GAITLEY

NEW!

Y55-33DML
ebook: **Y55-EB33DML**

33 Days to Merciful Love*
A Do-It-Yourself Retreat in Preparation for Consecration to Divine Mercy

Live the Jubilee Year of Mercy to the full! Get your copy of *33 Days to Merciful Love* by Fr. Michael Gaitley, MIC, the stirring sequel to the international sensation, *33 Days to Morning Glory*. Using the same 33-day preparation format, *33 Days to Merciful Love* journeys with one of the most beloved saints of modern times, St. Thérèse of Lisieux, and concludes with a consecration to Divine Mercy. So whether you want to deepen your love of Divine Mercy or have a devotion to St. Thérèse, *33 Days to Merciful Love* is the book for you. (216 pages.)

33 Days to Morning Glory*

Begin an extraordinary 33-day journey to Marian consecration with four spiritual giants: St. Louis de Montfort, St. Maximilian Kolbe, St. Mother Teresa, and St. John Paul II. (208 pages.)
Y55-33DAY ebook: **Y55-EB33DAY**

Consoling the Heart of Jesus*

This do-it-yourself retreat combines the *Spiritual Exercises of St. Ignatius* with the teachings of Saints Thérèse of Lisieux, Faustina Kowalska, and Louis de Montfort. (428 pages.) Includes bonus material in appendices.

Consoling the Heart of Jesus Prayer Companion (126 pages.)

Y55-CHJ

Y55-PCCHJ

'You Did it to Me':
A Practical Guide to Mercy in Action*

"[This book] blew me away. I believe it will become a spiritual classic, right up there with *33 Days to Morning Glory*."
— David Came, Marian Press

'You Did It to Me:'
Putting Mercy into Action
5-part DVD series. As seen on EWTN.

NEW!

Y55-2MEDVD

Y55-2ME

*Also available as a group retreat! See next page.

For our complete line of books, prayercards, pamphlets, and more, visit ShopMercy.org or call 1-800-462-7426.

THERE ARE THREE STAGES TO THE PROGRAM:

STAGE ONE: The Two Hearts

PART 1: The Immaculate Heart

We begin our journey to the Immaculate Heart with the book *33 Days to Morning Glory* and its accompanying group-retreat program.

PART 2: The Sacred Heart

Mary then leads us to the Sacred Heart, which begins the second part of Stage One with the book *Consoling the Heart of Jesus* and its accompanying group-retreat program.

STAGE TWO: Wisdom and Works of Mercy

We begin Stage Two with *The 'One Thing' Is Three* and its accompanying group-study program, which gives group members a kind of crash course in Catholic theology. Stage Two concludes with a program for group works of mercy based on the book '*You Did It to Me*.'

STAGE THREE: Keeping the Hearts Afire

The heart of Stage Three is the **Marian Missionaries of Divine Mercy**, which invites participants to concretely live everything they've learned in the Hearts Afire program and continue their formation with additional group programs such as the 33 Days to Merciful Love Group Retreat and the *Divine Mercy in the Second Greatest Story Ever Told* series. Become a Marian Missionary: MarianMissionaries.org • 413-944-8500.

Parish-based Programs from the
Marian Fathers of the Immaculate Conception

HAPP: 1-844-551-3755
Orders: 1-800-462-7426
AllHeartsAfire.org
HAPP@marian.org

MARIAN MISSIONARIES OF DIVINE MERCY

Level 1
Missionaries who give a year of service.

Level 3
Missionaries who actively serve our mission.

Level 2
Missionaries who support our mission.

Join us!

1. Get the FREE* *Missionary Handbook*
by Fr. Michael Gaitley, MIC
(Y55-MMDBK, 136 pages.)
Call **800-462-7426**.
*Limit one free Handbook per household.
Standard shipping rates apply. Continental
U.S. only.

2. Complete Stages 1 & 2 of the
Hearts Afire program.

3. Fill out and submit your
Commitment Form.
(Find it in the Handbook and
online at MarianMissionaries.org/cf.)

MARIAN MISSIONARIES
DIVINE *of* MERCY

MarianMissionaries.org
413-944-8500

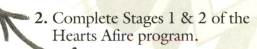